DAILY GUIDEPOSTS

365 SPIRIT-LIFTING DEVOTIONS OF *Comfort*

Guideposts

New York

365 Spirit-Lifting Devotions of Comfort

ISBN-10: 0-8249-3215-3
ISBN-13: 978-0-8249-3215-2

Published by Guideposts
16 East 34th Street
New York, New York 10016
Guideposts.org

Distributed by Ideals Publications, a Guideposts company
2630 Elm Hill Pike, Suite 100
Nashville, Tennessee 37214

Guideposts and *Ideals* are registered trademarks of Guideposts.

Acknowledgments
Every attempt has been made to credit the sources of copyrighted material used in this book. If any such acknowledgment has been inadvertently omitted or miscredited, receipt of such information would be appreciated.

All Scripture quotations, unless otherwise noted, are taken from *The King James Version of the Bible.*

Scripture quotations marked (GNB) are taken from *Good News Bible*, copyright © American Bible Society, 1966, 1971, 1976.

Scripture quotations marked (NAS) are taken from the *New American Standard Bible,* copyright © 1960, 1962, 1963, 1968, 1971, 1972, 1973, 1975, 1977, 1995 by the Lockman Foundation. Used by permission.

Scripture quotations marked (NIV) are taken from *The Holy Bible, New International Version.* Copyright © 1973, 1978, 1984, 2011 by Biblica, Inc. Used by permission of Zondervan. All rights reserved worldwide. www.zondervan.com

Scripture quotations marked (NKJV) are taken from *The Holy Bible, New King James Version.* Copyright © 1982 by Thomas Nelson, Inc.

Scripture quotations marked (RSV) are taken from the *Revised Standard Version of the Bible.* Copyright © 1946, 1952, 1971 by Division of Christian Education of the National Council of Churches of Christ in the United States of America. Used by permission.

Scripture quotations marked (TLB) are taken from *The Living Bible.* Copyright © 1971 by Tyndale House Publishers, Wheaton, Illinois 60187. All rights reserved.

Cover and interior design by Müllerhaus
Typeset by Aptara, Inc.

Printed and bound in China
10 9 8 7 6 5 4 3 2 1

Introduction

*L*ife is a blessing. And in that blessing sometimes lies difficulty. From petty annoyances to life-changing traumas, we all need the comfort that comes from our faith and from the people whose paths are intertwined with ours. The blessing of comfort reminds us that though it feels sometimes there is nowhere to turn, deep inside we know that there is; we just need a little help finding the way.

365 Spirit-Lifting Devotions of Comfort offers just that. This extraordinary treasury of devotions by people from all walks of life provides, day after day, a Scripture to focus your meditation, a true-life example of comfort, and a personal prayer to help you through the day.

365 Spirit-Lifting Devotions of Comfort commemorates the special days of the year, and the simple "holidays" that punctuate the year, from the true meaning of the groundhog's shadow to an April Fool's joke that teaches a college student to concentrate on her blessings. *365 Spirit-Lifting Devotions of Comfort* will bless you with a particularly apt devotion on your special day. Its wise and reassuring devotions make it a book to turn to daily, to assist you when you are troubled and to prepare you for what lies ahead. And since *365 Spirit-Lifting Devotions of Comfort* is not bound to a particular year, today is a perfect day to begin experiencing the comfort that comes from God, for all things that give comfort are gifts from our Creator.

January

January 1
New Year's Day

May God give peace to you, my Christian brothers, and love, with faith from God the Father and the Lord Jesus Christ.

—Ephesians 6:23 (TLB)

*E*arly in the new year when I take down the tree, the garlands, and the Christmas cards, it's become a tradition for me to prayerfully choose one of the greetings on a card and make it my inspirational focus for the year. This had been a somewhat nostalgic and sad Christmas, as I dearly missed my son Ian, my daughter-in-law, Melissa, and the grandkids. This was their first Christmas in Colorado; they phoned to tell me of the first snowfall with squeals of delight! Lovely for them but, oh, how I missed their hugs and cuddles.

The focus I chose for this year came by way of a letter from a pastor who has been one of my spiritual mentors. He reminded me of the wish sent by our mutual friend, the late Dr. Lew Smedes, who during his tenure as professor at Fuller Theological Seminary was always a great encourager: "We want you to be blessed with joys deeper than any sadness, gratitude happier than any regrets, hopes brighter than the shadows of any discouragement, and the vitality to make of every day what God on Christmas Day made for all days."

Joy, gratitude, hope, and vitality for every day of this new year.

The glow of Your grace warms my heart, Lord Jesus;
the power of Your love sustains me.

—Fay Angus

His work is perfect....
—DEUTERONOMY 32:4

I pride myself on having a very clear awareness of my failings. I keep a mental list under the heading "Fix These." I also know what I'm good at, and this much smaller list falls under the heading "Acceptable Behavior." I've filed "Good Organizer" in the "Acceptable Behavior" column, and I use my almost-daily walking time to hone this skill.

This past Sunday my husband, Charlie, accompanied me on my walk. At six feet, four inches tall, he's got quite a leg-span advantage over me, but he had to pay attention to match my determined stride. Where he might have meandered, I sped along, dragging him with me. As we passed ice-covered inlets, snow-brushed marshes, deserted winter beaches, and warmly lit houses, I plunged ahead with my agenda, talking nonstop about our budget. How much will our vacation cost? Will we have enough saved by then? Do we have enough frequent-flyer miles for a free ticket? What about two free tickets? Has he made the reservations yet?

Suddenly, Charlie interrupted me. "Marc, look at the Canada geese on the ice!"

Without even glancing to where he was gesturing, I snapped, "Are you even listening to me?"

Charlie gently took me by the shoulders and turned me toward the cove. I gasped in surprise: There were more than a hundred Canada geese waddling around on top of the ice as if waiting for the sun to melt it and restore order in their lives.

I put my arms around Charlie. When we got home, I would have to make a few changes to my "Acceptable Behavior" list.

Lord, You've given us so much! Open my senses to Your many gifts.
—MARCI ALBORGHETTI

Remember, O Lord, thy tender mercies and thy lovingkindnesses;
for they have been ever of old.
—PSALM 25:6

*R*ight after Christmas last year my wife Joy's dad went into the hospital with a flu that turned into pneumonia. For years he has had a condition called chronic pulmonary disease, so the situation was serious. Joy is a nurse, and she flew out to California to make sure he was getting the best care at the hospital and to help her family prepare for the long-term medical problems he might have.

After a few days the situation became worse, and each time I talked to Joy, I heard her professionalism taking over as she described working with her dad's doctors and nurses to take every step possible and monitor every response. Then one night she called, crying, and told me, "Today, when I went into the room, it wasn't a patient who was lying there dying, it was my daddy."

I felt helpless. I was three thousand miles away and unable to hold her or even think of the right things to say over the phone. We prayed, asking God for His help and entrusting Joy's father to His wisdom. When we finished, Joy said to me, "That old word in the Bible, lovingkindness, is what I feel right now. He will hold my father and my family in His hands, and whatever comes will be all right."

God has brought back Joy's dad, for now. But eventually he will leave us, as we will leave our children, to pass from life into lovingkindness. His life and ours are in God's hands, and we are safe there.

Lord, thank You for planning a life beyond this one, and for carrying us over
when we come to the doorway between the two.
—ERIC FELLMAN

JANUARY 4

There is a way that seems right to a man, but in the end....
—PROVERBS 14:12 (NIV)

I never dream about Chase. I dream about Lanea, but I never dream about Chase," I told my friend Portia over lunch—Chinese food with green tea. My daughter, Lanea, was eleven and my son, Chase, three. Divorce and death had taken their fathers from their lives. During Lanea's earlier years we had spent significant time together. Chase, however, had to compete with a job that held me in its grasp, sometimes ten or twelve hours a day.

"I don't think I'm spending enough time with him. I'm always tired. I'm always nervous. I'm always cranky. I'm always getting sick. If I could quit, I would."

"You can," Portia said.

I had my life all planned. By the time I was twenty-nine, I had already achieved my major career goal. After two years, I could not think of a single individual on my side of the corporate web who was happy. Smiles and calm, peaceful demeanors were in short supply. "Is this all there is?" I asked, paraphrasing a popular song.

I listened to Portia—and to the still, small voice speaking within me. Boxing up all our things, packing away my fears, we moved to rural North Carolina. We lived in a small trailer in the middle of the woods, with farms all around us. Poor in possessions, we grew richer in love. And we learned about one another.

When we returned to the city two years later, we returned with stronger faith, with the ability to find pleasure in small, simple things. We carried with us the personal relationship we had each developed with God. My career isn't what it was before I moved to the country, but I smile a lot more. My children, I believe, are more assured of my love and more courageous. They're less impressed with brand names and labels. And at night, when I dream, I dream of them both.

Lord, help me to hear Your voice and follow You.
—SHARON FOSTER

January 5

The God of hope fill you with all joy and peace in believing....
—ROMANS 15:13

The road ahead was dark and deserted. My car's wipers whined as they pushed a mixture of snow and ice back and forth across the windshield. I grasped the steering wheel with white knuckles and prayed silently. My daughter Keri and I were driving toward Birmingham, Alabama, where she was to participate in a scholarship competition the next morning. Winter storms are an oddity in the South, and I was terrified. I didn't want Keri to know.

She sat silently beside me, eyes straight ahead.

"If you want, you can turn on the radio," I said. Static followed, then a jumble of voices and music, and finally Elton John filled the car with a love song.

My heart melted, thinking of the child beside me. Then, in the midst of my anguished prayers for all the dark unknowns, the presence of God filled my heart with a confident knowing. "Keri," I said, "someday we'll remember this moment and everything I'm about to say will already be true. You are going to get a good scholarship. You are going to excel in college. Someone very wonderful is going to fall in love with you, and all the scattered, confusing pieces of your life will fit perfectly together. I know this because God has put it in my heart to say this to you. Someday we'll be dancing at your wedding, and we'll remember this night, and we'll laugh with happiness. Who knows? I might even get Elton John to sing this very song as you walk out onto the floor for the first dance!"

Five years later, I pick up the phone. Keri gives me a glowing report of her first class in graduate school. She speaks of the teenage girls she will be counseling and offers an update on her boyfriend, who attends another graduate school nearby. "Mama, have you written to Elton John yet?" she says with a chuckle. And with those words she tells me everything a mother needs to know.

Dear God, in my scariest moments, You point me to the place where, in Your time, You fit the pieces of my life together into a perfect whole. Thank You.
—PAM KIDD

January 6
EPIPHANY

Now when Jesus was born in Bethlehem of Judaea in the days of Herod the king, behold, there came wise men from the east.... And when they were come into the house, they saw the young child with Mary his mother, and fell down, and worshipped him: and when they had opened their treasures, they presented unto him gifts; gold, and frankincense and myrrh.

—MATTHEW 2:1, 11

oday is the feast of the Epiphany, or Twelfth Night, when many Christians commemorate the visit to Bethlehem by the wise men, bearing presents for the Christ Child. Only Matthew records the coming of the Magi and their gifts of gold, frankincense, and myrrh.

I read an article recently about the price of frankincense, which comes from the gum of a tree grown on the Arabian peninsula in Oman. Frankincense is used in one of the world's most expensive perfumes that sells for $220 an ounce. It is also an ingredient in cosmetics, anointing oils, and some embalming fluids. Myrrh has similar properties. The wise men's gifts were valuable and, according to legend, provided the wherewithal of the Holy Family's flight from King Herod into Egypt.

We don't know the route that Mary, Joseph, and Jesus traveled, their destination, the length of their stay, or who else helped them survive. The only thing of which we're certain is that God watched over them. No doubt they were frightened, worried, and unsure about how they were going to survive in a strange land, but God provided. He always does to those who trust Him. That's good to remember in whatever trials we face in the new year ahead.

Teach us, Lord, to trust You and wait.
Your timing's perfect, ne'er early or late.

—FRED BAUER

January 7

O give thanks unto the LORD; for he is good: for his mercy endureth for ever.
—PSALM 106:1

*P*lease, Lord, help me see the circumstances of this day as gifts from You," I prayed as I sat in a dreary motel room on a drab winter morning, far from home. For the last two days, I'd been at a conference and now it was my husband's birthday and I just wanted to get home. But because of airline problems, I couldn't get a flight until afternoon, and now it was snowing...hard.

So I packed my bags, caught a shuttle, and got to the airport early. Upon checking in, I found that all the flights were oversold, and even though I had a ticket, I didn't have a seat. "You're on the waiting list," the ticket agent told me. "I think you'll be fine."

I didn't want to be "fine." I wanted to be on the plane. I wanted to throw a tantrum. I wanted to talk about "being fair." But instead I merely sat down in the waiting area where I watched dozens of people board the flight. At least a dozen more waited, just like me, hoping for seats. Lots of names were called, and people went forward to get their boarding passes, including people who had checked in after I did.

Please, Lord, let me see these circumstances as gifts from You, I repeated, thinking maybe God hadn't heard me the first time.

At last my name was called, and I went up to the gate. "We're out of room in coach," the boarding agent said, "but we've found a seat for you."

An hour later, I was sitting on the plane with a white linen cloth covering my tray table, enjoying an elegant three-course meal, while stretching out to enjoy the extra space (and grace!) of my first-class seat. It seems they had run out of seats in coach and being last had made me first—for first-class.

> *Lord, even when my circumstances don't include first-class,*
> *may I see them as Your gifts, intended for good.*
> —CAROL KUYKENDALL

January 8

I can do everything through him who gives me strength.
—Philippians 4:13 (NIV)

I sat in a Chicago airport waiting for my flight. The gate was packed and noisy; a confusing jumble of voices spun around me and over the loudspeaker. In the seat next to me, a young mother held a child with curly, dark hair, who was wriggling to get down.

"You have your hands full," I said to the mother. She laughed and set the child down a short distance from her.

"Anna's just learning to walk. She's itching to practice." The mother held out her arms. "Come on, Anna. Come to Mommy."

But Anna's tiny sneakered feet froze on the strange floor. She looked around, her dark eyes growing large at all the noise. "Come on," the mother coaxed again, holding out her arms.

Back on track, Anna toddled a few steps. "Oh no, she's going to fall," a well-meaning lady called. Anna looked toward the voice and fell. She cried, a long, sobbing wail. Mother picked her up, kissed her, and put her back on track.

"You can do it, Anna," the mother insisted gently. "Come on. Just take a step." And this time she did. Squinting straight ahead, she walked the whole two yards right into her mother's arms.

I was embarking on a new project that both terrified and excited me. I was sure I could do it. Yet doubts pounded me till I stood frozen, listening to all the discouraging voices inside me. *Where is Your voice?* I kept asking God. *Why don't You show me how to do this? I don't even know where to start.*

But right here in this noisy airport, God did show me. Not how to do it, but how to know His voice. The child in me stood still, listening through the confusing jumble of doubt. Sure enough, His voice came soft and insistent: You can do it. Just take the first step.

Father, with each toddling step, help me to keep focused
on Your soft, encouraging voice.
—Shari Smyth

January 9

"While I was musing the fire burned; then I spoke with my tongue: Lord, make me to know my end and what is the extent of my days; let me know how transient I am.... My hope is in You."

—Psalm 39:3–4, 7 (NAS)

My family has gone to bed. I am alone in the darkened den, staring into the embers of this evening's fire. Sprawled in my easy chair, I have turned off the last light. It is time to reflect and remember, to be lulled into sleep.

Drifting into reverie, I am entranced by the glowing oak coals, their dry warmth radiating and soothing. For a moment I think of the generations of men and women who have finished their day this way: alone, draped in darkness, entranced by radiance, pondering the meaning of life.

I remember the years of my childhood, tucked away in the high, remote mountains of the Philippines. In the rainy season it grew cold and damp. Battered by fierce typhoons, our only heat came from a stone fireplace. I remember my father walking out of the night and through our front door, a load of split wood in his arms, pine kindling grasped in his hands. Dad would always light the family hearth, the place for our family to gather, to commune, to be.

And now, out of the same darkness comes a yearning for another Father. The embers of this night kindle a longing for God, a timeless longing that I share with the whole human race. As I slip toward sleep, my eyes closing, a blanket drawn around me, I know God is near. I don't know how I know: I just know. I believe, and I am a child again.

Father, in the darkness of this world,
enlighten me with the radiance of Your love. Amen.

—Scott Walker

January 10

Let not your heart be troubled....
—John 14:1

W hen loved ones die, we have a sense of loss. We know that we will have their companionship no longer. And it's easy to feel that their special qualities—their humor, wisdom, kindness, compassion—have vanished with them. But sometimes memory can bring those qualities back in unexpected ways.

In some old papers the other day I came across a letter written by one of my aunts more than half a century ago. This woman, who had already known more than her share of misfortune, had suffered a crushing blow when one of her children was killed in a tragic accident. To someone who had written her a letter of sympathy she replied, "Yes, you are right; I am deeply unhappy and distressed. But I try to remind myself that happiness is not the sum total of life. There are other important things and one of these, I think, is bearing pain bravely as one grows older."

There it was, the essence of this woman revealed in this quiet display of fortitude. I will try to remember her words as I grow older. And try, also, to pass along some of her courage to my own children.

Father, lend us Your strength in adversity always.
—Arthur Gordon

JANUARY 11

"Remember, therefore, what you have received...."
—REVELATION 3:3 (NIV)

*I*t's 7:00 AM, and I'm trying to be quiet as I rummage around for my razor in the bathroom I share with my wife and my stepdaughter Mara.

Everyone in New York City has space complaints, and after years of marriage, I'm used to the fact that the three of us might as well be living on a submarine. But the bathroom is the one place where I still lose patience. Papaya-scented clarifying solution, mango-essence rejuvenating cream. Each day I seem to be confronted with another new substance that Mara has decided is essential for her appearance. "For heaven's sake," I said to her recently, "you're fifteen! Why don't you at least wait until you're old and have some wrinkles to cover up before buying all this junk?"

Crash! In my haste I knock a big container of moisturizing lotion off the sink. It lands amid a phalanx of half-used shampoos and conditioners wedged up against the tub. Reaching down to retrieve it, my fingers touch something unfamiliar. I straighten back up and bring the object into the light: a Fisher-Price milkman with movable arms and legs and a hardy smile painted across his face. I haven't seen this figure in years, though I used to run into it just about every day. Instantly, I'm brought back to the first months of my marriage, when my new stepdaughter was seven and this bathroom was just as cluttered as it is now, but with altogether different items: plastic dinosaurs, animal-shaped sponges, and innumerable action figures like this one that Mara had long dialogues with as she sat in the tub. I look at that little figure and wonder at all the time that has gone by, and I pray:

Thank You, Lord, for the clutter in my life—every last piece of it.
—PTOLEMY TOMPKINS

January 12

For the Son of God, Jesus Christ, whom we preached among you...
was not Yes and No; but in him it is always Yes.
—II Corinthians 1:19 (RSV)

*L*ast January I went through a terrible three-week depression. Alaska is cold and dark at this time of year, which is enough to sabotage anybody's good mood. But there was more to it than that. With the children all out of the nest—and our oldest, Tamara, just married—I found myself wondering who I really was and where my life had gone. One afternoon I stood staring into the mirror, my face red and swollen from crying, calling out to the stranger in the glass, "Who are you? I don't know you."

During those bleak days, I buried myself at home. I vowed to get out of Alaska the next January, if that would keep the depression from happening again. Finally, with the arrival of out-of-town guests, I began to pick up my life once more.

Several months later, I listened to a "Celebrate Life" tape by Luci Swindoll. She advised, "Be involved. While you can, say yes to more things than you say no to." I re-inventoried my January melancholy and realized I had said yes to very little. I didn't meet with friends, complete any projects, work out at the gym, volunteer at church, or reach out to anyone in any way. My life was one great big "no."

January is here again. This time around I'm going to try out a lot more yeses and see where that lands me. Maybe I won't need to leave the state. Maybe there is joy to be found in my own backyard. Even in January.

God of the changing seasons, help me to say yes a dozen times over—
once for each month of the year.
—Carol Knapp

JANUARY 13

Whoever is kind to the needy honors God.
—PROVERBS 14:31 (NIV)

*W*hen our family lived in South Africa, we were approached almost daily on the street or at our door by beggars pleading for a job, food, clothing, or money. We were living in a small apartment with only the contents of our suitcases and little money, and I sorely felt our inability to help them.

One day I shared my frustration with the priest at the church we were attending. "Remember," Father Panteleimon said, "the greatest of all virtues is charity. Be grateful for any opportunity to show kindness to someone. See each request as a privilege, a chance to give to Christ coming to you in the 'least of His brethren.' Try to give what you can, even a few coins or a little food, a kind word and a prayer."

One evening shortly after our talk, I walked to the store "just to get milk"—and headed home with two bags. A woman in a maid's uniform, on her way home from work, approached me. "Oh, madame," she pleaded, "could you give me money for my children? I don't get paid until next week, and we have no more food."

About to say, "Sorry, I have no money left," I remembered Father Panteleimon's words.

"Here, take these." I handed her the bags, after pulling out a carton of milk. "This is all I really need tonight."

She protested, but I put the sacks in her hands. "It's not much," I insisted, "just bread, cheese, meat, and custard."

"Oh, madame, thank you, thank you!" Her face beamed. "My children will be so happy." I floated to our apartment, profoundly grateful that God had put her in my path.

Now I'm back home in the suburbs, and no beggars approach me for food. But God gives me other opportunities to make small sacrifices. A friend calls late at night needing to talk. Reluctantly leaving the recliner and my favorite TV show, I listen, offer some encouragement, and then head to bed renewed.

Lord, help me recognize each opportunity today to show You kindness.
—MARY BROWN

JANUARY 14

"I will send down showers in season; there will be showers of blessing."
—EZEKIEL 34:26 (NIV)

*B*less you!" a stranger said to me as I sneezed loudly in the supermarket once again. It must have been the tenth time I'd heard it that day as I suffered with yet another winter cold. *I don't feel all that blessed,* I thought, sniffling and reaching for another tissue. I appreciated her kindness, but suddenly the phrase seemed silly. Who's really thinking about God's blessings when somebody sneezes? I've read that the origins of this tradition go far back in history, to a superstitious belief that an evil spirit could enter the body to steal the soul or to the fear that a sneeze signaled oncoming illness, requiring God's protection for the sneezer. Whatever its origin, the average "bless you" is little more than a courtesy today.

Still, all those "bless yous" made me think about the many times each day when I do feel blessed in small ways. I was blessed when a truck driver let me in ahead of him to make my left turn, instead of speeding up to beat me to the intersection. And I was blessed when a woman held the door open and waited for me as I struggled with my arms full of boxes for a school project. These weren't big events, but little kindnesses that eased my way and brought much-needed help.

Yet I've discovered something about these small, everyday blessings. They seem to mean the most to me when I'm on the giving end. The other day I was waiting in the checkout line with my full cart, and I let a man with a huge box of diapers go ahead of me. "Thank you. You're a blessing to me today," he said. But instead I felt blessed, privileged to be able to pass on even the tiniest bit of God's love that might make someone's day go a little smoother. It's one of God's wonderful ironies: The more blessings I give others, the more blessed I am myself.

*Heavenly Father, show me the ways I might shower others with blessings
as You have showered me.*
—GINA BRIDGEMAN

"In a dream, in a vision of the night, when deep sleep falls upon men…
then He opens the ears of men.…"
—Job 33:15–16 (NKJV)

*I*t's almost as if he knew he didn't have much time. Young Martin Luther King Jr. was always in a hurry. Skipping grades of school, he entered college at age fifteen and became an ordained minister at age nineteen. He was only thirty when he saw the signing of the Civil Rights Act, and at thirty-five he was the youngest person ever to receive the Nobel Peace Prize. Just four years later his life was over.

How could one man do so much in such a short time? Maybe the answer is in a line from his speech at Selma, Alabama, in 1965. When asked how long it would take to win the reforms he was fighting for, he said, "How long? Not long, for mine eyes have seen the glory of the Lord."

I wonder how many good works I have neglected because I thought they would take too much time and effort. I can usually think of dozens of reasons why something can't be done:

"I'm too old to start."
"I'm not exactly rich, you know?"
"I'm a low-energy person."
"I'm too shy, not the leader type."

All of these may be true, but I think the real reason I don't accomplish more is that I don't have a clear vision of what I want to do, and I fail to include the Lord on my list of resources.

It stirs me to think of the possibilities for good if everyone learned to see with the eyes of a dreamer. Today, on the birthday of Dr. King, would be a good time to look up at the stars and ask God for a clearer vision of what needs to be done.

Thank You, Father, for men and women
who show us what we can do when we dare to dream.
—Daniel Schantz

They that had any sick...brought them unto him;
and he laid his hands on every one of them, and healed them.
—LUKE 4:40

*S*hirley and I belong to the contingent that believes, like the old evangelist, "It's better to stand on the promises than sit on the premises." Since coming to Florida, we've found two volunteer efforts beyond church service that are particularly rewarding: Meals on Wheels, and a pet therapy program for nursing homes and assisted-living centers. The philosophy behind pet therapy is that animals are wonderful expressers of love, capable of bringing smiles to the faces of people whose circumstances are often less than joyful.

Not long ago Shirley and I took a long-legged, sweet-spirited dog named Lady, a greyhound-Labrador mix, to a nursing home. We led her from one room to the next, and dozens of people enjoyed petting her shiny black coat, feeding her treats and getting hand licks in return. Then in the hallway we came upon a wheelchair-bound woman in her eighties.

"Would you like to pet Lady, Mabel?" I asked, reading the woman's name off a tag. She tried to talk, but her words came out in gibberish. The woman seemed unable to pet the dog, so I moved her hand for her. An amazing thing happened. With great willpower, Mabel slowly opened her closed fist until her palm lay on Lady's head, and in the slowest of motions she gently moved her hand from side to side. The smile that broke out on the woman's face rivaled the most beautiful sunsets I've ever seen.

There is great healing in touch. Sometimes it is as dramatic as it was for the ailing woman who touched the hem of Jesus' garment. Other times, as with Mabel, touch is a transitory heart healer. But I'm convinced God needs more agents willing to be conduits of His caring who with simple gestures—a spontaneous hug or kiss on the cheek—can help mend the ill, worried, lonely, aging, and depressed. If a dog can be God's instrument of love, so can we.

Remind me, God, when I stammer and words fail,
To study a dog and its wagging tail.
—FRED BAUER

Stand still, and see the salvation of the Lord....
—EXODUS 14:13

*K*athy Halpern could not have known about my dilemma. She lives in California, where I was visiting, far from the situation waiting for me back home in New York. Two of my closest friends had separated after forty years of marriage; now each wanted me to hear their side of the story. How could I be a friend to either one without being disloyal to the other?

It was a relief to escape for a few days to the West Coast, where Kathy's church had recently witnessed the near-miraculous recovery of one of its members. The young man had been pronounced brain-dead after a car accident. The church mounted a round-the-clock prayer vigil, and now, four months later, he was sitting up, talking, recognizing members of his family.

"Do you know what the hardest thing was for me?" Kathy said. "Not rushing to the hospital with everybody else on the night of the accident." That had been her first instinct—to jump in her car and get there as fast as she could. "I was on my way out the door when God simply stopped me." She thought she heard Him say that there would be a string of daunting medical negatives at the hospital. The role God had for Kathy was to focus on His power. *Keep your eyes on Me*, He said, *not on the problem*.

And so she had, contacting the young man's family the next day with a message of faith instead of fear.

As I say, Kathy couldn't have known about the situation back in New York, but of course, God did. Through her words shone God's wisdom for me as well: *You don't need to know the details of your friends' breakup. Right now, right here in California, you can lift them both to Me.*

When problems come, Lord, keep my eyes on the One Who has the answers.
—ELIZABETH SHERRILL

January 18

Teach me good judgment and knowledge: for I have believed thy commandments.
—Psalm 119:66

*T*uesday morning is garbage pickup at our country home. One Monday evening I hauled several heavy bags to the edge of the road. Wanting to make the lifting easier for the pickup man, I overturned a wheelbarrow and placed one heavy bag on top of it. Early the next morning the wheelbarrow was gone.

"Somebody stole our wheelbarrow," I fumed.

"Nobody stole your wheelbarrow," my brother said with a laugh. "Whoever took it thought you were throwing it out with the garbage."

"Well, then, I'll make a sign and ask for it back," I said.

"Mom, if you do that, I'm not coming home," my teenage son warned.

"Forget it," my brother said.

But I made a sign anyway. It read, "Please return our wheelbarrow. We need it. Thank you."

A couple of mornings later my daughter bounced into the kitchen. "Look, Mom," she said, pointing toward the living room window. There beside the road in the early dawn stood our wheelbarrow.

I never did find out who took our wheelbarrow or who brought it back. No matter. That wheelbarrow incident has taught me a good lesson: Sometimes what seems like mischief is just an honest mistake.

Lord Jesus, help me see others clearly, as You see them,
and to believe the best about them.
—Helen Grace Lescheid

JANUARY 19

"And if you greet only your brothers, what are you doing more than others?
Do not even pagans do that?"

—MATTHEW 5:47 (NIV)

*G*oing to church together on Sunday morning is very important for our family. One particular Sunday when our son Reggie was home from college, I was scheduled to preach at a church in a nearby town. We had never been to this church before, and as we walked in, no one spoke to us or reached out to shake our hands and make us welcome. In the midst of this cold environment, we felt out of place and unwanted.

As I went to the vestry to get ready for the service, I encouraged Reggie and my wife, Rosie, to take the initiative in breaking the ice. We could judge this congregation of strangers and stereotype them as self-absorbed folks who didn't want to like us, or we could trust God, treat them like brothers and sisters, and see what happened.

Reggie and Rosie sat down in a pew and turned to greet the people sitting around them. To their surprise, they discovered that here was a group of Christians who loved Christ and had nothing against us, but just didn't know how to reach out to us. If we had been unwilling to take the first step, we would have been confirmed in our uncharitable opinion—and we would have missed the chance to get to know some wonderful people.

Lord, thank You for revealing to my heart that nothing should stop me from reaching out to people from all backgrounds and cultures.

—DOLPHUS WEARY

"Shall we indeed accept good from God and not accept adversity?"…
—JOB 2:10 (NAS)

*F*or many years, I served on the boards of charitable organizations. One of the great delights of these assignments was the opportunity to meet many of the finest business men and women from across the country. I was always intrigued to hear how they found an idea or product that led to success. I was even more intrigued to discover how they handle adversity.

This recent recession has hit all walks of life, but I learned a valuable lesson about it from David Graebel, founder and chairman of Graebel Worldwide Movers. Starting with one used truck in Wausau, Wisconsin, he and his wife, Lois, built one of the biggest transportation and storage companies in the world. But in 1990, one of his biggest clients declared bankruptcy and left the Graebel companies holding an unpaid bill for $1.8 million. Soon gloom and doom spread through all the branch offices, and David had to do something quickly.

"I decided to call all the regional sales managers in from the field to a conference at headquarters," he recalls. "The first thing I did was exclaim, 'Isn't this fantastic!' Well, you can imagine they all thought I was nuts. But I continued by saying, 'Isn't God good? In just a few short years He has taken us from one used truck and one driver to the size where a single customer can hit us with a loss of more than a million dollars, and yet we are still in business the next day! In fact, we can afford to fly all of you in so we can sit down and figure out how we can get more business.'"

Isn't that a spectacular attitude toward adversity? As you might guess, the Graebel companies found more business, not just to cover the loss, but enough to make the following year their best year ever! From this, I conclude that when I'm hit with a big problem, the solution is to thank God I'm still around to face it! Then ask Him how to solve it, and watch how He handles adversity with a power that never fails.

Lord, let me feel Your hand holding mine in every dark place where I must tread. Give me the vision to see the solution at the center of every problem.
—RUTH STAFFORD PEALE

January 21

I must speak, that I may find relief....
—Job 32:20 (RSV)

I was amazed at how thoroughly Dr. Hughbanks, our veterinarian, knew how to treat Jamaica, our sick collie. "The hardest part," he said, as he gave our collie a pat, "is knowing where their pain or sickness is since they can't tell us."

I thought about that all the way home. Our ability to talk should make diagnosing human pain so much easier. Or does it? I recall a time when I was in terrible emotional pain. It was one more insensitive act by my boyfriend of five years. He was bright and well-educated but self-centered. Everything revolved around him; my needs weren't considered. I knew that if I wished to have self-respect, I would have to break it off, but...

Alone in my apartment, I cried out to God to send someone to comfort me. Surely, He knew and saw. Surely, He would provide. Yet my phone did not ring; nor did anyone stop by that weekend. I thought God had let me down. But He hadn't. I could talk. Unlike our collie on the vet's stainless steel table, I could speak about my hurt. Why didn't I tell someone? I believe it was pride. If someone could guess my ailment, I wouldn't have to admit anything or humble myself or confess shortcomings. I wouldn't have to appear needy.

Sometimes God does bring us unexpected help when we need it most. But I've learned to act now, instead of waiting for a miracle. I ask myself what is the reason for not simply telling someone my need? Fear? Laziness? Pride? Our loved ones and friends are just a phone call away, ready to demonstrate Christ's love and command to "bear one another's burdens" (Galatians 6:2, NAS). You know who they are. Tell them where it hurts.

Dear Lord, help me to understand the difference between "waiting on the Lord" and prideful procrastination. Give me the humility to speak to another of my hurts. Amen.
—Kathie Kania

"Take courage! It is I. Don't be afraid."
—MARK 6:50 (NIV)

I was physically and emotionally exhausted by 10:00 PM on moving day. My husband, Gordon, offered to stay behind to see the last items loaded onto the van while I got a head start with our six-year-old son, John, on the 120-mile drive to our new home. It was an emotional battle to start up the minivan and back out of our familiar driveway for the last time, hauling household chemicals that the movers would not transport. Just before I reached the interstate, I rounded a corner and heard an ominous hiss coming from somewhere inside the van. Fearing that something was about to explode, I swerved into a parking lot and screamed at John to get out of the car. I flung open the trunk and pawed through boxes of paints and cleaning supplies. At last I discovered the culprit—the vacuum cleaner wand had fallen on top of a spray bottle of carpet cleaner.

Shaking, I sank back into the car seat. Just then I saw a flash of lightning in the direction I would be heading. *I can't do this,* I thought. *I especially can't drive through a thunderstorm this late at night.* I gripped the steering wheel until my hands ached as I pulled back onto the interstate. The lightning became more visible as we sped into the countryside away from the interchange lights, but the darkness brought out something that the lights had hidden. Hovering just outside the top of my left-hand window was a single star. In the light of it, four ancient words spoken on another stormy night invaded my mind: *Courage. It is I.*

I took in a deep breath and repeated, "Courage. It is I." Each time I repeated it, I emphasized a different word, and the meaning grew. "*Courage.* It is I." (Karen, take heart.) "Courage. *It* is I." (This whole move is in My hands, a process that I will complete.) "Courage. It is *I.*" (I am here now, and I go before you.)

At 1:00 AM we finally arrived at the hotel, having gone through only a brief ten-minute period of mild rain. I found the Bible in the nightstand drawer and searched until I found the words, "Courage. It is I." Then, with a grateful heart, I closed the Bible and my exhausted eyes.

Father, this stormy journey is awfully dark. Help me
to know that You are really here.
—KAREN BARBER

January 23

And unto one he gave five talents, to another two, and to another one. . . .
—Matthew 25:15

*I*n 1944 I was a nineteen-year-old PFC living with thirty other GIs in a stable near Frome, England. One day the chaplain's assistant, PFC Lauck Crawford, a tall, soft-spoken Virginian who bunked with us, asked, "Can you help me on Sunday?"

"Sure," I said, wondering what I could possibly do for him.

On Sunday morning Lauck and I walked two hundred yards from our stable to a small, stone-walled, thatch-roofed church. Lauck pushed a huge iron key into the keyhole and unlocked the church's iron-hinged door.

Once we were inside, Lauck said, "Up there," and pointed to a hand-carved organ console with worn-down keys at the front of the church. Our combat boots clopping on the flagstone floor, we walked down the nave, which glowed with the light of stained-glass windows.

We squeezed between the ancient organ and the cold stone wall. Lauck pulled a hand bellows from a recess in the organ's back. "When I tap the organ twice," he said, "you pump this bellows. When I tap once, you stop." Then he stepped around to the front of the organ, leaving me and the bellows stuffed between the organ and the wall.

So this is what a one-talent person can do, I thought as I pumped the bellows and put air into the ancient organ. At the keyboard, Lauck accompanied the twenty or thirty soldiers who stood in the straight-backed wooden pews singing hymns. Hidden behind the huge organ, I wondered, as I listened to the music, if they were thinking as I was about the folks gathered at church back home.

It only took a little muscle-power to pump those bellows, but the singing would have been much poorer without them. Many years later, when I was asked to help out at another church and my first reaction was "I don't have the talent for that," I remembered that Sunday morning in England. And the Lord showed me I had two more talents: for pounding nails into wallboard and painting walls for our new Sunday school rooms.

You've given me a talent, Lord. Help me to discover it and use it in Your service.
—Richard Hagerman

The prudent see danger and take refuge....
—PROVERBS 27:12 (NIV)

*W*eary from a day of substitute teaching a large group of rambunctious teenagers, I settled into my seat on the bus, praying, *God, I could use a boost.* Just then I overheard two teenage girls talking about how they used Kool-Aid to highlight their hair. Cherry, they agreed, gave the best red highlights, while blueberry . . . I was intrigued. Kool-Aid was a lot cheaper than Clairol. Maybe this was the lift I'd prayed about—a new fashion twist.

As soon as I got home, I phoned Kool-Aid's information number. "This really sounds weird, but is it okay for me to use cherry Kool-Aid to color my hair?"

Apparently, this was not the first time the customer-service rep had been asked this question. She began reading through a prepared statement that went something like: "We do not recommend using Kool-Aid for anything other than ingestion as a beverage."

I persisted. "Have you ever heard of anyone using it on her hair?"

There was a pause, and then she lowered her voice and said, "Frankly, we get a lot more callers asking how to get Kool-Aid out of their hair than about how to put it on."

I laughed—which turned out to be the lift I needed—and hung up, deciding to stick with Clairol. But then I soberly considered the larger truth in her comment: How much easier it is to get into things than out of them. When I told my co-worker that I couldn't come to her bridal shower because I was "having out-of-town visitors that weekend," I had to invite people over so I wouldn't be a liar. And it was a lot easier for me to put those two pairs of high-heeled black pumps on my credit card than it was to work the seven hours at a substitute job to pay for them.

Over a tall glass of cherry Kool-Aid, I prayed:

God, let me look ahead a bit today and not "put the Kool-Aid in" before I think about how difficult it may be to "get the Kool-Aid out."
—LINDA NEUKRUG

And God said, "I will be with you...."
—Exodus 3:12 (NIV)

I stood in the kitchen and shuddered. It was nearly midnight, and we were experiencing one of our fierce winter windstorms that sweep across the front range of the Rocky Mountains.

"What's the use of going to bed?" I asked my husband, Lynn. "We won't be able to sleep." The words were barely out of my mouth when we heard an explosive crash. Our floor-to-ceiling corner window had blown in, spreading shattered glass everywhere.

"What shall we do?" I wailed in despair.

Lynn picked up the phone and dialed 911. Unfortunately, the dispatchers were swamped with calls and told us we'd have to "hold tight and wait until morning."

I looked at the awful mess and the gaping hole where dirt and dust continued to blow in and knew I couldn't "hold tight." Then I remembered Mike, the window repairman I'd called a few days earlier because we were concerned about the caulking around this very window. To my amazement, Mike answered. So I poured out our tale of woe.

"I'll be right there," he said simply.

I hung up the phone in shock. "He said he'd be right here," I told Lynn.

About ten minutes later, Mike and his wife showed up with a huge piece of canvas, a long ladder, a super-suction vacuum cleaner, and can-do smiles. As Mike pounded the canvas into place, his wife, Lynn, and I cleaned up most of the dirt and pieces of glass.

"We hardly know how to thank you," we told them about two hours later as they prepared to leave.

"Hey, this is our job," Mike said with a grin.

As Lynn and I fell into bed that night, the wind still howling around the house, we thanked God for bringing comfort into our chaos through a window repairman.

Father, thank You for being "right there" in my moments of fear and helplessness.
—Carol Kuykendall

January 26

May the Lord show mercy to the household of Onesiphorus,
because he often refreshed me....
—II Timothy 1:16 (niv)

*I*n a Bible study many years ago, I came across the name Onesiphorus and the simple statement of Paul, "He often refreshed me." I'm blessed these days to have a wonderful Onesiphorous in my life, an elderly lady called Sister Booker.

The other day, when I was feeling particularly tired and discouraged, the telephone rang. I picked up the phone and heard Sister Booker's voice, joyful as always, saying, "Brother Weary, God has chosen you as an eagle. An eagle has sharp vision and powerful wings. An eagle is one who rises above his troubles." Sister Booker seems to have a knack for knowing when I'm down. Then she calls me and reminds me to use the powerful aid of the Holy Spirit to rise above my circumstances and trust Him—to be like an eagle. Her messages are always uplifting and filled with a spiritual excitement all her own. Like Paul's friend Onesiphorus, Sister Booker has the gift of encouragement and is willing to use it for the benefit of others.

We all have special gifts from God, gifts He's given us to use for the good of the entire body of Christ. When we don't use them, the body suffers. Today, I want to make a commitment to use my gifts to brighten someone's life.

Lord, thank You for Sister Booker and all those like her who
use their gifts to help others. Help me to be like them.
—Dolphus Weary

JANUARY 27

*Where two or three are gathered together in my name,
there am I in the midst of them.*
—MATTHEW 18:20

*I*t was raining buckets when I walked through a side door into the Batesville United Methodist Church in Indiana. The rain was a fitting backdrop for the topic on which I was to speak: "Where do we go to draw spiritual water when our wells run dry?"

I had never been to Batesville before, and I didn't know a soul. I was nervous. When I looked through the double doors of the fellowship hall, I saw people everywhere, standing in groups, carrying food to long tables, looking at me. The minister appeared, a friendly man with crinkly eyes and a firm hand under my elbow. I was greeted, smiled at, and nudged to the head of the line for a wonderful meal.

By the time I got up to speak, the homegrown friendliness had eased my nerves. I talked about digging deeper into our faith and God's promises and finding hidden streams of water, thunderous even, like the rain hitting the roof.

When I was finished, the minister had the congregation line up in front of a table; on the table were a pitcher of water and paper cups. He poured; I handed out the cups of water. The line inched by me. Hands touched, eyes met, and smiles were exchanged as each person took a cup of water and drank. When the pitcher was empty, someone refilled it. Two people stepped forward to pour and give water to the minister and me: an unbroken circle of pouring, giving, receiving.

This silent, shared fellowship said something my talk hadn't: that the Water of Life also comes to us from each other, not in gushes, but in small cups. In smiles, in touches, in kind words and deeds, in little rituals we do together in Christ's name.

Lord, on this day, help me to give others to You in all I say and do.
—SHARI SMYTH

JANUARY 28

When we cry, "Abba! Father!" it is the Spirit himself bearing witness
with our spirit that we are children of God.
—ROMANS 8:15–16 (RSV)

I'm at my dining table, surrounded by all the candles I could find, during the most violent blizzard to hit Nebraska in thirty years. Roaring fifty-mile-an-hour winds are beating against the house, rattling the storm windows, splitting branches from winter-brittle trees. All power is out, so not even the furnace will come on. It's four degrees below zero, with a wind-chill factor of sixty to eighty below. I've closed all the blinds and drapes to keep in as much heat as possible, and I'm wearing three layers of clothes, but my hands, cheeks, and nose are beginning to get cold.

About an hour ago, I had picked up the phone to call my grown children to make sure they were all safe at home and okay, but the phone was dead! Up to that point, I was rather enjoying the storm and the involuntary cutback to simplicity. But that loss of contact with the outside world made me feel alone, isolated, cut off. So I went to my prayer chair and called upon my heavenly Father to protect those I love, to guide all who are stranded safely home, and to provide warmth, shelter, and food for those who are without them.

As I prayed, a great sense of connection with others by way of God came upon me, bringing with it a deep sense of peace and quiet protection. It's been a precious reminder to me that I'm never alone and that there's always an open circuit to my heavenly Father. It's a circuit by which I can be instantly connected with those I love and with all the other "children of God" with whom I share this planet.

Abba! Father! Thank You for creating this family of children,
and for being our always-available connecting circuit.
—MARILYN MORGAN KING

JANUARY 29

But whoever has the world's goods, and sees his brother in need and closes his heart against him, how does the love of God abide in him? Little children, let us not love with word or with tongue, but in deed and truth.

—I JOHN 3:17–18 (NAS)

I was caught red-handed this morning. I was feeding the birds, pouring seed into the ceramic containers that hang from tree limbs outside our kitchen window. Returning to the kitchen, I washed my hands in the sink and gazed out the window, smiling to see some small finches discover that their breakfast had been served. For a moment I basked in the knowledge of a good deed done. God was in His heaven and all was right with the world.

Suddenly, there was a blur of bright color as a red cardinal came whirring into view. Lighting on a bird feeder not five feet away from me, he thrust himself into the midst of the dull brown finches and started pecking at them. Drawing himself up to his full stature, he forced the finches to fly away. This cocky red baron now had the food to himself.

Indignant, I tapped on the window. "You rascal!" I hissed. "All of that food and you won't even share. You ought to be ashamed of yourself."

At that instant, God's Spirit tapped on the window of my awareness, and I got the message: That cardinal was really me, red hair and all. God has given me so many good things, and I need to share far more than birdseed.

Dear God, I know my selfishness breaks Your heart. Forgive me and transform my greed into love. Amen.

—SCOTT WALKER

"Blessed is the man who trusts in the Lord...."
—JEREMIAH 17:7 (NAS)

I was working in my office when the phone rang. It was my son Reggie. "Dad," he said, "I need your advice." Now, Reggie hasn't asked me for advice in quite some time. In fact, there had been a few times over the past few years when he thought I was giving him more advice than he cared to have. So I was both surprised and glad to hear his request. *Now that he's twenty-five years old,* I thought, *maybe he's growing up.*

Reggie wanted to talk to me about buying a car. We'd given him an older car when he graduated from college, but it had finally broken down. He needed a new one, which would be the first car he purchased on his own. We talked about the style and make of car he was interested in, the price range he was looking at, how large a monthly car payment he could afford, and how the car payment would affect his budget.

For the next few days, my phone rang off the hook. I didn't really give Reggie much advice; mostly I listened to him and asked questions. And when he finally bought a car, I knew that he'd considered his decision carefully, and he knew that even though the car he bought was not the one I would have purchased, he had my support.

Best of all, I'd been able to trust Reggie to make a good decision. It isn't easy for a father to let go, but I learned that I could be available to my son without trying to control him. Even if it meant biting my tongue once or twice, I could listen, ask a few questions, and let God go to work in Reggie's life.

Lord, help me trust You in all things, even in the decisions of my children.
—DOLPHUS WEARY

January 31

Ye shall do no unrighteousness in judgment...but in righteousness shalt thou judge thy neighbor.
—Leviticus 19:15

*L*ouise, who lives next door to me, is something of a recluse, keeping pretty much to her house. She was always cordial when I caught her in her yard, but my visits to her house were few, confined to the kitchen area via the back door. When I found out that she was in the hospital, I didn't visit. She had told me that when she was sick she preferred to be left alone—no visits, no phone calls, not even cards. Her husband and sons confirmed this every time I asked after her. *So just let her live in her house,* I told myself, *and I'll live in mine. If she doesn't want to be a good neighbor, I won't bother her.*

Then winter arrived and Louise came home from her long hospital stay. A few weeks later, my morning paper began appearing on the front porch, rather than at the end of my driveway, folded and laid flat against the front door. I'd tried to thank the early-morning walkers in our neighborhood, but they all denied doing it.

One cold, rainy morning I rose much earlier than usual and headed toward the front door. As I opened it, I saw Louise in her robe and slippers headed toward the porch, my paper in her hand. "So you're the one!" I called to her. "I wondered who was being so thoughtful of me." She shrugged slightly and smiled. "I go out to pick up my paper," she said, "and I just get yours, too. I know you sleep later than I do. It could get soaked, or a dog might take it."

How lightly she treated it! This dear woman, whom I thought cold and unneighborly, was quietly adding a bit of comfort to my life. Just because she wasn't an outgoing person, I'd failed to see—or even imagine—the sweetness of her spirit.

Father, help me open my eyes and my spirit to the goodness with which You surround me.
—Drue Duke

February

"My God, in whom I trust!" For it is He who delivers you from the snare....
—PSALM 91:2–3 (NAS)

I'd had it with Willie, our fat gray-and-white tomcat. If we let him sleep inside during the night, he'd wake me up around one o'clock with a constant *mmeeeeeeeoow* until I let him out. Then, promptly at four o'clock, he'd stand at the front door and demand to come back inside. When I let him in, he'd meow relentlessly at the side of our bed until I stomped upstairs and topped off his bowl with a few more pieces of dry food. During the day, Willie paced in my kitchen window boxes, trampling through my flowers, his wide eyes seeming to say, *Meet my needs. Meet my needs.*

I complained to Jamie, our twenty-year-old daughter, who had just finished house-sitting for us for a weekend. "I don't know what you're talking about, Mom. While I was in charge, Willie behaved like a perfectly normal cat. He slept at the foot of my bed all night. I fed him once each morning. He purred a lot, but I don't think he meowed much at all."

Is it just me, God? I prayed. *What am I doing wrong with Willie? Even our cat has begun to control me!* God's gentle Spirit seemed to impress an unwelcome truth on me: Too often I handled friends and family just the way I handled Willie. I'd zoom in to fix people's problems, until my constant "helping" made them think I was at their beck and call and left me feeling exhausted and irritable.

Then I came up with a simple plan: From now on, I'd shut our bedroom door at night and turn on the humidifier so I couldn't hear Willie. He could meow as much as he wanted. I wasn't going to jump up to get him more food. In a few days, Willie learned the new rules. So did I.

Lord, before I start trying to fix everything and everyone, remind me to pray and share my problem with You.
—JULIE GARMON

FEBRUARY 2

Ye are all the children of light, and the children of the day:
we are not of the night, nor of darkness.
—I THESSALONIANS 5:5

*A*s I walked down the driveway to the mailbox, Stevie from next door came shuffling by. He's usually a cheerful little guy, but today he frowned and his head was down.

"Something wrong?" I asked.

"Yeah," he replied as he kicked a chunk of icy snow into the street. "The groundhog saw his shadow and we're gonna have six more weeks of winter!"

So that's why he was so gloomy! And I realized there is a grain of truth in that superstition—a truth that has nothing to do with the weather. How often we let predictions of gloom spoil an otherwise sunny day. How many times I've looked in the direction of the shadow instead of in the direction of the sun.

If the world seems gray today, let's remember that a shadow is evidence that the sun is shining!

I'll turn my back on darkness, Father, by facing Your Son.
—MARILYN MORGAN KING

February 3

"How can I give you up, Ephraim? How can I hand you over, Israel?…"
—HOSEA 11:8 (NIV)

*M*y wife and I have two sons, Patrick and Ted. Patrick is my wife's son. When I met them, Patrick was two years old. We adopted Ted when he was seven.

Patrick, who is only eight months older than Ted, was excited about getting a younger brother, but Ted was—and is—much taller than Patrick. Patrick wanted someone who would obey his every command, and Ted refused to obey any. After about two months, Patrick came to me and announced, "It's not working out."

"What's not working out?"

"Ted. We have to get rid of him. We have to get someone smaller. And nicer."

"When?" I asked.

"Right now!" Patrick insisted. "I mean, we don't have to find a new brother right away. We just have to get rid of Ted."

"What if we got rid of you instead of Ted? He seems to like it here."

"Dad, don't be stupid! Mom would never do that. Would she?"

I pretended to ponder the matter.

"I'm sure she wouldn't," Patrick said. "Trouble is, she won't get rid of Ted either. That's why I came to you."

I had to disappoint Patrick. Despite the doubt in his mind, as a father, I could never be persuaded to keep one son and give up the other. God told the prophet Hosea that He could never give up on Israel despite the peoples' sins, and it's comforting to know that God will never give up on any of us either. He will never give up on Ted, and He didn't give up on Patrick…even when he wanted to get rid of his new brother.

> *Dear God, thank You for never giving up on us,*
> *even when we give up on each other.*
> —TIM WILLIAMS

FEBRUARY 4

For it is written, As I live, saith the Lord, every knee shall bow to me....
—ROMANS 14:11

*O*ne of my most vivid teenage memories is of my father, a pastor, kneeling to pray beside our living room sofa. For him, respect for the majesty and authority of God meant kneeling when he came into God's presence through prayer.

I, on the other hand, have taken a more informal approach to prayer. I encouraged my own four children to pray openly and spontaneously as they were growing up, but we never knelt to pray. Our son Philip developed an especially deep and meaningful prayer life, along with a hunger to study the Bible. I often thought how that would have pleased my father, who died when Phil was just two and a half years old.

After we moved from Alaska to Minnesota, Phil, then twenty-four, came to live with us for a few months. Every day he would shut himself away for a time of prayer in our upstairs guest bedroom. One morning, after he had left the room, I noticed that the bedspread was rumpled at the foot of the bed. I walked in, and as I bent to smooth it, I saw two distinct indentations in the soft rose carpet—the impressions of my son's knees.

Almost shyly, I knelt down on the same spot and settled my own knees into the carpet. With tears of joy and gratitude, I thanked the Lord for His generosity in giving me a father and a son who loved Him in the same way—on their knees.

Lord God, help me carry the blessings of prayer into my family's future.
—CAROL KNAPP

"I have come to bring fire to the earth, and, oh, that my task were completed! There is a terrible baptism ahead of me, and how I am pent up until it is accomplished!"

—LUKE 12:49–50 (TLB)

I'm not an autograph collector, but in our home we do have one framed autograph. I got it for my youngest son, Andrew, in 1991 when I was working for a radio station in Milwaukee, Wisconsin.

One day, baseball great Hank Aaron came to the station to promote his book *I Had a Hammer: The Hank Aaron Story*. During a commercial break, I asked Hank for his autograph. He smiled and wrote his name in big letters across a sheet from my radio station notepad.

Of course, Andrew was thrilled. After all, Hank Aaron still holds Major League Baseball's record for the most home runs hit by any player. Although I'm not a diehard baseball fan, I was even more thrilled than Andrew to have this man's autograph. Why? Because of the struggles Hank Aaron had during his career. He began playing at a time when few African-American athletes even made it into the big leagues. And because of racism, he had to struggle against the odds time and again, often facing taunts and jeers from the world outside the baseball field.

Do you ever feel you're battling a war against all odds? Do pressures in your home or job make you feel you're not accomplishing anything worthwhile? Next time you feel that way, think about Hank Aaron. For more than twenty years he just "hammered" away, facing the struggles head-on, until he beat Babe Ruth's record by forty-one home runs!

By the way, today is "Hammerin' Hank's" birthday.

Heavenly Father, when I feel as if I'm not accomplishing anything, give me the grace and determination to keep hammerin' away and remind me that someday, with Your help, I will have accomplished something great.

—PATRICIA LORENZ

And behold, there arose a great storm on the sea, so that the boat
was being swamped by the waves; but he was asleep.
—MATTHEW 8:24 (RSV)

*L*ike everyone else, I've been through a few thunderstorms in my life. The first I remember was when I was two or three years old, living near Chicago while my father attended Wheaton College. I remember the gentle touch of my grandfather's hands on my ankles as he coaxed me out from under a bed. Bundling me into something warm, he took me outdoors, sat me on his lap under the shelter of the front porch, and explained how "the big clouds can't see in the night and bang into each other and yell, 'Ow!'" Grandpa, I quickly realized, wasn't scared at all. Rather, he exulted in the fury of the skies. Soon I, too, caught his excitement and lost my fear.

Emotional storms have not been so easily resolved. While I've seen God's eventual provision and healing, I've never learned to appreciate biopsies or losing my house in the same way I do a raging wind. It's difficult to trust Jesus amid harsh emotional, physical, financial, or spiritual crises. Like His disciples, I tend to panic. I ask God, "Don't You care? Don't You see?"

At least I did until Pastor Sam came to our church.

"Has it ever occurred to you," he asked us when preaching about Jesus asleep in the storm-tossed boat, "that He slept because He had no fear? And that He slept, safe, unafraid, with those He loved?"

No, it had never occurred to me.

"He does us the same honor," said Pastor Sam.

This last observation was even more revealing. And so now, when life's storms overtake me, instead of "waking Jesus up" with the same old accusation, "Don't You care if I perish?" I feel a sense of honor, not abandonment.

Lord, help me to remain unafraid.
—BRENDA WILBEE

From childhood you have known the sacred writings which are able to give you
the wisdom that leads to salvation through faith which is in Christ Jesus.
—II TIMOTHY 3:15 (NAS)

I first met Father Bill Houghton in 1958. He was a young man in his early twenties, a recent seminary graduate and a newly arrived Episcopal missionary in the Philippines. Most important, he was the new Bible teacher for my second-grade class at the Brent School.

Few second graders liked Bible class; there was something about it that was always too serious for us. We would much rather be tormenting our reading teacher or playing. Then Father Houghton arrived. I remember what he was wearing the day I met him: khaki pants, a black clergy shirt, white clerical collar, and white bucks. White bucks! That's what Elvis Presley and cool teenage boys wore; even a second grader knew that. Suddenly, Bible class got a lot better.

Today, forty-three years later, I had lunch with Father Houghton in Waco, Texas. Now retired, Bill Houghton has stayed trim and fit. Silver and gray fleck his dark hair, and his handsome face is creased with the character lines of age. I was disappointed to learn he no longer owns a pair of white bucks.

As I watched Father Houghton stir sugar into his coffee, I asked myself, *What did this man teach me about the Bible? I don't remember a single lecture, story, or illustration. So what did he teach me?*

The answer came quickly. He taught a squirming second grader two things of immeasurable value: First, the Bible is important, important enough for a young man to travel far from home to teach Bible stories. Second, and most important, he taught me that you can love the Bible and wear white bucks, too.

Dear God, thank You for all of the people who have taught me that
the Bible is important, interesting, and always relevant. Amen.
—SCOTT WALKER

Lord, be thou my helper.
—PSALM 30:10

*G*od, help me to cheer up Mrs. Menina." She was the Russian woman I was tutoring in English. I'd already gotten her a plant and some upbeat musical tapes, but she still seemed down lately. The crimson sign of a pet store lured me in; she'd once mentioned admiring some goldfish. I'd buy her a fish!

Once in the pet store, though, I had second thoughts. Never having bought fish, I wasn't sure how expensive they'd be. The clerk said, "We only sell feeder fish."

Not knowing anything about goldfish, this sounded to me like some rare exotic breed. "I haven't got much money on me," I cautioned. "And I'll need two. I wouldn't want them to be lonely." Hoping to get some sympathy for my small purse, I added, "They're for an elderly woman I volunteer with. I want something to make her smile."

An odd look. "How about if I give you two for the price of one?"

I was stunned at his generosity. "God bless you," I said. "That's so kind of you."

He went in the back and eventually came out carrying a plastic bag with two large goldfish. *Uh-oh,* I thought, *they look expensive. I'll have to charge them.* Silently the man handed the bag to me, then punched in a few numbers on the big metal cash register. I handed him my Visa. He looked me in the eye. "That'll be twenty-four cents."

I stared at him and burst out laughing, and after a moment the man joined in. "Twenty-four cents!" I said, gasping with laughter. My prayer had been answered. I now had something to cheer up Mrs. Menina...the story of how I bought her the goldfish!

God, when I pray for something, let me trust that You will answer my prayer—although not always in the way I expect!
—LINDA NEUKRUG

41

FEBRUARY 9

I am the Lord thy God . . . which leadeth thee by the way that thou shouldest go.
—ISAIAH 48:17

*A*neighbor of mine is a highway surveyor and recently we were talking about one of his projects, a bypass being built around a nearby city. His assignment: to build the shortest route (for convenience and economy), the safest route (with rivers, woods, and terrain some of the considerations), and the least disruptive route (avoiding business and home sites as much as possible). "And your job is to show the road builders the way," I commented.

"Yes, my associates and I are the Lewis and Clark of the moment." We laughed at the comparison, but to anyone who knows of the 1803 assignment Thomas Jefferson gave Meriwether Lewis ("Find a safe passage to the Pacific"), it was good hyperbole. Except, of course, it was nature-wise Native Americans who guided the famous expedition, not surveyors. Otherwise, Lewis and Clark would have surely failed.

All of us have had guides in our lives—parents, teachers, pastors, relatives, friends—who took us by the hand and ushered us through unknown lands. And when we became adults, it was our turn to be the "way-showers" to those who came behind, wanderers and seekers in need of direction. St. Paul showed new disciples of Christ "the way" to a God-pleasing life with his letters, one of which I'm reading now. "None of us liveth to himself, and no man dieth to himself," St. Paul states (Romans 14:7). Poet John Donne was right when he wrote that "no man is an island." We are all dependent upon God and fellow journeyers—surveyors, if you will—who help us chart our path and find the best course for our lives.

> *Thank You, God, for Your Word and Your Son,*
> *Guides beyond compare—bar none.*
> —FRED BAUER

Then he took the cup, gave thanks and offered it to them....
—MARK 14:23 (NIV)

*H*oly Communion has always been a mystery to me. Probably because it is a mystery! Since childhood I've partaken in many different churches in a variety of ways: kneeling at the altar and dipping a wafer into a chalice of wine; or sitting in the pew and receiving spongy pieces of bread and little plastic cups of grape juice. As I child I would roll my tongue through the empty cup after drinking the grape juice so as not to miss a drop. It appalled the adults, but it satisfied a need in me to get it all.

Now, as an adult, I find a need to drain every drop of meaning from this sacred ritual. As I sit in the pew on our one communion Sunday a month, I must make myself fully present to this mystery, no matter how tired or distracted I am. For whether I know it or not, I'm hungry and need to be fed. And in front of me is the Food.

I look at the plain wooden table set with linen, the chalice, the plate. Gathered round are the ministers and elders. I listen to the words of invitation as I heard them in childhood, in simple faith, a child at the table with the family of God.

Jesus is the head of the family and is also the sustenance. Somehow, by receiving Him in this manner, my hunger is filled. I am being nourished, both body and soul, in a way nothing else could. I know it by faith. I know it because Jesus commanded it.

Jesus, thank You for feeding me at this table and making me whole.
—SHARI SMYTH

FEBRUARY 11

O taste and see that the Lord is good....
—PSALM 34:8

I knew I was over the flu yesterday when I could smell the coffee brewing. I lingered at the coffeemaker, inhaling that heady aroma. The sense of smell—how rarely I stopped to appreciate it!

I poured the coffee and sat down on a kitchen stool, hands wrapped around the warmth of the mug. Touch—another dimension I seldom gave conscious thought to. And taste! How often I ate mechanically, my mind elsewhere.

On hearing and sight I gave myself better marks: I'd often been grateful for those. I had seen my grandfather's face when he got his first hearing aid. "I can hear a clock ticking!" he said. And my father-in-law, who was blind by the time I entered the family, had said about the weeks of failing vision, "I'd never looked so keenly at things! Seeing everything for the last time, each object had an intense beauty."

But why had I never thanked God for the other three senses? Surely these were blessings, too!

I roamed through the house with broader awareness, delighting in the smooth curve of a wooden chair back, the coldness of a window pane, the nubby wool of my sweater. I peeled an orange, enjoying the sharp whiff of rind; sniffed the potted chrysanthemum on the windowsill; opened a dresser drawer to breathe in the balsam sachet.

My devotional life, I realized as I sat with a second mug of coffee, savoring each sip, has always been centered on the mind—on words and concepts. But worship in the Bible includes so much more! The joy of dance and song. The perfume of incense. The delights of food and drink. The involvement of all the senses. "O taste and see that the Lord is good," sang the psalmist. A drop of honey is still placed on the page as a Jewish child begins the study of the Torah, signaling that the senses, too, are doorways to God.

Help me worship You today, Lord, with my whole being.
—ELIZABETH SHERRILL

"My command is this: Love each other as I have loved you."
—JOHN 15:12 (NIV)

*A*braham Lincoln had a unique way of saying things. He could use words to make people think about issues, like slavery and states' rights. But he could use words to make people laugh, too.

One day a man came to Lincoln and asked, "How long should a man's legs be?" Lincoln looked first at the short man's little legs, then down at his own long ones. Slowly, he smiled. "Well," he said, "I reckon a man's legs ought to be long enough to reach the floor."

And that's the way God made each of us: with legs just the right length to reach the floor. And ears big enough to hear the song of birds and the laughter of children. With mouths wide enough for smiles and arms perfectly formed for hugs. Shoulders perfect for leaning on, backs meant to be patted. We've each got just the right equipment to help make the world a better place.

What better way to honor our sixteenth president than by doing something this very day to make the world a little more peaceful, a little less painful?

Creator of all perfect things, thank You for the opportunity to serve my fellow human beings.
—MARY LOU CARNEY

FEBRUARY 13

Train up a child in the way he should go: and when he is old,
he will not depart from it.

—PROVERBS 22:6

The organist had begun to play the opening notes of the first hymn of the morning worship service when I heard an unfamiliar couple and a small boy enter the pew behind mine. I turned to smile and handed them an opened hymnal. During the service, I became aware of the father holding a small white pad in his hands and writing or drawing something to entertain the child.

I must tell them about our children's programs, I thought. *A child that age should be in a class with other children.*

When the service was over, I turned, hand extended, to introduce myself and welcome them to our church. The man shook my hand, introduced himself and his wife, and said, "I hope we didn't make any noise or disturb you during the service."

"Oh no," I assured him.

"Daddy was drawing this for me," the little boy said, proudly handing the pad to me. The crude sketching I saw seemed to represent a person. There was a small circle for the head and a larger one for the body, with two long lines extending downward from it for legs. On each side of the body was a short line representing an arm. From each of these fanned five smaller lines.

"Oh?" I said, studying the sketch. Then, pointing to one group of the smallest lines, I asked, "And what are these?"

The child's face broke into a broad grin. "You don't recognize them?" he asked. "That's a drawing of Jesus and those are the fingers on His hands. Daddy says Jesus is always reaching His hands out to us."

I could find no words to speak. I simply handed him his drawing, put my arms around his shoulders, and gave him a big hug.

Dear Lord, bless all the parents who make sure their children know about Your
Son. May I never forget what my daddy taught me about Him. Amen.

—DRUE DUKE

Beloved, let us love one another: for love is of God. . . .
—I John 4:7

I inherited my aunt's Bible. Lovingly worn, it falls open to her favorite passages. With her Bible in my hands, it's impossible not to think of my aunt and the many times she turned to it for strength: when my uncle was missing in action during World War II and later when she learned he was a prisoner of war, after the war when they learned to make peace with their childlessness, and during my uncle's long illness when my aunt prayed for him to let go and go to heaven.

After my uncle died, my aunt spent many years in poor health. She often slept with her Bible on her lap. During those last days she spoke through tears about how she longed for her Phil and how she couldn't wait to see him again.

The first time I opened my aunt's Bible, I was awestruck at the beautiful cards tucked in the pages, reminders of my great-grandfather, grandfather, great-uncle, and uncle. Then, after having the Bible for almost a year, I found pressed deep in its pages a scrap of notebook paper folded into a tiny heart. It read:

Dearest husband,

I love you more than I will ever be able to express with pen and ink. You are my rock. My strength. My comfort. God bless you for your goodness. I love you always and forever.

Dear Lord, on this Valentine's Day, remind me that even though love isn't always perfect or easy, its strength and beauty are everlasting.

—Sabra Ciancanelli

FEBRUARY 15

My voice shalt thou hear in the morning, O Lord....
—PSALM 5:3

*I*t was 5:00 AM and all was quiet as I walked upstairs with my steamy cup of tea. I sat down in my chair in the study, flipped on the tiny lamp, opened my Bible, and began to read. My daily routine had been the same for months: tea, chair, lamp, Bible.

This morning, though, was different. My cat Smudge jumped into my lap and nudged my hand. When I didn't stop to pet her, she climbed on top of my Bible.

"Smudge!" I exclaimed. "No! I'm reading." I pushed her off my lap, but she refused to give up. She jumped back on my lap again and again.

"Okay, Smudge, you win," I said with a sigh. I put down my Bible and began petting her as I prayed.

In church that Sunday, my pastor shared a story. When he was a child, he had a good friend with whom he played soldiers and raced toy cars. When they grew into teenagers, they played the same sports. But after high school, they lost touch. Just recently they had run into each other at a restaurant. It was an awkward meeting; so much time had passed that they didn't have much to say to each other.

"We don't want our relationship with God to end up the same way," our pastor cautioned. "Prayer every day keeps us close to and in touch with God."

As I listened to the sermon, something clicked: I'd been so focused on reading my Bible that I'd been cutting my prayer time short! I wasn't taking the time to listen to what God was saying to me through His Word.

The next morning, after reading my Bible, I welcomed Smudge onto my lap while I prayed. Thanks to a persistent cat and a timely story from my minister, those wee hours of the morning have a new routine: tea, chair, lamp, Bible—and prayer.

Remind me, gracious God, that knowing You is more than just reading about You.
—MELODY BONNETTE

FEBRUARY 16

Seek and read from the book of the Lord....
—ISAIAH 34:16 (RSV)

*B*efore leaving the house this morning I picked up my grocery list and glanced at the calendar: "11:30, dentist." *Better stick a paperback in my purse—there's always a wait. Better look up the phone number of that lampshade place, too.*

An ordinary day...with an extraordinary gift in constant use. The gift of reading. So much a part of daily life, I usually accept it without thinking. But because this morning's newspaper had featured a story on illiteracy around the world, I found myself aware all day of this taken-for-granted skill: the street signs as I drove, the flyer of specials at the grocery store, the letters I scooped from the mailbox on my return, the e-mail waiting on my screen.

Reading is an essential component of daily existence, but also my daily joy! A morning without *Daily Guideposts* is an impoverished one, bedtime without a book unthinkable. Once my husband and I spent a week in a house where there was not a single book or magazine, not even a seed catalogue, though the family were farmers. So starved were we for anything in print, we found ourselves opening the kitchen cupboard and reading the labels on the cans.

Literacy—how much of the world is still without it! I remembered the day I took a stack of nutrition leaflets to the school where I taught in Uganda. "Take them home to your parents," I urged the students. Next day the leaflets were still there; the kids explained with embarrassment that their parents could not read.

What does the gift of reading bestow? Information, ease of communication, the past and the present at the turning of a page, the knowledge of God. From the Jews comes our heritage of Holy Scripture—sacred writing, the Bible passages with which I begin each day. But sacred reading as well, without which even the greatest book of all is only little black marks on a page.

Lord Jesus, Who asked so often, "Have you not read?" guide my reading today.
—ELIZABETH SHERRILL

The blessings of your father are mighty beyond the blessings of the eternal mountains, the bounties of the everlasting hills....

—GENESIS 49:26 (RSV)

*H*olding the sleeping infant, I compose a silent speech to him, trying to impart some important matters by osmosis.

Listen, son, above all things, be straightforward with your love. Tend to the generous; admire mettle in the small; try to be awake to miracles, whether they are rivers or lovers or beggars. There is more beauty in this world than we can handle.

Tell the truth. Be gentle. Be open. Work hard. Choose joyful work, which is better than money. In games, find joy and milk it. Praise light, as it comes from the Maker, like truth and music.

Savor the old, as they have lived furiously and helped make your world. Pay them with love, and bring your children to them to bless and be blessed, for children are pure, closest to the light, freshly made.

Know that God has the same face everywhere, if not the same name. The search for what is true and kind will lead to God.

Touch what you love, your mother's face, your father's beard, and never be shy with a kiss. Listen: Time eats everything, so hold your family close to heart and hand, while heart and hand you have, and time to sing.

Dear Lord, for this sleeping miracle, and all miracles, which is to say every second and every breath, thanks.

—BRIAN DOYLE

FEBRUARY 18

We give thanks to God always for you all, making mention of you in our prayers.
—I Thessalonians 1:2

Mable Sharpston, who helps my neighbor Ina, was driving the three of us to the grocery store. As we turned into the parking lot, Mable asked me, "Mrs. Duke, will you pray for my son and me?"

From the backseat, I answered, "Of course I will. Is there something in particular I should pray about?"

"I want to hear from him," she said. "He's moved, and I don't know where he is. I just need for him to call me." She parked the car and turned to face me. "I want to hear from him," she repeated, "and know that he's all right."

"Have you put him in God's hands?" I asked her. On her face, I saw the anguish of a frightened mother. "I will pray constantly," I promised her, "but you must pray, too. And you should stop fretting. You could make yourself sick."

As we shopped, I prayed silently. And at home, the rest of that day and the next, I talked to God—over the dishpan, the vacuum cleaner, with everything I did.

Bright and early the following morning, the telephone rang, and I heard Mable's voice ringing with joy. "He called me!" she said. "He didn't realize it had been so long or that I would be so worried. Thank you very much for praying for me!"

"I feel honored that you asked me," I told her. "Now let's both remember to thank our Lord."

Thank You, Father, for this and the many prayers You hear and answer. Let me always be ready to come to You when there is a problem. Amen.
—Drue Duke

FEBRUARY 19

Let brotherly love continue.
—HEBREWS 13:1

*E*very morning before work I like to sit in the clouds. I mean, I sit in the men's steam room at my gym. You hear amazing things in the clouds of steam: men's voices bragging or complaining about work, bragging or complaining about their wives, bragging or complaining about their children. There's something therapeutic in sitting in a room where you can barely see your hand in front of your face, like sitting in white darkness and sounding off about life.

Today there were just three of us, three dim, fleshy outlines. Perhaps because he felt comfortably anonymous, the man on my left suddenly said, "I haven't had a drink in over a week."

I sat wondering what I was supposed to say to this, or if I was supposed to say anything at all, when the man on my right volunteered, "I haven't had a drink in five years."

"How do you do it?" the man on my left asked softly. "It's the hardest thing I've ever tried. But I know if I keep drinking I'm gonna lose everything. I saw my dad go through it, saw him lose it all. Still, I want to drink."

Then the man with five years of sobriety told an amazing story of how his life was nearly destroyed by alcohol. He talked about his recovery, the faith that he had found, and the life that he rebuilt. His voice flowed with gratitude. When he had finished, he asked the man on my left which way he was going when he left the gym. "Uptown," the man replied.

"I'll walk with you," the man said. "Maybe we'll grab a cup of coffee."

With that they were gone. Later, as I dressed in the locker room, I wondered who they were. But I couldn't tell, and it didn't matter. What did matter is that I had seen God working in a most unusual place, as is so often the case.

You never know what you'll find in the clouds.

Make me ever vigilant, God, for signs of You at work.
—EDWARD GRINNAN

For we wrestle not against flesh and blood, but against principalities, against powers, against the rulers of the darkness of this world, against spiritual wickedness in high places.

—EPHESIANS 6:12

My husband, Bill, and I stood by the elegantly curtained ten-foot window, looking out through the white columns of the portico at the lights of cars passing on Pennsylvania Avenue. The air around us was charged with power. I shivered with excitement.

We had entered the White House on the lower level, passed the China Room, and slowly climbed the marble stairs to the main floor. We wandered wide-eyed from the East Room through the Green, Blue, and Red rooms to the State Dining Room. The Air Force Strolling Strings played softly from room to room, complementing the Marine Band performing in the center hall.

Soon the president would come downstairs and, because he knew and loved my in-laws, we would have personal messages to take from him back to them in Ohio. For now, we had paused in a quiet place just to collect our thoughts on being where we were.

"Your first time?"

We turned to find a famous columnist grinning at us. We nodded.

"Well, this is my thirty-fourth one of these. And I still get goose bumps."

Ever since that first electrifying evening at 1600 Pennsylvania Avenue more than twenty-five years ago, I have prayed regularly for each of our presidents, regardless of party. I have sensed firsthand how great is the power that surrounds them, and how deeply they need our prayers.

How good it is on this Presidents' Day to pray for those in authority. If only we remember every day!

Lord, may You always be the Power behind the throne for this nation. Please grant both knowledge and wisdom to our leaders, from the top down.

—ROBERTA ROGERS

FEBRUARY 21

They that dwell in the land of the shadow of death,
upon them hath the light shined.
—ISAIAH 9:2

*A*s I walked down the corridor of the second floor of the nursing home where my dad has lived for the past three years, I noticed the silence. Usually there were residents in wheelchairs along the way, and by this time I knew many of them by name. Then I realized that those who could get around were probably downstairs at an Ash Wednesday worship service conducted by several churches in our area. My dad always used to attend, but this year he wasn't well enough to spend much time out of bed. Poor guy—although he was in the advanced stages of Alzheimer's and sometimes didn't even know who I was, he did remember every word of the Lord's Prayer. Would he realize what day this was and wonder why he wasn't a part of it? What would he think when he saw the ashes on my forehead? I wasn't looking forward to the visit.

A man and a woman came out of his room. I didn't recognize them, but they stopped and smiled. "Are you Ray's daughter?" the woman asked. When I nodded, she told me they were ministers from one of the local churches, and while the regular service was going on downstairs, they were visiting residents who were confined to bed.

"Thank you!" I said. "This means a lot to both of us."

When I walked into Dad's room, he was sitting up in bed and smiling. He pointed to my forehead and said, "Hey, just like you!" And there on his own forehead was a smudgy cross. He was part of the worship service, after all, and he knew it.

In that moment I understood that God never excludes any of us from His love and concern. Even if we can't get to Him, He comes to us—wherever we are.

Dear Lord, when times of darkness lie ahead of us, let us remember that
the light of Christ's love shines through them. Amen.
—PHYLLIS HOBE

Thou didst gird me with strength for the battle....
—II SAMUEL 22:40 (RSV)

God bless my seventh-grade history teacher, Mrs. Weaver, for turning the dollar-bill figure of George Washington into flesh and blood for us. She walked him into our lives with descriptive tidbits told with dramatic flair.

We knew, for instance, that Washington had red hair covered with a powdered wig, that he had false teeth that gave him fits, that his face was scarred from smallpox, that he was a farmer ahead of his time in rotating crops, that in the French and Indian War he had two horses shot out from under him, that he was shy but learned to be sociable, that he wrestled a bad temper, that during the crushing winter of Valley Forge he knelt in the snow to pray.

And we knew that when, in the throes of victory over the British, the people were ready to crown him king—King George—he penned a hasty reply from his Mount Vernon home: "Banish the thought from your minds!" Instead, he submitted to the Constitution, and with Congress launched a republic, under God, with liberty and justice for all.

On this day, Washington is rightly honored as the father of our country, a larger-than-life figure. But, as Mrs. Weaver would tell you, he was also a person with foibles and faults like all of us, whose virtues are not just to be admired. They're to be imitated.

Lord, help me to have faith in You and stay the course through wins and losses.
—SHARI SMYTH

Now may our Lord Jesus Christ himself, and God our Father, who loved us and gave us eternal comfort and good hope through grace, comfort your hearts and establish them in every good work and word.

—II THESSALONIANS 2:16–17 (RSV)

*D*avid Allen is a man with cancer. He was told he had one year to live, but he continues in his dry cleaning business with a full-time workday. Through the years David has helped friends and acquaintances with their personal hardships. He continues to do this. He calls himself a "silent evangelist" and finds many ways to give practical help to people in his community. For instance, he arranged music lessons for six children and provided pianos for some of them. When he learned that a family could not bury a relative because they could not afford to buy a cemetery plot, he saw to it that they got the money.

David is a man at peace with God. His philosophy is "If you give the world the best you have, the best will come back to you." David has already lived two years since the doctor gave him his one-year verdict. The Lord is blessing him as he gives to others.

Dear Lord, may I look for ways to help others today. Amen.

— RUTH STAFFORD PEALE

FEBRUARY 24

Let them now make intercession to the Lord....
—JEREMIAH 27:18

*S*t. Mark's Church, Mount Kisco, New York, where my wife and I have belonged for forty years, happens to be located down the street from the village fire department. It often seems to us that emergencies wait for Sunday morning. With devastating timing, the minister will reach the climax of the sermon when a window-rattling blast of the firehorn will drown him out. Long. Short. A brief silence. Then another teeth-jarring blare. The effect inside St. Mark's is always the same: paralysis of the service.

Different preachers have handled the intrusion in different ways. Some simply wait patiently until the interruption is over. One assistant rector, I remember, tried to outshout the horn. Another squeezed snatches of her sermon into the pauses. One Sunday not long after our current rector's arrival, just as he began to preach, the deafening firehorn stopped him short. *How,* I wondered as the air vibrated to the din, *will Stephen handle this introduction to St. Mark's noisy neighbor?*

As the first blast quivered into silence he said, "Let's pray right now for whatever crisis lies behind this call for help." I followed Stephen's lead. Instead of waiting out the interruptions with irritation, I pictured possible scenes—a burning house, an overturned oil truck on Interstate 684. I had no idea what the need was, only that someone was in trouble and that rescuers were being summoned to help. *Go with the emergency crew, Father. Give Your calm to anyone in danger.*

Intercession! What a creative response to interruptions, whatever form they take: a traffic tie-up, a power outage, a broken appointment, a snowstorm. Each one is a chance to assume our God-given role as intercessors.

Thank You, Father, for the interruptions in my agenda that make room for Yours.
—JOHN SHERRILL

Suffer the little children to come unto me, and forbid them not....
—MARK 10:14

*M*y arms were filled with groceries as I entered the house. On the floor just inside the door, I spotted a piece of paper covered with what looked like a child's drawing. I put the groceries down and picked up the paper. It was an invitation, designed by our six-year-old neighbor, Billy, to attend a school play at nine thirty the next morning.

Billy was in kindergarten, and he was playing the lead role in Peter Rabbit. I wanted to go, but June was my busiest month, and I had two appointments scheduled for the next morning. I didn't want to disappoint Billy, but I had responsibilities. Anyway, I was a little annoyed that I'd only been invited at the last moment.

The next morning, as I reached for the cereal, these words seemed to leap from the front of the box: "The greatest gift you can give a child is your time." I picked up Billy's invitation from the counter where I'd left it and then glanced back at the box. I got the message. I would reschedule my appointments and attend the play.

At nine thirty, parents and children were squeezed into the hall where the kindergartners sat in a circle. Our Billy was brilliant as the naughty Peter Rabbit who ran away from home, ate too much, and suffered a terrible tummy ache, while a chorus of children admonished him, "Peter, mind your mother!"

After the play, when I shook Billy's hand and thanked him for inviting me, his face beamed with pride. And I silently thanked God for using a cereal box to nudge me to do the right thing.

Heavenly Father, thank You for Your nudges. Please keep me always willing to encourage the very young.
—OSCAR GREENE

He that believeth and is baptized shall be saved....
—MARK 16:16

On a balmy Sunday in early June, my husband, Robert, and I attended St. Luke's Episcopal Church, my former church home in Kearney, Nebraska, where we had the great joy of seeing my little granddaughter Saralisa baptized into the family of Christ.

As we stood at the baptismal font behind Saralisa and my daughter Karen and heard Father Park speak those precious words, "I baptize you, Saralisa Christine, in the name of the Father and of the Son and of the Holy Spirit," tears of joy started flowing down my cheeks. Then I looked up and saw Anita, Beth, and Verna, members of the prayer group I belonged to when I lived in Kearney, beaming smiles at me. We had prayed for this moment and our prayers were now being answered in the most lovely way. How beautiful Saralisa and Karen looked, happy in their new church home.

I think I hadn't realized until that moment how valuable my membership in this church family had been to me and, yes, how much I missed my friends there. I even felt the presence of my dear friend and prayer partner Carolmae, who had died shortly before I moved away. And a deep truth rang in my heart like a bell. Those who are baptized into Christ's family can never be separated.

I will return to St. Luke's many times in the years to come, both in person and in thought. And I know, too, that Carolmae will keep her promise to "meet me at the river."

Lord Christ, thank You for this family that bears Your name,
this family that is our true and lasting home.
—MARILYN MORGAN KING

Hear my cry, O God; attend unto my prayer.
—PSALM 61:1

*I*t was a bad day. A really bad day: tension headache, dirty house, work deadline, a class to teach that night. With a sinking heart I remembered I'd promised to pick up a manuscript that morning from one of my students, an elderly woman who wanted my advice on a short story she had written for a contest.

Begrudging the time it was taking, I drove to Ellen's house, which I had never visited before. It proved to be a homey place filled with her needlework, including an old-fashioned sampler on one wall: *When your day is hemmed with prayer, it's less likely to unravel.*

Following my glance, she said, "That message has gotten me through many a bad day."

So, had I stopped to pray that morning? No, all I'd done was wallow in misery. I sat back and relaxed while Ellen fixed me a cup of tea. *Lord, take me into Your stillness,* I prayed. The tension in my neck and shoulders gradually lessened.

As we sipped tea together, I answered some of Ellen's questions about her story, and in so doing I found the answer to a problem with my own work. By the time I left her house thirty minutes later, the day had turned into a good one after all.

Lord, any day is good when I hold You near. Amen.
—MADGE HARRAH

February 28

The Lord is nigh unto all them that call upon him....
—Psalm 145:18

*O*h no, not again! I'd thought when the doctor scheduled my second breast biopsy within a year. The first time I had been lucky. This time I wasn't so sure. Too many of my friends had developed cancer recently. Poor Kim had died.

As I lay in the pre-surgical area, now so dreadfully familiar, Rita, the nurse, smiled as she glided around my bed. She took my vital signs, snapped on my plastic ID bracelet, and attached the patch that would reduce the side effects from the anesthesia. Rita was a longtime friend from our church. Every morning she cycled for forty-five minutes to get to the early service, her two little sons tucked in a wheeled tandem. Seated in her pew, juggling her babies, plastic bags full of cereal and storybooks, she prayed fervently yet serenely. Best of all, her smile said, *Today is absolutely the best day of my life!* She smiled like that now.

Rita patted my arm. "Gail, would you like me to pray with you?" Words wouldn't come—I bit my lip and nodded. Still smiling, Rita clasped my hand, closed her eyes, and prayed that God would guide the surgeon's hand and keep me in His perfect care, no matter what. Her confidence assured me that I was in good hands—my Maker's, and my "fixer's" too.

She clanked up the sides of the gurney and adjusted my hair net. I was smiling as we cruised into surgery.

I awoke about an hour later to good news: no cancer, no nausea. Yet even now, years later, the calming "side effects" of Rita's tender prayer still linger in my life.

Dear Father, thank You for Your Son, the Great Physician, and for all those You send to heal us, in body and soul.
—Gail Thorell Schilling

February 29
LEAP DAY

This is the day which the Lord hath made; we will rejoice and be glad in it.
—Psalm 118:24

*S*uppose an eccentric but benevolent millionaire told you that at the stroke of midnight he was going to deposit in your bank account a gift of $86,400. What would you say?

You'd probably say, "What's the catch?"

And he would say, "The catch is that in the following twenty-four hours, you will have to spend it all. If you don't, it will vanish."

Eighty-six thousand four hundred dollars? Not very likely. But how about 86,400 seconds? That's the number of extra time units that this Leap Day brings to all of us. And when the hands of the clock close on midnight tonight, all of them will be gone. What should one do with these bonus minutes and hours? Not an easy question, is it?

I put it to an old friend much wiser than I, and this is what he said: "There's a little game I play with myself on Leap Day. I call it 'Suppose.' Suppose all the little pleasures and satisfactions we take for granted happened to us only once in four years? Little things like the smell of bacon frying or the song of a bird or the laughter of children playing in the yard. If such things happened only on Leap Day, how precious and marvelous they would seem. If you play this little game, even half seriously, it will intensify your awareness and your appreciation for all the days that the Lord has given us. Use this extra day to remind you how wonderful life really is on all the other days. It may sound a bit foolish, but it works for me. Maybe it would work for you."

For the magical gift of time granted to each of us in exactly the same measure,
we thank You, dear Lord.
—Arthur Gordon

March

*B*y the time I left Ohio and got to Princeton, New Jersey, in the early 1960s, one of its most famous citizens, Albert Einstein, was already gone. He died on April 18, 1955, but stories about the celebrated scientist were told over and over by townspeople who had seen him walk the streets (sometimes in house slippers, oblivious to his surroundings).

A trainman who served the Dinky, the Toonerville-like shuttle that runs from town to the Princeton Junction railroad station, once related a story about Einstein to me. The famous man often traveled by train to meetings in New York, Washington, and points in between. It was the points in between that apparently tested his memory.

On one trip, the conductor came by collecting tickets, and Einstein couldn't find his. Recognizing the illustrious scientist, the conductor said, "That's all right, Dr. Einstein. I know you've got a ticket."

"No, it's not all right," Einstein replied. "Without it, I don't know where I'm going."

It's not forgetfulness as much as bad compasses that plague many of us today. I read in today's paper about a successful businessman who had lost his fortune and committed suicide. He didn't know where he was going. Neither did the rich young ruler who came to Christ, wondering what he needed to do to inherit eternal life. Jesus told him to sell all that he had, give the proceeds to the poor, and follow Him (Luke 18:18–25). But the cost was too much. It always is for people who don't know where they're going.

*Teach us, Lord, to discern siren's song from angels singing,
Lest too late we learn, to wrong things we've been clinging.*

—FRED BAUER

MARCH 2

I thank my God upon every remembrance of you.
—PHILIPPIANS 1:3

I'd been carrying it around with me for at least a couple of months, a smart, handsome, new pocket address book, all ready to replace the dilapidated one I'd clung to for several years beyond its natural lifetime. All that remained was for me to transfer the old addresses and numbers into the new book.

The book I'd used for years—a promotional freebie from an early Internet company long since defunct—was disintegrating, its cover gone, its spine reinforced by tape, and many of its crowded pages tattered and stained.

Yet the book had served me well through some very good years. It gave me a pleasant feeling to look at a name I'd scrawled into my book and to think that that person had grown, sometimes quite unexpectedly, into a friend, someone whose life was now a part of mine. Of course, there were names and numbers that were a complete mystery, as well as those I had transferred the last time I changed books and probably hadn't called or contacted once. Should I edit those people out? It was all causing me a great deal of anxiety and a bad case of procrastination.

Finally, one rainy weekend, I got down to business. It turned out to be not so bad, partly because I discovered a little trick: I said a prayer for each name as I worked, usually just a simple prayer of thanks to God for bringing that person into my life. It wasn't long before I felt the stirrings of gratitude. How blessed could a person be to have all these remarkable people in his life?

Yes, I know, I could probably do the same thing with a Palm Pilot. Maybe next time. For now I'll stick with my little address book.

Lord, from A to Z, I am profoundly blessed with friends.
—EDWARD GRINNAN

March 3

Always seek to do good to one another and to all.
—I Thessalonians 5:15 (RSV)

*I*t was March, and I was feeling downhearted. Christine, our insurance agent, would be here Tuesday seeking eight hundred dollars for long-term-care insurance. The Internal Revenue Service was asking for an unexpected four hundred dollars in taxes. And last Monday, while I was attending a Bible study, a hit-and-run driver damaged our car. The repair costs were five hundred dollars. I felt put upon and discouraged, and I walked into church carrying my burdens.

We had a guest preacher that morning, and his message was about reaching out to others. He suggested that we should be willing to sacrifice some of our personal time to become involved in service. He called it "freedom swapping."

Then he held up a golden loaf of bread, which he called "the ministry of nourishment." "This beautiful loaf could be placed on display and admired forever," he said. "but to be useful, the bread must be cut, torn, or broken to release the nourishment. We, too, must be broken before our goodness and our comforting can reach others."

Suddenly, my cloud lifted. Each of my financial obligations was for something that benefited me: The insurance lessened the worries of loved ones; taxes paid for services that protected my way of life; the car needed to be repaired if I was to get around. To meet these obligations, I was getting out and becoming more involved in the community through the work I had to do. In a way, they represented opportunities, blessings. All that remained was for me to accept them and smile.

Gracious Lord, I thank You for using Your minister to open my eyes to see.
—Oscar Greene

MARCH 4

*On either side of the river, was there the tree of life ... and the leaves of
the tree were for the healing of the nations.*

—REVELATION 22:2

*C*ollins, huh? That would be ... English? Irish?"

It's a game we play, reckoning heritage based on the sequence of
consonants and vowels in surnames, like some kind of ethnic crossword.

"Irish. Used to be O'Collins, I think."

Our answers, of course, are misleading. We're not Irish, but Irish-American
or German-American or Japanese-American. But our nation has accumulated
so many, accommodated so many (or, in some cases, compelled so many), that
we often drop the hyphen and cut to our roots—a sort of cultural shorthand.

We may boast of the tough alloy forged from our melting pot, but these
same immigrants are the sons and daughters of long memories. Despite their
allegiance to all things American, they can't easily retract their ethnic passions
when troubles brew in their homeland. It's not whether you're "from Ireland,"
but which part of Ireland? Or Yugoslavia: Bosnia, Serbia, Montenegro—
the homes of highly developed cultures, of musical and artistic achievement,
the cradles of many diverse and colorful folk traditions. Now the only color we
see is scarlet red, bled in quantity on the evening news.

Nationality is a complicated concept. Maybe that's why I like twelve-step
meetings even though I don't have any addictions (that I know of). I like a
roomful of strangers—first names only, please—who admit they're powerless,
who admit that only a Higher Power can help. This is the country I want to live
in—one nationality, the country called Hope and Salvation and Reaching Out
and Reaching Up, where arms are only used for hugging. I'm no geographer, but
I suspect that if God had a nationality, it would be among these folks—the tired,
the poor, the wretched, all yearning to be free.

*Father, let it be as John Oxenham's hymn has it: "In Christ there is no
East or West, in Him no South or North, but one great fellowship
of love throughout the whole wide earth."*

—MARK COLLINS

March 5

But the Lord has been my stronghold, and my God the rock of my refuge.
—Psalm 94:22 (NAS)

*T*his has been a "butterflies in the stomach" morning. After driving my thirteen-year-old daughter, Jodi, to school, I dropped by a bagel shop for breakfast. Sipping a hot cup of coffee, I began to read the morning paper. As I scanned article after article, I felt my anxiety level spiking.

There was news about the fight against terrorism, the spread of biological warfare, and mounting tensions in the Middle East. I thought about my nineteen-year-old son, Drew, and I tasted fear. Then I looked at the financial section of the paper. Like most Americans, I have seen my retirement funds shrink as our economy has plunged. And I have watched our savings for college tuition dwindle. *How am I going to put three kids through school?* I wondered.

When I arrived home, I sat wordlessly at my desk as my eyes focused on a small, round rock sitting on my bookshelf. The rock is an old stone from a river, given to me by a friend. There is a handwritten note by the rock that reads, "Sometimes we have to hold the rock of ages and have faith."

I picked up the smooth stone and cradled it in my hands. I closed my eyes and thought of all the millions of years the rock has existed. Slowly, the words of the psalmist formed on my lips: "Lord, thou hast been our dwelling place in all generations. Before the mountains were brought forth, or ever thou hadst formed the earth and the world, even from everlasting to everlasting, thou art God" (Psalm 90:1–2). Suddenly my distress began to ease, and a quiet peace filled my heart.

Every generation faces challenges. My task is not to fear, but to be faithful; not to be swayed by the swirl of current events, but to be made strong by the age-old promises of God.

Dear Father, Thou hast been our dwelling place in all generations. Help me to rest in Thee. Amen.
—Scott Walker

*Do not conform any longer to the pattern of this world, but
be transformed by the renewing of your mind....*
—ROMANS 12:2 (NIV)

*T*he other morning as I drove to the monthly men's breakfast at
church, I thought how pleased I was to be back living in sunny
Southern California. Here I was, dressed in shorts and a polo shirt, going to a
function at church. One of the things I like about California is the casual social
climate. I could go to the worship service on Sunday morning dressed in shorts
(as some in fact do) and feel perfectly at home.

But I recalled with embarrassment another church function my wife, Carol,
and I had attended after moving from California to New Jersey more than twenty
years ago. Of course, we realized the East Coast is more formal, and we dressed
up for Sunday services like everyone else. But when we went to a church family
retreat at a rural conference center, we wore casual clothes. Imagine our chagrin
when we arrived for the Friday night dinner to find everyone else wearing his or
her Sunday best! No one commented on my sport shirt and slacks, but I was ill
at ease all evening.

I guess I'm something of a conformist—I like to fit in. When we lived in
Manhattan in the 1960s, I felt out of place if I left our apartment without a
coat and tie. During our ten years in Hawaii I enjoyed wearing colorful aloha
shirts, and Carol often wore long muumuus to church. Everywhere we've
lived, we've adapted to local customs.

But as I got out of my car in the church parking lot and tucked my Bible
under my arm, I thought how wonderful it is that God accepts me just as I am.
Whether in coat and tie or polo shirt and shorts, I am accepted by the One Who
loves me unconditionally.

*Lord Jesus, thank You for becoming one of us, so that
we can become part of Your family.*
—HAROLD HOSTETLER

MARCH 7

Your beauty ... should be that of your inner self, the unfading beauty of
a gentle and quiet spirit. ...
—I PETER 3:3–4 (NIV)

I had stopped at a local fast-food restaurant to read the newspaper and drink a cup of tea before heading into the office. As I walked toward the building, something caught my eye. The van next to me had a mini-chandelier hanging from its rearview mirror! I looked past it and saw that the whole vehicle seemed to be filled with boxes and ribbon and bright splashes of cloth. *I'd like to meet the person who drives that,* I thought.

Inside the restaurant, I spotted her. She was at the counter, ordering. She was wearing wonderfully sparkly bracelets, half a dozen on each arm. Around her neck hung an antique necklace, amber stones set in shiny black. "I like your necklace ... and bracelets," I said.

She turned and smiled. "Thanks. I have a store in Chicago, but I'm off to Grand Rapids to give a jewelry show for a friend." I remarked that I'd wanted to meet her when I'd seen inside her van. "Want to see my stuff?" she asked. She grabbed her breakfast sandwich and coffee, and I stepped out of line.

Outside, we pawed through the back of her van. Such beautiful things! The morning sun caught green crystals, elaborate marcasite, black glass beads. I tried things on as she pulled one pretty item after another from plastic bags. We chatted about the artists who had designed the pieces and which ones were made from antique jewelry. Suddenly, she turned to me and said, "I bet you are a Christian."

I was surprised, since all we'd been talking about was jewelry. "Yes," I said, "I am."

"I knew it!" She laughed, slipping yet another bracelet on her arm. "I could just tell."

In another few minutes, we parted ways. I left with a big smile, the address of a new friend—and a really gorgeous bracelet.

Father, may Your love and gentleness be the real adornments of our lives.
And may they sparkle every day!
—MARY LOU CARNEY

MARCH 8

Blessed are they that mourn: for they shall be comforted.
—MATTHEW 5:4

A couple of years ago, I took the training course for hospice volunteers so I'd be able to help the terminally ill and their families. If you know about hospice care firsthand, I don't have to tell you what a fantastic service it is. Not only can volunteers be supportive of those at the end of their journey, they can also give relief to caregivers who sometimes become exhausted and ill themselves from the strain of watching over a loved one.

When the instructor asked our class why we wanted to be hospice volunteers, there was a wide variety of responses. Not surprisingly, many were church members who thought hospice work would be a way for them to be God's hands and feet. Some were people whose dying loved ones had been beneficiaries of hospice services, and they wanted to give something back. "I don't like the thought of anyone dying alone" was my answer.

Today I got a phone call from Eleanor, a member of a family I had served. Her husband had died a few months earlier, and she thanked me again for my help. In truth, I did little more than listen to her and her husband talk about their long life together. I began my writing career as a newspaperman, and one of the things interviewing people taught me was how to listen. Sometimes I had to ask a few leading questions, but the key to extracting the facts of a story is listening. Eleanor and her husband had a wonderful faith story. Both had been active Christian workers who believed they'd meet again in the hereafter.

Dying is never easy, but our faith in God will help us cope. If we listen to His still, small voice, we will hear His reassuring words even when the shadows grow long and life grows short.

Teach me, Lord, the holy art
Of hearing others with my heart.
—FRED BAUER

MARCH 9

They pierced My hands and My feet.
—PSALM 22:16 (NKJV)

*E*ven more than the suffering described by the psalmist, the piercing of Jesus' hands is a horrible scene. It seems to fire the imagination of artists and moviemakers like no other torment Jesus endured. I think there was something unspeakably dark about the deed, even beyond the pain. Without free hands, Jesus could not rub sweat from His eyes or shoo flies from His mouth or adjust His position. He was utterly helpless.

Furthermore, to puncture those hands was to mock His whole life. After all, those hands had healed the blind and blessed children. Those hands had raised the dead, animated His talks about heaven, and passed along miraculous gifts.

When I was just a boy, I attended a Christian camp where the chapel speaker described the Crucifixion in graphic detail. When he got to the part about Jesus' hands, I began to cry. I rubbed my palms and felt overwhelming gratitude for the Lord's sacrifice. Afterward, I asked my father if I could be baptized.

Hands are unique, with their amazing blend of sensitivity and strength. My mother could read one degree of fever with the back of her fingers, and she could thread a tiny needle faster than a magician. Although she complained about her tired back and tired feet, she never once mentioned tired hands.

I'm really not surprised to find that hands had something to do with our redemption. I use my hands to teach my grandson to build a birdhouse. I show my love to my wife, Sharon, by holding her hand. Hands seem to have infinite possibilities for good when I dedicate them to God.

My Lord and my God, when I think of Your hands, I know that You really do love me. I give You my hands to be used for good.
—DANIEL SCHANTZ

MARCH 10

He hath made every thing beautiful in his time: also
he hath set the world in their heart....

—ECCLESIASTES 3:11

*T*he night before my husband, Robert, and I left on our trip to Japan, we received a fax from the owner of Amherst House, where we were to stay during our week in Kyoto. "The weeping cherry tree in the backyard is in full bloom!" We'd tried to plan our trip to coincide with cherry blossom time, but that time varies from year to year, and the blossoms last only a very short while. So we were indeed fortunate to arrive at just this brief season of fullest blooming.

On our first day there, we walked the three-kilometer "philosopher's path" under an archway of gorgeous cherry trees, their boughs gracefully bent by hundreds of vivid pink blossoms. Everywhere we went during that week, we were awed by the beauty and lingering scent of these gorgeous flowering trees. But near the end of the week, it seemed as if the trees were raining blossoms. And by the day we left Kyoto, their branches were nearly bare. I thought, *How swiftly the pink blossoms fade into winter snow!* Suddenly I was deeply aware of the shortness of human life, of my life! Then I remembered an admonition once given to me by a spiritual teacher: "What will you do with your remaining breaths?"

So what's my answer? I want to grow spiritually, enjoy my grandchildren, savor Robert's companionship. But perhaps, as much as anything, I want to appreciate the simple things: the tang of fresh Texas grapefruit at breakfast, deer tracks in the new snow of our backyard, a surprise call from my son John, the satisfaction of a clean house, and the scent of dinner cooking in my warm kitchen. I want to use my remaining breaths to be fully alive in each moment.

What will you do with your remaining breaths?

How precious is this life You have given me, Lord!
May gratitude grace each remaining breath.

—MARILYN MORGAN KING

And I John saw the holy city, new Jerusalem, coming down from God
out of heaven, prepared as a bride adorned for her husband.
—REVELATION 21:2

*I*t's such a big church, Mom," said my daughter Charlotte as we looked around St. Bartholomew's, the beautiful and spacious city church where we worship. "We'll need so many flowers—that'll be really expensive."

Weddings are like that. It's hard to keep one's mind on the holy and profound nature of the event when florists, dressmakers, and caterers keep tripping across the stage in the most distracting way. And then there's money. Of course, it's not supposed to be important in approaching this sacrament, but there aren't many families who aren't concerned about the amazing expense of a simple wedding.

Charlotte is both sensible and loving. "St. Bart's is beautiful, Mom. We don't need lots of flowers," she decided briskly. "Just an arrangement on the altar. The church will do the rest by itself." And I certainly wasn't going to argue.

The big day was in April, and as we stepped out of the car in front of the church, I suddenly noticed that the cherry trees along New York's Park Avenue had flowered almost overnight. They were all covered with a glorious mass of white blossoms.

As we entered the church through the big bronze doors, I gasped. This was the Saturday after Easter; for Easter, the church had been filled with flowers, including spectacular white hydrangeas high above the nave. I had assumed that their day of glory was past and they would have been swept neatly away. But now I saw that the hydrangeas were live plants, not bouquets, and they brought the springtime into the whole church.

All I could think, as my husband and I walked carefully and sedately down the aisle with our daughter, was that God had sent His own florist to the city streets and to the church—especially for Charlotte.

Lord, help me to appreciate Your divine generosity.
—BRIGITTE WEEKS

*"By this all men will know that you are My disciples,
if you have love for one another."*

—JOHN 13:35 (NAS)

I stood there at home plate, wearing a baseball cap on my bald head and just ten years of life experience under my belt. My cancer-ridden leg had been amputated only a month before, and now I was trying to prove that a disability wouldn't hinder my life by attending a church softball game. At the encouragement of the group, I had come up to bat.

Learning to balance on one leg was hard enough, but swinging a bat without falling over was a different story. With each successive strike, the pitcher stepped up a little bit closer and tried to throw a little bit slower.

I continued to rack up strikes, and everyone from my church watched expectantly. Since I was still a little shaky on my crutches, my "runner" was positioned behind me to take off when I hit the ball.

"You can do it, Josh!" I kept hearing people yell.

Looking around the field, I could see several kids on both teams whose hair was very short. They seemed to have normal buzz cuts, but I knew they were among the twenty kids who had attended a "head-shaving party" at my house when I first lost my hair to the chemotherapy.

Another kid in the game was wearing a T-shirt that read "Covenant Kids for Joshua." My church, Covenant Presbyterian, had designed the shirts and handed them out to fifty-four kids at Vacation Bible School.

Sometime after I had passed the ten-strikes mark, I hit a short grounder. The infielders threw the ball to first base, but I had chosen a fast runner and he was safe.

The entire church seemed to want to give me a high-five afterward, and I certainly felt victorious. But I also knew that everything—from the unlimited strikes, to my fast runner, to the bald heads and T-shirts—was from God, and was given to me through the body of Christ.

Lord, thank You for the love You give to the body of Christ.

—JOSHUA SUNDQUIST

MARCH 13

*I*t's amazing how something as simple as an old-fashioned tea cake can mean so much and be so encouraging. My wife, Rosie, loves to visit the elderly, and she uses tea cakes as a means of ministry to them. They look forward to her dropping by and sharing those tasty delicacies with them—and some prayers, too.

One morning, Rosie met an elderly lady at the grocery store and started a conversation with her. Sobbing intensely, the lady (we'll call her Mrs. Johnson) told Rosie that she had a serious illness and was afraid of dying. Rosie walked Mrs. Johnson to her car, and somehow the conversation got around to the subject of tea cakes. Mrs. Johnson loved tea cakes, but she was unable to bake, and it had been quite awhile since she had had any. She perked up when Rosie promised that she would drive the thirty-five miles to Mrs. Johnson's house to bring her some.

My wife now takes tea cakes to that dear lady regularly. On days when Mrs. Johnson is at the doctor's office, Rosie will open the screen door of her house and put a bag of tea cakes between the doors. Mrs. Johnson says she often goes to her front door and looks down, hoping that Rosie has left more tea cakes.

It's amazing how things that may seem insignificant to us can be a special blessing for others. A smile and a friendly greeting can bring comfort to a lonely heart—and so can a plate of tea cakes.

Lord, every day, help me to use the gifts and abilities You've given me to be a blessing to others.

—DOLPHUS WEARY

MARCH 14

God saw every thing that he had made, and, behold, it was very good....
—GENESIS 1:31

*W*hen I was in high school, I worked at a neighborhood grocery. It was a valuable experience, because I learned to do many things—deal with the public, order merchandise, figure prices, keep the books, write advertisements, cut meat, run the cash register, and, at the end of the year, take inventory. That meant counting everything on the shelves, in the storerooms, and in the freezers. The store owner explained that without an inventory of goods he wouldn't know his financial status.

"Of course, I could operate like old Jake Thomas, a hardware store owner I once knew." My boss chuckled. "He never made an accounting, and it didn't seem to matter until he decided to sell the business. The prospective buyer was taken aback. 'How do you determine your profit or loss at the end of the year?' he asked. 'All I know,' Jake responded, 'is that I always have more cash in the drawer at night than I did in the morning.'"

Some people, myself included, like to take personal inventory each year, not so much financial as spiritual. Questions I ask are: Am I using my time more wisely? Am I a better listener—to God and others? Am I more Christlike, more giving, more loving, more understanding? Am I kinder, gentler, more thoughtful of others? Am I more helpful to people (especially strangers) with needs (especially silent ones)? Some day at the final accounting, I wonder how I'll measure up.

Remind me, Lord, when my spirit wills, but my flesh won't,
that the things I count, often don't.
—FRED BAUER

You do not have, because you do not ask.

—JAMES 4:2 (RSV)

*T*he first—and most embarrassing—discovery I made about why I don't hear God's instructions is that I haven't asked for them. My friend Demos Shakarian learned this lesson the hard way.

Demos was a California dairyman who spent 75 percent of his time volunteering for Christian causes. "I sort of took for granted," he told me, "that since I was attending to God's business, He would look after mine." A dairyman's first priority is feeding his animals. With three thousand cows, Demos often bought grain "futures," committing his dairy to a specific price for feed long before harvest time. When a bumper crop came in one year, grain prices plummeted to half what Demos had agreed to pay. "I took delivery with a sick heart. It was a huge financial blow, when I was spending my time and money the way I thought God wanted me to." The words Demos addressed to God that night were more a complaint than a prayer: "I sure wish You'd told me!"

"And as clear as though He'd spoken aloud," Demos said, "I heard Him answer: *I sure wish you'd asked Me!* I realized then," Demos went on, "that I hadn't prayed at all before making that disastrous decision. I figured God knew my cows had to eat—why bother Him with the obvious?"

Why do we have to ask, since Jesus assures us, "Your Father knows what you need before you ask him" (Matthew 6:8, RSV)? Because, I've come to think, asking is entering into relationship—and relationship with Him is always God's purpose, beyond all the decisions, large and small, of our lives.

Before each decision today, Father, remind me that the journey with You is more important than the destination.

—ELIZABETH SHERRILL

MARCH 16

However, I consider my life worth nothing to me, if only I may finish the race and complete the task the Lord Jesus has given me—the task of testifying to the gospel of God's grace.

— ACTS 20:24 (NIV)

This morning, I woke up with Craig Virgin on my mind. For the past few months, off and on, I've thought about Craig.

In high school, I participated in every activity I could think of and attended school sports events from football to track and field. It was at a track meet in 1973 that I first saw Craig.

It was cold that day, but I didn't feel the chill as I stood on the sidelines cheering for one or another of our school's track stars. Then Craig blazed by. I don't remember much about his appearance except that he was pale and had brown hair.

What I do remember clearly, more than twenty-five years later, is the elegance with which he ran the long-distance race, not his runner's gait, but his style. At one point, he began to dominate the race. I fell silent—all I could do was watch him. With little effort he seemed to pull away from the rest of the pack, first a few steps, then yards.

I don't recall whether a whisper sent his name through the crowd, or whether it was the PA announcer. I do remember that we all started cheering for Craig Virgin to pull ahead of the other runners by one complete circuit of the track, to lap the pack. Even though he was yards and yards ahead of them, Craig was running full out right up to the end, when he passed the rest of the group and crossed the finish line.

That day, I knew he was going to the Olympics. He did, three times. This morning I prayed that he is still running full out.

Dear God, help me to do the things You have set before me.
Give me strength and courage to run the race to win.

—SHARON FOSTER

MARCH 17
ST. PATRICK'S DAY

"Yes, I have called him. I will bring him, and he will succeed in his mission."
—ISAIAH 48:15 (NIV)

I like celebrating St. Patrick's Day—I'm not sure if it's because I consider St. Patrick my patron saint (although there is a St. Patricia) or if I like celebrating the smidgen of Irish in my Scotch-Irish-English-French-German ancestry. It may be because, as a single parent, I've always identified with St. Patrick as someone who had a mission to do and did it, in spite of great difficulties.

St. Patrick was actually born in Britain and sold into slavery in Ireland, where he turned to religion. After six years, he escaped back to Britain, but when he was twenty-two years old he returned to Ireland, determined to convert the Irish to Christianity. He eventually became a priest, then a bishop. In spite of great difficulties in life, he succeeded in making many converts, even among royal families.

St. Patrick is a great saint to identify with if you're going through hard times. I know when I was raising my four children, I was often lonely and fearful as I struggled to keep everything together. Like St. Patrick, I knew I had a tough job to do and that if I persevered and used my faith in God as a shield, I would be successful.

It wasn't easy, but St. Patrick taught me that the struggle itself is often the thing that makes us strong, gives us good character, and makes us more interesting people.

Heavenly Father, thank You for saints who inspire me. Give me courage to face my problems head on and the strength to endure hardship along the way.
—PATRICIA LORENZ

MARCH 18

And the light shineth in darkness; and the darkness comprehended it not.
—JOHN 1:5

More than half a million visitors come annually to see the Book of Kells at Trinity College, Dublin, but my hotel's concierge assured me there would be no crowds this time of year. "Ah, 'tis a lovely thing to see, sir," he said, pointing me in the direction of Trinity.

The Book of Kells, dating from AD 800, is a copy of the four Gospels. It was painstakingly transcribed and illuminated—that is, illustrated—by the monks of St. Columba on the island of Iona before it was removed to Kells in County Meath to protect it from plundering Vikings.

My eyes took awhile to adjust to the dim lighting of the Old Library's East Pavilion where the manuscript is kept. Tourists were indeed in short supply, but there were several groups of Irish schoolchildren, and I kept bumping into them in the russet gloom. "It's so dark in here I can hardly see my own foot," I remarked to a studious-looking older gentleman bent over one of the display cases.

"Light can damage the paper," he remarked. "None at all would be best but then..." His words trailed off as he gestured to the milling children. My eyes followed his back to the fragile but magnificent pages beneath the glass, bathed in soft light. The breathtaking beauty of the manuscript shone through as if it had light of its own.

The monks labored over their manuscripts during what we call the Dark Ages. Their rich and ornate embellishments emblazoned the pages of Scripture, the words of Jesus that lighted the way through the chaos and darkness that followed the fall of the Roman Empire. All these centuries later we are protecting the Light of the World from—literally—the light of the world.

We may not consider ourselves as living in a dark age, but you never know. One Light burns a path of beauty and brightness when all seems dark. And it burns brightest when the world seems darkest.

Lord, Your Word is our light.
—EDWARD GRINNAN

MARCH 19

Fear not them which kill the body, but are not able to kill the soul....
—MATTHEW 10:28

*W*hen I tell people my mother suffers from Alzheimer's, they invariably ask if she still recognizes me. I am relieved to say she does, for now, though this will probably not continue to be the case. Yet the question I increasingly ask myself is: Do I recognize her?

This was a woman who continued to jog well into her seventies. Her favorite pastimes included shoveling snow and mowing the yard. When the time came to take away her driver's license, I will never forget my brother and sister and I standing guiltily around Mom's kitchen table while she shook her head defiantly, much too stubborn and proud to cry or plead—after all, who were we, her children, to tell her what she couldn't do? After that, she walked the three miles to church nearly every morning. She counted the money from the collection basket, though someone always quietly recounted it after Mom began slipping.

My mother will still tell you she has never been sick a day in her life. She told me that very same thing this morning, in fact, from the hospital where she had been taken when she couldn't get out of bed. She is failing physically now. The ravages of osteoporosis, a stubborn intestinal disorder, high blood pressure—these are the wolves that circle her. At eighty-five and barely able to understand what is happening and why she is in pain, Estelle Grinnan is not the person I once recognized as my mother.

But then there is that strange but nonetheless resounding declaration of health despite the tubing that invades her, the cumbersome back brace that is supposed to relieve the pressure on her crushed vertebrae, the x-rays and blood tests and CAT scans and sonograms, the whole unnerving high-tech arsenal of modern medicine. There is, after all, somewhere in all of that corporeal wreckage of a long life well-lived a woman who has never been sick a day in her life.

Lord, at the end of our journey, we are still the people You made us.
—EDWARD GRINNAN

Ye shall be witnesses unto me . . . unto the uttermost part of the earth.
—ACTS 1:8

*S*pring in New York City is a very short season. Chilly April seems to give way suddenly to hot May. But today, the first day of spring, is beautiful, so I'm taking an after-lunch stroll down Fifth Avenue from the Guideposts editorial offices on 34th Street.

Five blocks downtown, on the corner of 29th Street, I come to Marble Collegiate Church. To the right of the entrance, there's a life-size bronze statue of Guideposts' cofounder, Dr. Norman Vincent Peale. Feeling a little guilty for being away from my desk, I duck my head and walk by, trying to look inconspicuous.

The next dozen blocks go by quickly. With a sigh, I hurry by the big bookstore on 18th Street. If I stop there, it'll be hours before I get back to work. Then, blocks south at 10th Street, I see the open door of the Church of the Ascension. I stop in to look around.

On the wall above the altar is an enormous painting by John Lafarge of the event for which the church is named. Surrounded by a circle of angels, Jesus rises into a cloudy sky, while His disciples gaze up at Him in amazement. But there's something odd about the picture: The curving green hills in the background seem somehow out of place. On receiving the commission for the mural, I learn, Lafarge made a trip to Japan. The Far East, not the Middle East, provided the landscape for his painting.

I take my eyes from the painting and glance at my watch. It's almost two. I'd better head back to the office. As I walk back up Fifth Avenue, surrounded by strollers whose roots are in a hundred different countries, Lafarge's odd choice suddenly makes sense: Japan and Galilee are equally close to heaven—and for the believing heart, so is New York City.

Lord, renew us in Your Spirit and make us one in You.
—ANDREW ATTAWAY

MARCH 21

Break forth into singing, O mountains....
—ISAIAH 49:13

I gloomily surveyed the thick white powder coating the back of my clothes dryer. At least the fire was out, and it hadn't been my fault. The air vent had been installed backward, trapping lint.

"Remember, don't use it until an appliance repairman takes a look," advised my friendly volunteer fireman. No, I certainly wasn't ready to risk another fire, but with three teenagers in the house, I sure would miss the convenience of a dryer.

Oh well, at least it's spring, I thought as I ducked under branches to tie one end of a cotton clothesline to a Russian olive and the other to a willow in the backyard. After I had hauled the first load to the new line, I began the classic, rhythmic routine: bend to the basket, stretch to the line, squeak the clothespin over damp cloth. Bend. Stretch. Squeak. The movement began to lull me.

A light breeze fluffed my hair and set the aspens quivering. Sunlight filtering through their leaves in a dozen shades of green cast dappled shadows along the edge of the swift-running creek near the end of the clothesline. The water lapped at branches trailing in the twinkling stream. As I pegged out each sock and towel, my contentment becoming deeper and deeper, I gazed up at a panoramic view of the Wind River Mountains, snow glistening on the ten-thousand-foot peaks. I took a deep breath of cool mountain air. When puffy clouds drifted overhead in a postcard-blue sky, my daily tensions drifted away, too. I have a better view from my clothesline than most tourists have from their resorts. Who needs a dryer?

Even after the dryer was repaired, I found myself using the clothesline until snow began to fly. What had begun as an inconvenience had become a refreshing interlude—and a perfect setting for "fresh air prayer."

Father of all Creation, keep my eyes open to the marvelous works of Your hands.
—GAIL THORELL SCHILLING

MARCH 22

God is love. Whoever lives in love lives in God, and God in him.
—I JOHN 4:16 (NIV)

*I*n the Makapa Valley outside Nairobi, Kenya, thousands of homeless families live in a vast shantytown that begins to assault eyes, ears, and noses from high atop the surrounding ridge. The ankle-deep mud, open sewers, and hungry, hollow-eyed children overwhelmed me within minutes. Sensing my discomfort, my guide, an Ethiopian friend, said to me, "You see only the despair. Come and see the hope."

Down an alleyway and around a corner we came to an open courtyard about ten yards square, surrounded on all four sides by lean-tos. Two of them were for sleeping, one was for cooking, and one was a classroom. Small children filled the courtyard. A dozen old women sat on benches along the outer edges.

"What do you see now?" my friend asked.

What struck me the most were the smiles and energy; only a few paces away we had been surrounded by despair and listlessness. "What makes the difference?" I asked.

"Love," he replied. "These children are the outcasts—orphans with no one to care for them. And these old women thought they had nothing to live for until they began to look after the children. The orphans had no hope until they were touched by such love. Look around you. The shacks here are no better than those elsewhere, the ground is no cleaner, the food no more plentiful. The only difference is God's love reaching out through human hands."

Lord, help me to use my hands to show Your love's power over every sort of evil and despair.
—ERIC FELLMAN

MARCH 23

Blessed is a man who perseveres under trial....
—JAMES 1:12 (NAS)

*T*he assignment was proving to be too much for me. I stormed out of my home office and decided to go grocery shopping.

"That caller from Connecticut phoned again," my husband, Gene, told me when I got home. "Won't leave a number." As I set down the grocery bags, the phone rang and I picked it up.

"Is this Marion Bond West of Watkinsville, Georgia?" a small but resolute voice asked.

"Yes. Are you the caller from Connecticut?"

"I am. Did you write about a duck that died?"

"Yes."

"Is it true?"

"Yes."

Big sigh. "Oh, I'm so glad! I loved your story. You see, I love ducks, too, and I had pet ducks—three. I raised them from babies. One day after school they didn't meet me at the bus and I found a pile of feathers ... and sure enough, the neighbor's dog had killed them."

"Oh, I'm so sorry. How old are you?"

"Twelve."

"Won't your parents be upset by your calling down to Georgia so many times?"

"No. I'm paying for the calls myself. I wouldn't dream of letting my parents pay for my calls. I have money. I work in people's yards, plus I sell eggs."

And that's how a determined Jake Hendrickson from Woodstock, Connecticut, and I became friends. After our conversation about ducks, I marched right back to my typewriter and decided to give that impossible assignment one more try.

Thank You, Lord (and you, too, Jake), for teaching me not to give up. Amen.
—MARION BOND WEST

MARCH 24

Speak to the earth, and it shall teach thee....
—JOB 12:8

In March 1938, when I was a college student in Virginia, Mr. Perkins, my math teacher, told the class about the Hoosac Tunnel. "You may feel math is unimportant. But the Hoosac Tunnel, between Greenfield and North Adams, Massachusetts, was built by digging simultaneously from opposite sides of Hoosac Mountain. The engineer's calculations were so accurate that when the tunnels met at midpoint, they were off only a little more than a half-inch."

That July I took my first train ride through the Hoosac Tunnel. I left Williamstown and passed through North Adams on my way to Boston. Then, without warning, I was plunged into pitch darkness! For 4.7501 miles I felt as if I were trapped in an elevator between floors. It was frightening. Finally, the train broke into daylight.

Over the years many significant events in my life were marked by trips through the Hoosac Tunnel. I went through the tunnel from Williamstown to Boston for induction into the US Army in 1944. I returned through the tunnel after my discharge in 1946. I traveled through the tunnel to attend my brother's graduation from Williams College in January 1948 and my sister's wedding in June 1950.

On November 30, 1958, the last passenger train left Williamstown for Boston, ending eighty-three years of service through the Hoosac Tunnel. Freight trains still use it, however, and in 1997 work began to carve an extra fifteen inches of clearance into the tunnel's roof.

Sometimes my life resembles a long, dark tunnel. When illness strikes or I'm burdened with responsibilities, the darkness seems endless. But my trips through the Hoosac Tunnel remind me that there's always light ahead.

No matter how hopeless things may seem, Father, You are the light at the end of all the tunnels of my life.
—OSCAR GREENE

MARCH 25

Charge them that are rich in this world, that they be not highminded, nor trust in uncertain riches, but in the living God, who giveth us richly all things to enjoy.
—I TIMOTHY 6:17

*J*ust across the street from where I live in New York City lies Central Park. I go into the park about four times a day to walk my dog, Shep, and I've come to know it in each of its seasons. We've wandered far afield to Belvedere Castle and to Strawberry Fields, to the Ramble, the Dairy, the Sheep Meadow, the Mall, and more.

The one walk that is a constant with us is the one around Summit Rock. It's the highest point in the park, 137 feet. We go there early every morning, sometimes in darkness, when few, if any, people are there. Down below, I remove Shep's leash, and she runs while I huff and puff my way up. I sit on a bench, and eventually Shep comes along for me to refasten her leash. We move down and around, the squirrels scurrying out of our way, until we come to the memorable part of the walk, Our Tree.

It isn't much, considering the twenty-six thousand trees in the park, some grand and of great age. It's a simple spruce pine, conical, sitting all alone, with a three-foot fence surrounding it for protection. Of course it isn't ours—how could it be?—it's just that we have silently adopted it ever since it was planted several years ago. We were there at a distance when we saw people gather, and we watched as someone read from a Bible while the people stood reverently. When they had gone, Shep and I went up to the tree. There was no marker for it, nor has there ever been. Who the person was that it memorializes doesn't matter; what better way to remember than with a living thing. We silently pay our respects every morning.

We have watched Our Tree grow and prosper. One day soon they will remove the wire fence and it will be on its own, just one more object in the cosmos called Central Park.

Another wondrous thing You have given me, Lord. Let me protect it.
—VAN VARNER

March 26

The greatest of these is love.
—I Corinthians 13:13 (RSV)

*A*ll writers know, or should know, that there is power in simplicity. I was reminded of this the other day when I came across a passage in a book called *Views from the Publisher's Desk* by a Minnesota newspaperman named Elmer Andersen, who also served as governor of his state.

Mr. Andersen told of being at a dinner party where people were asked to guess the world's most popular song. Everyone tried, but no one came up with the correct answer: "Happy Birthday to You." As Mr. Andersen says, it is sung countless times every day. The tune was composed by a Kentucky school teacher named Mildred J. Hill; her younger sister, Patty Smith Hill, wrote the lyrics.

How amazing that such a simple handful of words and notes has touched and continues to touch so many lives! And the message is simple, too: We love you and we wish you well, on this day that is so special to you.

Every minute of every day, all around the world, somebody is sending that musical greeting to a relative or neighbor, colleague or friend.

Comforting thought, isn't it?

Lord, teach us not only to feel love, but to share it.
—Arthur Gordon

March 27

The earth which drinketh in the rain that cometh oft upon it . . .
receiveth blessing from God.
—Hebrews 6:7

*E*very time my car turns the corner from my street into the adjoining one, my eyes see the entire yard of the house there. I never noticed it much until last summer, when an ugly mound of weeds and dirt was dumped near the street. My first thought was that the man who lived there would probably use it for fill dirt around the yard.

But that wasn't done.

Perhaps he needs some flowerbeds and will remove the weeds and use the dirt for that, I thought as the summer came along. No flowerbeds appeared.

As I watched winter frost cover the unsightly mass, I found myself quietly fuming about that offensive blot on our nice neighborhood. I was tempted to express my feelings to the owner but decided to keep quiet.

And then it was spring, a beautiful warm morning. I turned the corner expecting to see the same pile of dirt. Instead, the entire mound sparkled with white blossoms, a beauty to behold! I couldn't resist stopping my car and getting out for a closer look. The blooms of wild strawberries bobbed on fragile stems, cushioned by a thick layer of the plant's dark leaves. My heart thrilled at the beauty that had transformed an eyesore, and my soul was filled with praise for God.

Lord, when I make a mess of my life, forgive me and transform me with
the beauty of Your love. Amen.
—Drue Duke

Bearing with one another in love....
—EPHESIANS 4:2 (NIV)

*L*ast week, while cleaning the house, I found a pair of my husband Leo's old shoes stashed away in a corner. "I'll just throw these out, okay?"

"Not yet. They might come in handy."

"But look at them!" I protested. "They're turned up at the toes, run down at the heels, there's a hole in the sole, and the laces are broken."

"So? I could still use them for gardening." He grinned sheepishly.

Mumbling and grumbling about useless old shoes taking up prime storage space, I stuffed them back into the cupboard.

The following Sunday, I held the church door open for Alice as she brought her husband to the worship service in a wheelchair. He was smartly dressed in a gray suit, white shirt, and maroon tie, but it was his black shoes that caught my attention. They looked so shiny and new, with not even the hint of a crease across the vamps. *That's because he hasn't walked since his stroke ten years ago,* I thought.

The very next morning, I was about to complain about another pair of Leo's old work shoes littering the back entrance when I stopped short in my tracks. *Thank You, Lord, that he has been healthy enough to take thousands of steps in these wrinkled old shoes. He has worn them to carry in the groceries and carry out the garbage. By the look of the mud on them, he has even tilled the garden in them and dug my flower beds. Thank You for the man who wears these shoes.*

I surprised myself by what I said next. "Is it okay," I called to Leo, "if I park your gardening shoes right here on the welcome mat?"

*Father God, help me appreciate my loved ones more and fret about
their petty annoyances less.*
—ALMA BARKMAN

MARCH 29

And the ears of the deaf shall be unstopped.
—ISAIAH 35:5

The tiny, curtained cubicle in the doctor's office was freezing. I'd just had my mammogram. Until now, these hadn't worried me, but this year I was still reeling from the fact that my mother had had breast cancer. A friend had been diagnosed with early-stage cancer, too. And my own doctor was away, and this one seemed new—and brusque.

So I sat in the cubicle and waited. And waited. And waited, getting more nervous as each moment passed. "Keep your gown on," the mammogram technician had instructed me earlier. "Doctor will be in to discuss your results shortly." Why was he taking so long? What was wrong?

Twenty minutes later, I finally pulled the curtain back and tapped a passing nurse with my sweaty-palmed hand. "Excuse me. If he's with another patient, that's fine, but I've been waiting for my results." The young nurse's eyes widened. "Are you still here? Oh, I think he forgot you!"

In less than a minute, the doctor stuck his head in the curtain, snapped, "You're fine. You can get dressed and go," and strode off. I was fuming. What nerve! He forgot me, and all I get is a two-second, brusque "You're fine." And I waited so long, and it's cold in the paper gown, and all he says is "You're fine."

I closed my eyes and stopped mid-thought. What would my mother or my friend have given to hear those words, spoken brusquely, spoken in pig Latin, spoken at all? I rolled the words around in my mind: *I'm fine. I'm fine. Thank You, God.*

Today, God, let me give up my petty grievances and rejoice in the good in my life.
—LINDA NEUKRUG

MARCH 30

Hereafter ye shall see heaven....
—JOHN 1:51

*I*n heaven," says my four-year-old son, with the confidence of a man talking about his native country, "everyone is one hundred inches tall." He goes on at some length about the geography and nature of heaven, what sort of boots people wear there (red ones), what the angels do all day long (play basketball), what's for breakfast (cookies).

These pronouncements draw guffaws and scorn from his brother and sister, but he holds forth with undiminished verve. "Yeah, I remember that heaven," he says with affection. "God was there all the time. He really big guy. He laughing all the time. He funny guy. He have really big hands. He bigger than Daddy. I was not scared because He was laughing."

More scorn from his siblings and a grin from his mother, but his father is moved to ruminate on the topography of heaven, and not for the first time, either. *Did not this boy come to me from God? Didn't his long-legged sister and his exuberant brother? And the lovely woman sipping coffee and smiling across the table? And the air we all breathe and the vast country outside and the crow on the fence cocking a curious eye at the heavenly boy in the house? None would be but for the Maker. And who is to say that this boy does not remember a place he was a mere four years ago?*

So I listen with care, and hear of a country filled with joy and peace and light and laughter. Many days I think that I am in heaven right now, right here, in the sea of love that is my family. But listening to the little prophet at the head of the table, I dream for a moment of the world to come, the world we work for, in the end an ocean of love in which there are no islands of lovelessness.

Lord, give me ears to hear Your voice and Your music, to savor the heaven around me every moment. And give me the grace never to shush a child telling tales.

—BRIAN DOYLE

MARCH 31

Over all the glory there will be a canopy.... It will be for a shade by day from the heat, and for a refuge and a shelter from the storm and rain.
— ISAIAH 4:5–6 (RSV)

*J*t was one of those days when storms raged outside and inside of me. Outside, a blue norther was settling in. The wind was picking up, and the temperature was dropping. Deep within me, I felt a tempest of anxiety and depression, the result of too much work without rest. I yearned to hear a gentle voice from God, to be reassured of His guidance and presence. I put on my running shoes, picked up a small New Testament and slipped it into my jacket pocket, and set out to run my blues away.

I decided to jog around a small, picturesque lake, one of my favorite routes. The strong wind was kicking up short, choppy waves, and the gray sky threatened rain. Usually wood ducks skirted the sandy shore, bobbing and quacking at one another. But today they were nowhere to be seen. *Where do ducks go when it storms?* I wondered.

Finally tiring, I stopped and pulled out my New Testament. The brisk gale blew its thin pages back and forth. I looked around for a windbreak, a place to sit down, and saw a thick clump of trees nestled in a shallow cove by the water. Entering the leafy shelter, I leaned back against an oak. Dozens of ducks huddled together in front of me in the cove. They, too, had sought shelter from the storm. They knew where to find still water.

I sat down under the oak tree and read from my New Testament. Quietly I savored the safety and security found in the Scriptures, the shelter that God provides for all of us in the midst of storms.

Father, thank You for always being with me in Your Word.
—SCOTT WALKER

April

APRIL 1
APRIL FOOL'S DAY

"Will all your worries add a single moment to your life?"
—MATTHEW 6:27 (TLB)

One year not so long ago when I was in college, our dormitory council decided to sponsor an April Fool's Day contest. Each of our floors was to submit a prank that, if selected, would be played on one other floor. The winner—whose identity was kept secret—got to choose the floor that would become the butt of the joke. My floor was it.

For seven long hours my floormates and I kept a wary eye out for preparations or secret meetings. We sent spies to other floors looking for anything that might betray the perpetrators of the forthcoming dastardly deed. Then on April Fool's Day, our every step was taken with extreme caution, looking out for short-sheeted beds, sewn-up pants legs, or buckets of water cascading from booby-trapped doors. But nothing happened. The whole day passed with no atrocity. Finally, at the 11 PM dorm meeting, the winner was announced. His gag?—not playing a gag at all. He simply wanted to make us sweat and worry for nothing. His joke had worked to perfection!

My worry has not been limited to that one April Fool's week. Often I seem to fret about problems, like the April Fool's gag, that never materialize. It is only when I concentrate on the blessings I receive each day, rather than on the problems I may never experience, that I know the comfort of my God.

On this April Fool's Day, Lord, help me to admire beauty,
cherish friendship, count blessings, and laugh.
—JEFF JAPINGA

APRIL 2

He hath put a new song in my mouth....
—Psalm 40:3

*M*y work often takes me overseas. This time the writing seminar was in Singapore and I was exhausted from the start. The flight had been endless, the thermometer stood at one hundred degrees, and I found my group's Singaporean English hard to follow. When Sunday came, I took a break by visiting a park where, I'd been told, people brought their caged birds for a weekly airing.

I heard the twittering songs as I stepped from the bus. There they were, hundreds of tiny birds in dainty cages hung from long horizontal poles. Singapore apartments are small, and birds are the pets of choice. Exclamation points of green, blue, yellow, they hopped excitedly from perch to perch.

And the cages! Each one was a work of art: bamboo, brass, teakwood, with hand-carved ivory swings and ladders, and exquisite porcelain water dishes. *That must be,* I thought, *why people bring their birds from every corner of the sprawling city to this one spot—to show off these miniature palaces.*

But there was a more important reason, an elderly bird owner explained. "We bring them together," he said, "to learn each other's songs."

Each other's songs...

I'd come to Singapore to share my own song. Now, through this stranger, Jesus was reminding me to listen more closely to the songs of my students. *Every person has a melody of his or her own. When I bring you together, it's to learn new melodies for the universal chorus.*

What new song, Lord, will someone teach me today?
—Elizabeth Sherrill

With weeping they shall come, and with consolations I will lead them back.
—JEREMIAH 31:9 (RSV)

When Bonnie, my best friend of more than forty years, died in April 1998, she left me her almost brand-new car. She'd teased me for years about my old car, a 1981 model with more than 150,000 miles on it. She also used to tease me about other things, one of which was how much I cried at the movies we saw together. "You cry at the end of every movie we've ever seen," she insisted.

"No, I don't," I said. "Only at the ones that are sad or touching or joyful."

"You cried at the end of *Seven Brides for Seven Brothers*," she accused me scornfully. That was an exaggeration.

But when we saw *Beaches* together—the story of a lifelong friendship between two women, one of whom dies at the end—I wept buckets, especially when Bette Midler sang "The Wind beneath My Wings" while Barbara Hershey died.

Bonnie eyed me with a profound forbearance, as if to say, "Well, you're my friend, so I suppose I have to put up with this sort of thing."

After Bonnie died, the lawyer handling her estate told me I would need to fly up to Portland, Oregon, to pick up the car. I had a fairly smooth flight, a quick trip to the lawyer's office to sign papers, and a cab ride to what had been Bonnie's condo, where the car waited. I took the keys, started the car, and began the two-day, thousand-mile drive back to Los Angeles. As I headed for the interstate, I flicked on the radio. A song was ending. There was a short pause, without an announcer. Then the next song started. It was "The Wind beneath My Wings."

I knew that Bonnie was still teasing me, but I also knew that I would not be making the drive to Los Angeles alone. I thought that she probably expected me to cry, but I called her names instead.

Thank You, Lord, for the friends You give me throughout my life.
—RHODA BLECKER

Whosoever shall do the will of my Father which is in heaven,
the same is my brother, and sister, and mother.
—MATTHEW 12:50

I walked into my mother's room at Claussen Manor, where she was an Alzheimer's patient, to find her bed surrounded by people I thought were strangers. The night before, my sister had called me from Michigan. "You'd better come," she said, and I didn't have to ask why.

Mom looked unimaginably frail and parched. A woman with blonde hair held Mom's hand in both of hers while an aide dribbled sugar water from a dropper through Mom's lips, making rivulets of the deeper wrinkles on her chin. I noticed Mom's buddy Pat standing guard at the end of the bed. I now recognized the blonde woman, Colleen Burke, whom I'd met once not long after she'd taken charge of the unit. "Hey, green eyes," she said softly to Mom, "look who's here." My mother turned her head weakly and gave me that goofy Alzheimer's grin that had taken so much getting used to. The movement caused more sugar water to run down her chin as she made a sound that substituted for "hi."

The hospice nurse and a social worker slipped in, and Mom's eyes brightened even as she tried to fend off the hovering dropper. "Hi, Estelle," whispered the nurse. Mom waved as if she were in a parade.

For an instant, I felt like an intruder. My mom had always been so profoundly devoted to her family. Yet here she was, surrounded mostly by young strangers. Dying.

I made myself go forward. Colleen transferred Mom's hand to mine. Her grip was surprisingly strong, and she was pulling me closer even as she closed her eyes. I knew then that I was exactly where I was supposed to be, surrounded by my mother's new family, the people who cared for her on a daily, hourly basis. They were not strangers but helpers, and in the coming days I was to learn how much they cared.

God, I thank You not only for the help You send, but the people who bring it.
—EDWARD GRINNAN

APRIL 5

"If I do not wash you, you have no part in me."
—John 13:8 (RSV)

W e have been told that it is more blessed to give than to receive. What we have not been told is that it is also safer.

When Marilyn and I began to make a life together, we discovered we had many wonderful things in common. We like to take walks together in the evening, listen to the sound of a mountain stream, read aloud to each other, and sometimes just sit in silence together. We also like doing things for each other. I like to do the dishes after Marilyn has prepared a meal; she likes to reassure me whenever I express a momentary disappointment.

But our desire to help each other eventually became a point of contention. I didn't always want to be reassured, while she would frequently respond to my offers of help by saying, "You don't need to do that." It soon became evident that both of us were more comfortable in the role of giver than receiver.

I was reminded of the story of Jesus washing His disciples' feet on the eve of His death. Peter objected, saying, "You shall never wash my feet." But Jesus replied, "If I do not wash you, you have no part in Me." Like Peter, Marilyn and I each wanted to be the giver. It was a safer position, one in which we were less likely to be hurt. Yet it also kept some distance between us—and kept us from being fully receptive to God's love.

We are gradually learning to be receivers as well as givers in expressing our love. In the process, we have found that we are more vulnerable, but also more at-one with each other. While we continue to delight in the many ways we are alike, we have come to realize that in this regard we both needed to change. We needed to allow the One Who came in the form of a servant to wash our feet, so that we could in turn wash each other's.

May I be like the transformed Peter, Lord, graciously receiving,
authentically giving.
—Robert King

April 6

Show yourself ... a model of good deeds....
—Titus 2:7 (RSV)

I signed up for duty at a children's hospital in Manhattan with hopes of saving the world—only to discover I was the world's worst volunteer. Every Tuesday night, I joined twenty other women to lead craft time for young kids who lived at the hospital year round. My sheltered, Alabama childhood had certainly not prepared me to work with city kids from broken homes. I colored and painted with them, but their emotional outbreaks and battles for our attention made me a nervous wreck. I didn't know how to reach out to them—even hugging was against the rules because most of the children had been abused. After a few months of failing to connect, I was just about ready to give up. Surely someone else could love them better than I.

On what was to have been my last night, eight-year-old Victor wanted help drawing a tiger. "Please, somebody," he pleaded, as one by one the volunteers turned him down. "How about you?" He stood right in front of me with a brown crayon. I didn't want him to be disappointed, but it was only fair to warn him: "It won't be perfect, Victor."

He frowned and pointed right between my eyes. "Nothing in life is perfect, but you have to try." I looked at that child, whose life had been anything but perfect, and knew he was right. I might never be the best volunteer, but I could be a willing one. So I tried. And for weeks to come, a goofy tiger with a lopsided grin hung over my favorite second grader's bed.

Lord, I know I'm not perfect, but with my trust in You, I'll try.
—Allison Sample

April 7

I am come that they might have life, and ... have it more abundantly.
—John 10:10

> t was the day before Easter, and I was on a train from Fort Worth to Houston to fill in for a pastor who was recovering from a heart attack. I had prepared a standard Easter sermon—the certainty and centrality of the Resurrection, the reality that created the Church, and our hope for life after death. Somewhere between Cleburne and College Station the train slowed to a crawl to let a northbound train pass, and I looked out the window at a small farmhouse with its swaybacked barn. What caught my attention were three gravestones in the yard by a flowerbed. As the train picked up speed that scene stayed in my mind and I wondered what stories went with those stones—who was buried there and who tended the graves so lovingly.

As I thought about that private burial place, I was reminded that there are more kinds of death than physical dying that each of us experiences—death to friendships, to marriages, to belief in people, to integrity, to ambition, and even to hope. In those private places of the heart, each of us tends graves where we have buried things that were precious and whose loss we grieve often all by ourselves. I wondered what Easter had to do with all these deaths.

During the rest of the trip and that night in the hotel, I reworked my sermon for the next day. What I had already prepared was true and was the basis for our Christian hope, so I made it the introduction to a more relevant message for myself and for those who would hear me. Easter is not just remembering our hope for life after the grave. It is a celebration of the fact that the living Christ comes to us in all the deaths we experience in this world and seeks to bring us life.

> *Father, thank You for the hope that brings the promise of real life*
> *both here and hereafter.*
> —Kenneth Chafin

APRIL 8

"Your grief will turn to joy."
—JOHN 16:20 (NIV)

*O*ur new church in our new state was dressed in lilies, arrayed in the glory of Solomon. Pastor Kidd, in his white stole, announced, "The Lord is risen!"

"Please give me faith," I'd begged on that night in South Salem, New York. And God had said, *Use the faith you have.*

Impossible, I'd thought. But here I was. We'd moved to Tennessee in winter, chased by spring, a spring I viewed from the porch of our new cedar house, perfect for rockers. Our finances had turned around. Best of all, my daughter had graduated from rehab. She was working and saving money to go to school to become a therapist. As I sat next to my husband, Whitney, on that Easter, I thought of her visit a few weeks back. We were approaching the church door a few minutes late and heard the strains of "Amazing Grace."

Face radiant, she grabbed my arm. "Mom, that's my favorite song because of what I was and what I am now." We both cried. Resurrection life is planted deep in our souls. The same power that raised Jesus from the dead pushes us up to new life. But first we must die in whatever dirt we find ourselves in, and reach out and wait for God.

Living Lord, thank You for the gift of Your risen life.
—SHARI SMYTH

APRIL 9

A blizzard scooped up snow from the Ukrainian steppes and hurled it against the small windowpanes of my childhood home, but inside our small kitchen, my mother had prepared a happy Easter surprise. An awestruck six-year-old, I gazed at the red, blue, green, and yellow Easter eggs nestled among a forest of rye shoots, five inches high, growing in a rusty old dishpan.

Not until I was an adult did I grasp the significance of my mother's creativity. During the early 1940s, I was too young to be worried by the privations that World War II had brought into our lives. Food was scarce. Carefully Mother rationed potatoes, beets, and flour. Fuel was almost gone. The dried cow dung and cornstalks carefully gathered in fall were almost used up. Such luxuries as egg coloring could not be found. Mother had used boiled onion skins for yellow, cooked moss for green, a bleeding piece of red fabric for red, and a few drops of ink for dark blue. Despite our hardships, she had created a joyous Easter celebration for us children.

Two years later, my mother and we four children fled from our home in eastern Europe. We survived the war and eventually immigrated to Canada. In time, life became easier; we no longer had to worry about food and fuel and egg coloring. But the joy of that Easter celebration in war-torn Ukraine has remained with me through the decades. At times, the chaos of my own life threatens to overwhelm me, and it's hard to see how I'm going to keep going. Then I remember Mother and the maxim she lived by: In a world of chaos, find a corner where you still have control and fill it with beauty. Then share it with others.

Lord Jesus, help me find the treasure of joy You've scattered throughout this day.
—HELEN GRACE LESCHEID

APRIL 10

Seek the Lord and his strength....
—I Chronicles 16:11

*E*ven before it sailed into theaters as a multimillion-dollar blockbuster, I had an avid interest in the *Titanic*. I've read dozens of accounts that attempt to solve the riddle of the great ship's sinking. Of course, it struck an iceberg while traveling at a high rate of speed. But questions have arisen regarding the construction of the vessel and the role that construction may have played in its destruction.

So I was particularly intrigued with a recent headline in a Chicago paper: "Two Weak Rivets May Help Explain 1912 Sinking of the *Titanic*." According to the story, experts believe they have evidence suggesting the *Titanic* may have been done in by two wrought-iron rivets from the hull. The rivets were riddled with unusually high concentrations of slag and, consequently, were very brittle. One theory is that they popped and allowed the plates to separate, letting water in.

I'll remember that the next time I'm tempted to neglect my own "spiritual rivets"—the unseen things like early-morning prayer, solitary walks dedicated to praise, time spent memorizing Scripture. After all, life—like ships—needs to be held together with strong supports.

Support me, God, as I sail the seas of life. Hold me together in the midst of storms. Bring me safely into heaven's harbor.
—Mary Lou Carney

APRIL 11

J once lost a valuable coral-and-silver bracelet at a concert in a large auditorium. I went back the next day and searched the auditorium and the parking lot, but I didn't find the bracelet, nor did it ever turn up at the lost-and-found.

When I bemoaned my loss to my friend Elsie, she said, "Nothing is ever lost. You don't have the bracelet anymore, but somebody does. Bless that person and let the bracelet go."

Following her suggestion, I thought of the bracelet on another woman's arm and said a short prayer: "Lord, let that woman wear the bracelet in health and joy." A weight lifted from my heart, replaced by a feeling of peace.

Father God, Ruler of the universe, I release all my losses to You
as I proceed toward the future. Amen.
—MADGE HARRAH

APRIL 12

A time to be born, and a time to die....
—ECCLESIASTES 3:2

*H*i, Mom. I just thought I'd let you know that Cheryl's in labor." My son Paul sounded quite nonchalant on the phone, but after all, this would be their seventh child. I arrived at the hospital only five minutes after little Haley Sierra was born, and was greeted by my beaming son, who was now anything but nonchalant. "Just look at her, Mom—isn't she the most beautiful baby you ever saw? Perfect in every way!"

She was. She really was. But, of course, I've felt that way about each one. The excitement and sense of wonder at the birth of a baby never diminishes. What a miracle a new life is! Every birth has had its own uniqueness. Yet a mysterious thread has been weaving in and out among the members of our extended family, a thread I've not told about before. It's this. It often happens that soon after the death of an elder family member, a new baby arrives.

Grandmother Morgan died just before Karen was born; John was born shortly after my father died; Joshua, our first grandchild, arrived a few days after the death of my husband's father; Saralisa was born shortly after her paternal grandmother died; and little Haley's maternal grandfather died only a few days before she was born.

So what do I make of this? I don't think it's cause and effect (although when my father died, while I was pregnant with John, a friend consoled me by saying, "Your dad is with God, picking out just the right little angel to send into your family"). For me, the message has always been: Every ending is also a beginning. Whenever I find myself grieving a loss—a friend moving away, a cherished possession stolen, a death in the family—I see the faces of all those beautiful babies, and I give thanks for new beginnings, yet unseen, that are just a life-breath away.

Thank You, great Creator of all life. Thank You for
the continual promise of new beginnings.
—MARILYN MORGAN KING

APRIL 13

A prudent wife is from the Lord.
—PROVERBS 19:14

I couldn't believe it! After fifteen years of talking about it, my husband was sorting through and clearing out the boxes stacked in the stairwell of the garage.

Then he found the letter. "What about this?" he asked as he came into the kitchen for a glass of iced tea.

"What is it?" I asked.

"You know, Aunt Belle's letter," he said.

How could I ever forget! Aunt Belle lived on a farm on the White Horse Plains, about a hundred miles west of Winnipeg, Manitoba, Canada. She was a God-fearing, no-nonsense woman. The strength of the prairie ran in her blood. It had to. She took her family through hail, grasshoppers, rust blight, and drought, and then through the crippling Depression of the thirties.

Her letter came after we became engaged and John had written telling her about me and enclosed a picture. "Well now," she wrote, "at last you have found someone willing to marry you. She seems like a sensible girl; should make you a good wife."

I had bristled at the word.

"She's given you the best compliment ever," John assured me. "A farm wife has to be sensible."

Unimpressed, I frowned. "Well, I don't like her, and that's that."

Little did I know then how much Aunt Belle's word *sensible* would focus me through my life. As problems came up, I'd think, *Now what would be Aunt Belle's sensible way to solve this?* When the bills kept coming in and our money kept running out, I'd sit down and tell myself, *Aunt Belle says I'm sensible. There must be a way to cut the corners.* I found them.

When our son got engaged, I said to my husband, "Melissa's a pretty girl, and"—with a knowing wink—"she seems sensible. Should make him a good wife."

*Thank You, Lord, for those who through the living of their lives
have given me gems of wisdom.*
—FAY ANGUS

I have called daily upon thee, I have stretched out my hands unto thee.
—PSALM 88:9

*M*y wife, Carol, has a group of friends on the Internet, most of whom she's never met face-to-face. They are part of a network set up by our college where alumni from different classes get to know each other. In her group the primary bond is parenting—all of the alums are rearing children—and over the years they have come to know one another well, discussing everything from homework problems to soccer camp. Inevitably, they have also talked each other through some tough times.

One of the toughest came when one member was diagnosed with breast cancer. Advice flew through cyberspace—what treatments to try, what doctors had said, which hospitals were best. In this case, the family made the decision to move across the country to be near a fine hospital in Texas. Progress reports kept the e-mail group well informed. But then, at a crucial moment, someone came up with an idea as good as any medical science had provided. "12:00 tomorrow, Central Time, let's meet for prayer," said the e-mail message.

The next day, Carol logged on at one o'clock our time, noon in Texas, and opened her e-mail. She scrolled down. "I'm here," "Ready," "Waiting," came the litany of responses, and from office buildings in New York to kitchens in California, people prayed through the great electronic silence. "Amen," they signed out.

No one who first heard Christ say, "Where two or more are gathered in my name," could have guessed at a gathering encompassing thousands of miles. But then again, the mystery and power of prayer is more profound than cyberspace. And our communities of prayer need only be a password away.

May I be tireless, Lord, in Your community of prayer.
—RICK HAMLIN

APRIL 15
TAX DAY

Render therefore unto Caesar the things which be Caesar's....
—LUKE 20:25

O h, the misery of income tax time! It's not so much paying out the money to Uncle Sam (although that's bad enough), it's the agony of doing all the arithmetic, scouting around for misplaced receipts, and fumbling through umpteen canceled checks. But the worst part (and this always happens to me) is when you've added everything up, made all the calculations, and completed your return, you recheck it once more only to find that your totals don't match. You have to do your whole return again!

The other night, trying to find where I had gone wrong in a column of figures that I'd added three times with three different results, I remembered something that C. S. Lewis once wrote about the nature of sin. He said that it wasn't enough to admit your sins and be sorry. He said that you have to go back, make restitution, and set things to rights exactly at the point where they went wrong in the first place. He likened it to a mistake in arithmetic, explaining that you'll never come up with the right answer until you retrace your steps, locate the original error—and correct it! I know all too well that that's true when I've made a mistake in addition. And I'm willing to wager it's just as true when I've made a mistake in life!

*Lord, give us the honesty to admit past mistakes and the courage
to go back and correct them.*

—ARTHUR GORDON

I can do all things through Christ which strengtheneth me.
—PHILIPPIANS 4:13

ake a running start and dive forward, allowing your body to fly headfirst toward the ground. Now, just before you land, pull your chin and feet up and slide to a stop on your chest."

Our high-school volleyball coach was teaching my teammates and me this maneuver so we could dive for balls without cracking our ribs on the gym floor. The only problem was, it was 100 percent counterintuitive. We'd grown up trying to avoid ever having to hurtle toward the earth upside-down. Now we were being told we had to do it. Guys were landing with a thud on their knees, sprawling on their bellies, coming within inches of chipping their metal-braced teeth. Some guys would just stand there for minutes at a time, frozen, without the foggiest idea of how they were going to get their chests to hit the floor before their faces.

Finally, I got the hang of it. And it really wasn't a matter of mechanics. It was a matter of trust. If I listened to the instructor and didn't listen to the inner voice telling me it was impossible, I could indeed experience the freedom of letting myself fly through the air and land like a seaplane on a lake of still water.

I learned a lesson that day. There are some things that seem completely impossible, but with a little trust, I can do them. I can forgive somebody who has hurt me. I can sit next to somebody I don't know at church and start up a conversation. I can extend a hand and a heart of friendship to someone of a different color. It's all in the letting go.

Lord, when I think I'm trapped by my limitations,
help me to surpass them by trusting You.
—DAVE FRANCO

"The Lord will fight for you while you keep silent."
—Exodus 14:14 (NAS)

I was fighting an overwhelming desire. I longed to urge my thirty-three-year-old son, Jon, to enter a drug rehab program. I knew he was close to making the phone call. Surely there was something else I could say. But God seemed to insist, *You can't help him. Be quiet.*

As I entered our local pharmacy at five o'clock that afternoon, my eye caught a slight movement in a piece of crumpled newspaper resting against the building. The tip of a bird's tail protruded from it. Inside, I asked the cashier, "Do y'all know there's a baby bird outside?"

"Oh my! Is it still there? It's been there since early this morning." The temperature was in the mid-nineties and the humidity was intense. *I don't need a bird today*, I thought as I left the store. Even so, I stooped down and removed the newspaper. The little swallow didn't struggle when I cupped a hand over it and slid my other hand underneath. From the top of a building high above us, the frightened mother bird called loudly.

I gazed up at her and at the relentless May sun. *You aren't going to be able to help him, Mother Bird. You have to trust me.*

Back at home, I phoned the wildlife department at the University of Georgia. An hour and many calls later, someone on the other end of the phone asked, "Do you know about Elizabeth? I have her number somewhere."

Elizabeth confirmed that she rescued wildlife as a volunteer for the state of Georgia. But she was sorry; she couldn't help today. She was already feeding quite a few birds and she was expecting company. The birds had to be fed every forty-five minutes. Despair closed in quickly. First Jon and now this bird.

Suddenly Elizabeth said, "Listen, Marion, I'm supposed to take this bird. I don't know why."

Three long days later, Jon made that life-changing phone call.

Oh, Father, teach me when I should remain silent, so those I love
can hear Your powerful voice.

—Marion Bond West

*The Lord recompense thy work, and a full reward be given thee
of the Lord God of Israel....*
—RUTH 2:12

*T*he minister who married my husband and me is a very interesting man. Not only is Jerry Lites cominister of an active and growing little church in northern California, he's also a local law enforcement officer and, in his spare time, he travels with a crisis team to hot spots all over the world to teach people how to deal with potential terrorist and hostage situations.

I didn't learn about Jerry's other life until after I got to know him as a caring, faith-filled minister. Frankly, it was a bit hard for me to reconcile the gentle servant of God with the vigilant cop and the cool crisis negotiator. When we walked out to the parking lot after our wedding rehearsal, Jerry told us a story that closed the gap.

He had been on patrol the night before in what was apparently a very cool unmarked car. When the youngster who had just gotten his license decided to impress his friends by trying to race the gentleman in the great car, he didn't know whom he was tangling with—until Jerry pulled him over. After admonishing, ticketing, and sternly lecturing the youngster, Jerry noticed how unhappy the boy was. He put his arm around the boy's shoulders, handed him his cell phone, and said, "Now, I'll stay here with you while you call your mom."

As we drove away from the church that night, I understood that Jerry was a good minister because of, and not despite, his wide range of experience. His knowledge of human nature—the good and the bad—had taught him how to nurture the one and forgive the other.

*Father, help me to follow Jerry's example in all my relationships
and in all my work.*
—MARCI ALBORGHETTI

All the ends of the world shall remember and turn unto the Lord.
—PSALM 22:27

*A*pril 19 is an important anniversary for me. I like to celebrate it with my friend Ray, because it's important for him, too. He calls me or I call him and we schedule lunch. Initially we don't talk about why we happen to be celebrating. Maybe I'll be conscious of it in a noisy restaurant as I try to seat myself close to his right side because he's been deaf in his left ear since his operation. Or I might scratch my left ear and think of it because of the lingering numbness in my nerves there ever since my operation. Otherwise we talk about our kids, our wives, our work.

At the end of lunch, when I'm taking a bite out of his slice of chocolate cake and he's taking a spoonful of my apple pie, it will come up in an oblique way. I'll remember that morning when we were both recovering from surgery, when the best distraction from my discomfort had been to pray for him because I was too afraid to pray for myself. That we both had tumors in similar places and that we both were operated on—in different hospitals—on the same day was the sort of coincidence that we would have been happier without.

But then came the good news. My surgery was successful, so was his. Both our tumors were benign. In the five years since, our other news has been good. So we schedule this annual lunch to remind ourselves of our blessings. We have a lot to be grateful for. No one knows that as well as Ray and me, two guys in business suits at a thanksgiving feast. Just what an anniversary is for.

Let me never forget all the good reasons I have for celebrating, Lord!
—RICK HAMLIN

APRIL 20

I well remember them, and my soul is downcast.... Yet this I call to mind and therefore I have hope: Because of the Lord's great love we are not consumed, for his compassions never fail.

—LAMENTATIONS 3:20–22 (NIV)

oday marks an anniversary indelibly imprinted in many of our hearts, the day the tragic Columbine High School shootings occurred. Two armed students killed thirteen people and injured more than twenty others before killing themselves in the school library. Here in the Denver area, we absorbed many of the painful shock waves because this struck so close to home. I work with a mom whose son hid for hours as a captive in the school that day and with another woman whose teenage babysitter was critically injured.

Where is the hope in the midst of this horror? I wondered.

A few days after the tragedy, while getting some bedding plants at a local nursery, I spied a packet of columbine flower seeds. On the front was a beautiful picture of these blue-and-white blossoms, a hopeful vision of what could grow out of the dead-looking seeds inside. I purchased a packet and placed it on the windowsill above my desk at my office to remind me that the seeds of hope could grow something beautiful out of this tragedy. And sure enough, as the days wore on, I began to see some of those seeds of hope. At local blood banks, people stood in line for hours to donate. Young people all over Denver committed their lives to Christ. Church attendance grew and many congregations reported incredible revivals. A high school student in California raised eighteen thousand dollars to help pay for a victim's medical bills. Students broke down the barriers between cliques, and some victim's families lived out amazing examples of forgiveness.

I still have that packet of columbine seeds on my windowsill, and today, as the media again review the horror of that day, I will remember how little seeds of hope can blossom into great blessings.

Lord, today please comfort and bless the families of those touched by tragedy.

—CAROL KUYKENDALL

So we, being many, are one body in Christ, and
every one members one of another.

—ROMANS 12:5

s a five-year-old growing up in a small New Hampshire village, I knew exactly how a church should look: white, with a white steeple. So I felt stirrings of frustration that morning in Sunday school when I couldn't find a white crayon in the sharing box. I was too shy to ask my classmates to borrow theirs. And why bother? Since all the other five-year-olds knew that churches were white, and the coloring project was large, I would never have time to finish even if I waited for a white crayon.

So I did the next best thing. I poked around in the sharing box, found my favorite colors, and concentrated on staying within the lines. After a few moments I paused to survey my church: purple roof and steeple, pink front. Why stop there? Blue side, green door, a dash of yellow on the entryway. The innovative color scheme of my church did not at all reflect the way I wanted it to be, but I had done a pretty good job, even crudely cutting the front door so that it opened. I felt strangely pleased with my colorful project. Not perfect, but the door opened. It worked.

My wise mother saved my creation.

Today I worship in a modern church of beige brick. I'm not very shy anymore and can ask for what I need, but my church still isn't all I want it to be. I try to adapt to the inconvenient schedules, the irritating personalities, the startling innovations that knock me out of my comfort zone. That's when it's good to reflect upon my yellowing pink-and-purple church, and remember that my congregation reflects my imperfect personality, too. My church isn't always the way I want it to be, but it works. And the door is always open.

Lord, help me to do my best and not waste energy criticizing myself or others—
in and out of church. Amen.

—GAIL THORELL SCHILLING

APRIL 22
EARTH DAY

"Go, walk through the length and breadth of the land, for I am giving it to you."
—GENESIS 13:17 (NIV)

My little girl Maria and I were waiting for my mom to finish a doctor's appointment, and rather than try to keep a lively toddler busy in the waiting room, I took her for a walk. We wandered across the street to a church with a huge, wide lawn. Maria ran as fast as she could up the grassy hills, then rolled down, smiling and laughing.

Just then a woman began walking toward us from the church office. *Uh-oh!* I thought. *Did I overlook a "Keep Off the Grass" sign?*

"You know," she said as she reached us, smiling at my little girl, "I've worked here quite awhile and I've never seen anyone play on this lawn. I think it's because we're a church and people think they have to show reverence for the whole place, even the grass."

The woman was correct. If Maria hadn't been with me that day, I would have walked on the sidewalk and appreciated that lush green lawn only from afar. But Maria had the right idea. I can't imagine God intended His great natural wonders merely to inspire reverence and awe. So to the popular slogan, "Reduce, reuse, recycle," I'm adding another word, *realize.* For me that means getting up close to realize fully the world's wonder and appreciate its treasures.

Here are some new ways to celebrate this Earth Day. Stick your nose in a flower. Lie down in wet grass. Get some dirt under your fingernails. Bury your toes in the sand. Play in the water. Bite into a fresh apple and let the juice run down your chin. Care for the earth in the simplest way: Spend some time with it.

Giver of all life, help me to embrace Your earth like a little child, with more enthusiasm than reverence and more love than awe.

—GINA BRIDGEMAN

April 23

The Lord is near to the brokenhearted, and saves the crushed in spirit.
—Psalm 34:18 (RSV)

When my daughter was married two years ago, I discovered a reservoir of sadness over my own failed marriage. At the time, God provided friends to help me cope with my pain, and I thought it had gone. But my middle child, Phil, is to be married this summer, and my pain, I'm discovering, is still there.

When I was a child, my sisters and I were each given a large chocolate pencil. I hadn't had mine long when it broke. I was disconsolate. When my father came home, I went to him in tears with the two halves of my broken treasure. He sat me on his lap and, when I was all cried out, told me to fetch the matches and a candle from the mantel.

"Why?" I wanted to know, sniffing through my lingering tears.

"Watch and see."

Dad melted the broken ends of my pencil over the flickering flame, then quickly pressed the sticky chocolate together. A few slow spins over the flame and he was able to smooth the lumpy joining. When he handed me back my pencil, it was wondrously repaired and, although not as good as new, all the dearer to me. What had once been broken, my father had made whole.

Today, while praying again for the healing of my sadness, I remembered my father and that chocolate pencil and I prayed:

Heavenly Father, I bring You the pain of broken dreams, knowing that whatever is broken, You can make whole.

—Brenda Wilbee

APRIL 24

This is my comfort in my affliction....
—PSALM 119:50

*T*he word *comfort* is scattered all through the Bible, as well it should be, because there are times when all of us need it, especially when a loved one dies.

Recently an eighty-four-year-old friend named Edna Hawkins sent me a note from Smyrna, Georgia, where she lives. "Here's something I found on a tombstone in a North Carolina cemetery," she wrote.

Spring will come again to the valley.
Flowers will grow on the mountains.
And the Shepherd will return for His sheep.

Just twenty-one words. I don't know who wrote them. But it seems to me that there is an enormous comfort in them. My friend recognized this, and passed them along to me. Now I am passing them along to you.

Lord, teach us to comfort the afflicted in any way we can.
—ARTHUR GORDON

APRIL 25

*And some of the parts that seem weakest and least important
are really the most necessary.*
—I CORINTHIANS 12:22 (TLB)

*I*t was April of my freshman year at Oklahoma State University. My father had died that January, and I needed a summer job to help with next year's college expenses. But what could I do? There were no jobs available in my town of 350 people and I didn't have a car. Then I spotted an announcement posted on the Student Union bulletin board.

Female Counselors, Red Rock Canyon Girl Scout Camp, nine-week position. Preference given to former Girl Scouts with both wilderness and traditional camping experience.

That job would be an answer to my prayers. Red Rock Canyon was only thirty miles from my home. There was only one hitch: I wasn't qualified.

My mouth went dry when Maryellen, the camp director, asked if I could remain calm around poisonous snakes. The only question I answered with an enthusiastic "Yes!" was "Do you know how to cook?"

When Maryellen called a week later, I was amazed to hear I'd landed a job. "Almost everyone had basic scouting skills," she said, "but you were the only girl who could cook. Counselors prepare meals on the wilderness trips, and they also teach campers about food preparation and safety."

That summer I skinned snakes and dried the skins with borax. I survived four-day wilderness trips without washing my hair or brushing my teeth. And, yes, I mastered the art of the jungle hammock.

It was the most valuable summer of my life, for I learned something that has helped me in every job since: God can use my everyday skills to answer my prayers and to build His kingdom on earth.

*Lord, You have come to the lakeshore, looking for neither wealthy nor wise ones;
You only asked me to follow humbly.*
—PENNEY SCHWAB

APRIL 26

The prayer of faith shall save the sick....
—JAMES 5:15

*W*hen I was helping the late poet Helen Steiner Rice write her autobiography many years ago, she told me something that I've never forgotten. "What happens to you in life, Fred," she counseled, "is not as important as your attitude toward it."

Her words came back to me when I was diagnosed with non-Hodgkin's lymphoma. My first thought upon hearing the doctor's verdict was, *I am going to die soon.* My chest tightened and my heart raced. My second thought, a calming one, was, *Your life is still in God's hands, the same as it was when He gave you your first breath. Nothing can separate you from His love.*

And it was that faith and positive mindset—along with the prayers of many others—that sustained me through the chemotherapy. As I am writing this, my cancer is in remission, the length or permanence of which I do not know. What I do know is that Mrs. Rice was right about the importance of attitude. There are many things that we cannot control, but with God's help we can control our thoughts, and triumph over anything.

When troubles mount and worries grow large,
Remind me, Lord, of Who's in charge.
—FRED BAUER

Lay not up for yourselves treasures upon earth....
—MATTHEW 6:19

*E*ver wonder what happens to people who have a lot of talent yet never make it to the top? Well, I know one of them.

A few months ago I came across a notice on our library bulletin board. It announced a new Saturday morning program for children featuring a storyteller named Eleanor Booth. "I know her!" I said to my friend. "We were in high school together."

Even as a teenager, Eleanor seemed destined for stardom. She loved to act and had the lead in every school play. She was beautiful, too. We all expected to see her name up in lights someday, but she went on to college, got married, had a child, and then I lost track of her. That was a long time ago.

Naturally I was curious, so I went to the first storytelling hour. The room was so crowded that some of the parents and children sat on the floor. When Eleanor was introduced, I saw that she was still lovely—a tall, slim woman who moved like a dancer. And for the next hour she took us all on a journey to a magical world of children, talking trees, singing waterfalls, and exciting chases up and down mountains. She acted out every part, lowering her voice to a growl for the villains and chirping birdcalls that sounded like the real thing. She made us see the story and the characters in it, and when she finished we all stood and cheered.

"Thank you," she whispered. Except for being older, she looked exactly the way she did when she used to take a bow after a school play—happy and a bit surprised by all the fuss. She was surrounded by excited children asking questions, so I waited to say hello. But I could see that Eleanor hadn't missed out on anything by missing the big time. She used her God-given talent to make people happy. And maybe that's why God gives us our talents—not to put our names up in lights, but to bring light into the lives of others.

Thank You for my gifts, Lord, and give me opportunities to share them.
—PHYLLIS HOBE

APRIL 28

Therefore I will look unto the Lord....
—MICAH 7:7

J did something today that I dread doing: I went to the doctor for my annual physical. I procrastinate even making the appointment, and when I do, it's mostly out of guilt and fear, because we all know that once we reach a certain age, an annual physical is advised. Making the appointment reminds me that I've reached that certain age.

I woke up today feeling apprehensive. I didn't eat breakfast because of the weigh-in. Instead of taking the elevator, I walked up the three flights of stairs to the office. When it came time to step on the scales, I quickly removed my shoes, watch, and earrings, but still I winced at the results, fearing the nurse might demand to see my driver's license, just to see how badly I lied about my weight.

Next came the finger-prick for blood. I watched the nurse take out the pricker, squeeze my finger, and pause. In that split second, I anticipated agonizing pain, and sure enough—*ouch*! With a Band-Aid wrapped around my throbbing finger, I was ushered into a little examining room. The nurse told me to remove my clothes and put on this teensy triangular piece of cloth, and then she left me alone. A few minutes later, I sat perched on the edge of the examining table, with nothing to do but think about how much I dreaded the next part of the examination. I leaned back on my elbows, looked up at the ceiling, and then laughed out loud. There was a drawing of a silly-looking worm, laid out stiff as a board, with a grimace on its face. Underneath was just one word: *Relax*.

The ceiling picture helped me lighten up, but it also made me realize that I needed to change my focus. I'd been looking down at everything I dreaded—the scales, the finger-pricking, the teensy triangle of cloth. In the midst of my angst, I'd forgotten to look up, which is where I'd find the strength to relax.

Relax. I know the word comes from You, Father. Thank You.
—CAROL KUYKENDALL

April 29

Mercy triumphs over judgment!
—James 2:13 (niv)

*M*y wife, Rosie, and I were driving to a speaking engagement at a church not far from where Rosie grew up. It was a wonderful opportunity for me. I would be the first African-American to speak at this church. The pastor had become my friend and he wanted the people in his church to learn about our ministry.

As we drove along, Rosie said, "Dolphus, this is the town where I was taken to a doctor for the first time. I was an eleventh-grade student then, and the experience really scared me. I wish you hadn't accepted the invitation to speak here." I was nervous enough about speaking at the church, and Rosie's words made me uneasy. By the time we got to within a few blocks of the church, Rosie's pulse was racing. "I don't know what good can possibly come out of our being here. I wish we could just turn the car around and go home!"

When we drove up, the pastor and some of the members of the congregation were waiting outside for us. We were warmly greeted, and when it was time for me to speak, I felt an incredible sense of freedom. Afterward, in the fellowship hall, I could feel the love of Christ through the love the people showed us.

As we drove back to Mendenhall, Rosie was thoughtful. "You know," she said, "when we drove into town, all I could think of was my bad experience here. I wasn't willing to live in the present. I wasn't ready for God to do something really new here. But He didn't care if I was ready. He just wanted me to feel His love."

Lord, teach me today to let go of the past and experience Your love.
—Dolphus Weary

April 30

"The time of the singing of birds has come...."
—Song of Solomon 2:12 (TLB)

One day, twenty years ago, jostled about by a family of four getting ready for school and work, I felt overwhelmed, trapped by the myriad responsibilities of motherhood. And then, among the sounds of alarm clocks ringing, showers running, children squabbling, and dishes clattering, I heard a robin sing. I still remember that melody filtering through the cracks of that hectic spring morning, challenging me to slow down, relax, enjoy life more.

A robin's song spoke of spring rains, clean air, and lilac blooms, a brook running meekly within its banks, earthworms surfacing in the garden, fish swimming upstream. It meant water bugs sprinting on the surface of the river and fiddlehead ferns uncurling along the banks. A robin's song meant apple blossoms white and pink as sugared popcorn, and a nest with four blue eggs holding promises of new life.

Today, the house seems almost deathly still, the brooding silence broken only by the monotonous ticking of the clock. I feel lonely, unmotivated, depressed— until a robin's song penetrates the quiet. That cheerful sound means it is time to resume daily walks, take the fishing tackle out of storage, build a trellis, round up the garden tools. The label on a packet of flower seeds boasts "spring's best promise." How dare they plagiarize a robin's song!

God, thank You for that harbinger of joy that tells my soul "the winter is past, the rain is over and gone."
—Alma Barkman

May

MAY 1

Sing unto the Lord a new song, and his praise from the end of the earth....
—ISAIAH 42:10

O ne day I told my dentist, "I like to hear you sing while you work." He laughed and resumed the tune he had been humming. The Bible is full of accounts of people singing with joy and happiness—but it also tells of another kind of singing. Singing when there is no reason to sing. Paul sang while he was in prison. After the Last Supper, Jesus sang with His disciples. Knowing of the ordeal He faced, He still sang! Surely the sound of song in all its manifestations is dear to God.

Recently I heard a minister give voice to song in a most difficult situation. At the graveside of his son, as the young body was being lowered into the ground, the father started to softly sing his favorite hymns—songs of praise!

Is there a joyful occasion in your life today that you can celebrate with song? Is there a pain that you must work through? Why not offer Your Father a sacrifice of singing praises in His name?

Alleluia! Alleluia! Alleluia! Alleluia!
—MARION BOND WEST

MAY 2

"Bring my sons from afar and my daughters from the ends of the earth—
everyone who is called by my name, whom I created for my glory,
whom I formed and made."

—ISAIAH 43:6–7 (NIV)

I was sitting in our prayer group one Sunday after a week of especially grim news stories: murders, child abuse, corruption in government. Our tiny circle felt weighed down by these and by all the problems we ourselves had brought into the room. In despair, I said glumly, "How does this world keep going? It seems like all these problems would overwhelm it."

A middle-aged grandmother leaned forward, eyes suddenly sparkling. "Why, we're forgetting how large our circle really is. There are millions of us who follow God, who each day, in His name, pick up the jobs we've been given and do them to the best of our ability. All over the world, this very minute, people like us are sending up prayers. There are more of us than you think when you're reading the papers."

Her reminder brought sighs of relief. The mood shifted. Our load had lightened. We smiled at one another, fellow laborers in a world where God still reigns, despite the bad news.

The next time I feel outnumbered, weighed down and weary, I'll remember this truth. And when I read the paper, I'll keep the bad news in perspective.

Lord, help me to do my part and leave those who don't do their part to You.

—SHARI SMYTH

MAY 3

Accept one another....
—ROMANS 15:7 (NAS)

*L*ovey, our golden retriever Labrador, wags her tail at everything that moves—squirrels, butterflies, strangers, even cars whizzing by. Most of the time, they don't respond. But that doesn't faze Lovey. She keeps wagging her tail as if the whole world loved her.

Maybe dogs don't worry about being rejected, but I do. I'm afraid to make friends because I'm afraid I'll lose them. Whether it's a gradual cooling of friendly feelings, a change in circumstances that forces someone to move away, or the forces of life over which we have no control like sickness and death, something will happen to take my friend away from me.

As we walk, Lovey pulls hard on the leash and begins to wag her tail furiously. A neighbor we hardly know is approaching her mailbox. She bends down to give Lovey a pat. Lovey looks back at me, panting with wild delight, as if to say, "See, she accepts me. I am loved!" Then I remember that this neighbor is going through a family crisis. Reluctant to get involved, I say a polite "hi," planning to move on quickly. But Lovey drags me to within inches of the woman. I can see the agony in her face. I'm startled, shocked. "Are you okay?" I ask her.

She starts to cry right there by the mailbox. Not neat little tears, from the corners of her eyes—the kind you can dab away—but deep, racking sobs. Even as she cries, her gentle eyes hold mine. "Listen, let me put the dog in the house and I'll be right back, okay?" She nods and stands there and waits for me at the mailbox. I hurry.

Father, help me overcome my fear of rejection and get on with the things
You have for me to do.
—MARION BOND WEST

Your lips have spoken lies....
—Isaiah 59:3

I was having trouble with the A-drive of my new laptop and had brought it in for analysis by my computer mentor and friend Sven Jarvis. Sven has spent years struggling with these wonderful/awful machines and I was sure he could help. But even Sven was stumped by the problem. He thought that perhaps the trouble was with the diskette I had been using. Sven took the disk out of my laptop, put it into his own equipment, and hit the Enter key. Suddenly, a voice boomed out, filling his entire shop. *You have made a fatal error. Nothing can be done!*

Dismayed, I stared at my friend, but he was unconcerned. Then he explained that his computer will talk to you when you do something wrong. "You learn, though, not to panic," Sven said. "The computer gives false messages all the time." So often, when I blunder, I can hear a voice inside telling me I've made a fatal error and nothing can be done. I can be frightened into immobility unless, like Sven, I know better. My errors are not fatal. They are opportunities for Jesus to redeem.

*Father, help me to discern voices that are bringing messages
that do not come from You.*
—John Sherrill

He will be the sure foundation for your times, a rich store of salvation and wisdom and knowledge; the fear of the Lord is the key to this treasure.
—Isaiah 33:6 (NIV)

When my dad was dying, I wondered how my mom would react after his death. In her eighties, would she choose to move on, or would she be unable to adjust to his loss after more than fifty years of marriage? The first months were a struggle, but then Mom did something new. She went to a women's retreat at her church. I talked to her after she got back.

"We each had to bring some small item and tell why it symbolized our life at this moment. I took my key chain," she said to me. "I showed them the car keys and said that they symbolized a new independence. I told them how I had to start driving all over again after Daddy died. He had done all the driving for ten years! I still don't like driving much, but I can get to the store and church by myself at least. And I showed them the house key and told them how hard and sad it was to come back to an empty house. I told them that this key also was a bit scary to me since I am probably going to have to sell this house. I wondered what door key will replace it."

Mom made her choice to move on. She sold the house, and within another year became president of the residents' committee at an active retirement complex. In facing reality through the eyes of faith, she had found the keys to surviving her great loss.

Lord, when I face great loss, help me to remember Mom's keys to survival. Help me to grieve, to accept, and then to move on.
—Roberta Rogers

MAY 6

Surely he has borne our griefs and carried our sorrows....
—ISAIAH 53:4 (RSV)

I curled in a red vinyl hospital chair, blue-jeaned knees against my chest, watching my daughter under the bedcovers. She was sleeping with tubes in her arms, dark hair spilling over the pillow, so thin she hardly seemed to be there. "She's lucky she's alive and there's no damage to her major organs," the doctor had told me earlier. After three months of struggling with sobriety, she'd binged on drugs and alcohol.

Whitney and I had rushed her to the hospital. Now he was at work. I was alone with memories only a mother knows. Carrying her. Birthing her. Nursing her late at night when the house was quiet and I'd given her to God. Watching her grow into a child with bobbing curls. Tending her dolls and later her pony with a simple faith that God would take care of all.

The covers stirred. I knelt by her bedside and watched her awaken, enormous dark eyes searching for, then finding me. "I'm sorry, Mom," she said, shame filling her face. Never had I felt so helpless, wanting to take her shame, her sickness upon me. *I can't bear it,* I cried inwardly. From across the centuries I felt the touch of another mother, reminding me that she'd watched as her Son bore the shame and sin of the world. I felt her whisper, *You can bear it because He bore it for you.* I hugged my daughter, feeling the awesome strength of love. Bigger than any addiction, deeper than any shame. My daughter hugged me back. Tubes and all.

Thank You, Lord, for a love that will not let me go.
—SHARI SMYTH

"Whose confidence is fragile, and whose trust a spider's web."
—Job 8:14 (NAS)

s I planted the garden, the weather was unseasonably cold, the soil lumpy. And oh, my aching back! Gardening under such conditions was not just a workout for my muscles. Sowing tiny seeds in the hardened ground was a real test of faith.

But as I worked, I noticed the hollyhock plants leafing out along the foundation on the east side of our bungalow. Last year, a summer storm had bent one of the hollyhocks almost double. I expected the plant to die, but within a very few days the crippled stem was mysteriously standing upright again. The strong multiple strands of a spider's web had drawn the broken hollyhock back up into position and anchored it to the foundation of the house. With its injured stalk supported by this silken splint, the hollyhock soon recovered, its pink blossoms eventually inching up its entire length.

The memory of that spider's web supporting a tall hollyhock reminded me that even fragile faith can be effective. I resumed my planting. *This garden shows very little promise now, Lord, but these are mountain-moving mustard seeds of faith I'm sowing here.*

Lord, I believe, but help my unbelief.
—Alma Barkman

MAY 8

For God alone my soul waits in silence; from him comes my salvation.
—PSALM 62:1 (RSV)

No one else was within five miles of Laity Lodge that night. The lodge was a new Christian conference center, cantilevered over the edge of a canyon deep in the hill country of southwest Texas. The first official conference was scheduled to begin in two days.

The huge tan flagstone floor of Great Hall reflected the full moon beyond the fifteen-foot glass wall where I sat and looked down at the same moon mirrored in the silent lake far below. This lodge was a place to tell people about God, people who might never listen in a church. I was to be the first director.

I was frightened. I didn't know what to do except tell them my own story: how I'd always sought God, but also run from Him, until I ran out of places and ways to run. And finally, one day on a roadside in east Texas, I surrendered to God as I saw Him in Jesus. But that was years ago, and now I was afraid that I was powerless to help anyone. I felt tears coming to my eyes. I wanted to run away, to hide where no one could find me.

I was sitting in a beam of moonlight coming from the sunroof window in the vaulted ceiling far above my head, with the rest of the cavernous room in shadows. Now I began to feel a reverence, a presence almost, in that beam of moonlight, splayed in an elongated square around me on the flagstones. Excitement, fear, joy flashed through me as I wondered if it could be true, or if it was another trick of my mind. But it didn't matter what my mind thought in that moment. God was with me there, and I with Him. I let go, surrendered, and I was chastened, calmed, and filled with a sure knowledge that everything would be all right.

I wept tears of gratitude. Somehow, God had filled that empty place and washed my fears away in a silver beam of moonlight.

Lord, thank You for reaching out to us, even where there is no preacher or church spire. Amen.
—KEITH MILLER

MAY 9

But if we hope for what we do not see, we wait for it with patience.
—ROMANS 8:25 (RSV)

Another wedding invitation had arrived from the South. As I headed to the post office to mail my regrets and a silver serving spoon, I wondered when my turn for marriage would come. Most of my college friends were celebrating third and fourth anniversaries. Some had babies. What about me? "How much longer?" I asked God.

It was the same question that had wearied my parents during my childhood on our annual eight-hour drive from north Alabama to the Gulf of Mexico. Ten miles from our driveway I was ready to jump out of the station wagon and feel sand between my toes. So I nagged my mom all the way to the coast. "Have we gone halfway? Are we there yet?" Mom suggested I entertain myself. I tried to play the alphabet game or read a book, but they soon lost their charm.

After more than a decade, dating was getting old, too. Fun, yes, but hard work and heartache were part of the long haul. I began to wonder: *Am I really getting closer to a lasting relationship?* My family always made it to the beach by supper time, I remembered as I posted my package. Above the creaking mailbin door I thought I heard God say, *You'll make it, too. You're just not there yet.*

Grant me patience, Lord, when my dreams feel far away,
and help me to enjoy the ride.
—ALLISON SAMPLE

MAY 10

Now there stood by the cross of Jesus his mother, and his mother's sister,
Mary the wife of Cleophas, and Mary Magdalene.

—JOHN 19:25

*S*tanding in church one day, I noticed an older woman across the way. She was around seventy years old. There were two younger women with her—in their forties, I guessed. They seemed like family—two sisters with their mom, or their aunt, perhaps.

It was pouring cars and boats outside, and all three women were wearing rain slickers. The older woman reached up to brush back the younger women's gleaming hoods, and as she did so, the two younger women just stood there quietly. Then she brushed back their hair, and the young women stood there obediently, like small children. I realized slowly that something was strange—the younger women were too calm. They didn't seem quite alert, quite all there.

During services, the younger women held hands, and they watched the older woman to see when to rise and when to kneel. The older woman was calm, her gestures deft. She led the two younger women gently and efficiently down the aisle and out the door when the service was over.

I sat there for a moment amazed and abashed and astounded at the strength of women, the mountains that mothers are, the way mothers carry their loads all their lives, and who knows what those loads are? For some mothers, it is too-placid children who will never really grow up; for another, her own son bleeding and broken above her as she stared up into His face.

Dear Lord, every one of Your children must bear his or her load, well or ill. Lend
us Your sinew, Your broad shoulder, Your capacious heart, Your sudden joy.
This we ask, this we beg, this we pray.

—BRIAN DOYLE

You guide me with your counsel....
—PSALM 73:24 (NIV)

My friend Jeanie's father died after a lengthy illness. Jeanie had always been close to her father, and I knew this would be a difficult time for her. I decided to send flowers to the memorial service, but as I reached for the phone to call the florist, I stopped. I had the distinct impression not to order flowers. "Lord," I prayed, "show me how I can comfort my friend."

The following day I passed an open-air produce market and my thoughts returned to Jeanie. *What is it, Lord? Should I send a basket of fruit?* I tried to dismiss the thought. It didn't seem appropriate. The idea, though, refused to go away. The next day I returned to the produce market. As I walked through the aisles, the pungent fragrance of ripe peaches, sweet strawberries, and tangy oranges filled my nostrils. I purchased a large wicker basket and filled it with fresh fruit for Jeanie. A fragrant breeze blew through the aisles, and I felt my spirit lift. I prayed that this gift of God's goodness would lift her spirit as well.

I received a note from Jeanie a few days later. "During my dad's last days he spoke of picking peaches. As I held his hands, I thought of our life together. Dad was a chef, and each week when I was growing up, a produce man would leave fresh fruit in a box on our porch—juicy oranges, sweet apples, and fragrant peaches. Your gift of fresh fruit was more than a coincidence, it was a sign from my dad."

Thank You, Lord, for Your gentle guidance.
—MELODY BONNETTE

MAY 12

"As a mother comforts her child, so will I comfort you...."
—ISAIAH 66:13 (NIV)

My husband, Whitney, and I had just come home from an overnight trip, and our pet sitter wore a long face. "That wild kitten got in the house," she said. "He's upstairs and won't let me near him. I'm so sorry."

The kitten belonged to a stray named Babe who lived on our porch. She had given birth to him in the woods. He'd never seen a human until the week before, when she brought him home to us. He was as wild as could be, and now he was in the house. I hadn't a clue how to catch him.

I climbed the stairs in dread. There he was, his little yellow face poking around the corner. When he saw me, he hissed and raised his back, unsheathed his claws, and sprang for my face. I ducked just in time. He ran to the bedroom. I ran in after him and closed the door.

The kitten was hunched in a corner under the bed, panting with fear. I thought about ways to trap him. The butterfly net! *If I chase him long enough and tire him out, I can put the net over him. Then I'll cover the net with a towel and...* But, no. The little guy would never get over the trauma if I used such force. *Think, Shari, think. If you were that kitten, what would take away your terror?* I closed the door softly, went out to the porch, picked up the mother cat, and carried her up to the bedroom. She sniffed at the rug. *Meow*, she called. I heard a rustling from under the bed.

The kitten's taut little face appeared, draped with the dust ruffle. He raced to greet his mother. She washed his ears and talked to him in soft meows. He purred. Ever so gently I nudged them both into the crate I had waiting and carried it downstairs to the porch. When I opened the crate, kitten and mother strolled out. I bowed my head and said:

Thank You, God, for comfort and comforters.
—SHARI SMYTH

MAY 13

My son... forsake not the law of thy mother.
—PROVERBS 1:8

A few years ago, after my mother moved into a nursing home, I spent a melancholy weekend boxing up her things, trying to decide what should be saved and what should be tossed out, and resisting the urge to donate it all to Goodwill and let them deal with it.

Then, in the big bottom drawer of her old oak wardrobe, I discovered a collection of stuff in a beat-up Hudson's department store box: all the childhood gifts I'd given her for Mother's Day. I didn't know whether to cringe or cry.

There was the shamrock key chain with the illegible "Mom" I had engraved on it myself, and the Jean Naté Fleur de Versailles bath set I saved my lawn-mowing money to buy at the five-and-ten. She still had the awful blue Wedgwood candy dish with the poodle head cameo in honor of Pete, our dog. There was the pot holder that said "#1 Cook" (Mom didn't really like to cook), a chintzy picture frame with my fifth-grade class shot still in it, taken the day after I got a front tooth knocked out playing tetherball, a snow globe of the Mackinac Bridge from my smart-aleck gag-gift phase (crossing that huge span always made her dizzy); and the cards with my earnest attempts to put my feelings into words. I was amazed I ever passed spelling, let alone penmanship.

Yet what I felt most keenly as I went through those Mother's Day gifts of mine was the joy with which each and every one was received, the delight Mom took in the act of giving, especially when practiced so imperfectly by a little boy. No, Mom never cringed, not even at the sight of the Wedgwood poodle dish, and sometimes, I remember, she did cry. So did I that day over the old Hudson's box. No one will ever love you like your mother, they say, and I had found proof of that.

Lord, You give us mothers for countless reasons. I think
the most important is this: They teach us to love.
—EDWARD GRINNAN

MAY 14

For the Lord seeth not as man seeth....
—I SAMUEL 16:7

*E*very morning Tib and I walk to the village of Hawkshead, some forty-five minutes away.

We follow public footpaths that wander down lanes and cross farmers' fields. Most of the way, the footpaths are hedged with stone walls. My mind struggles to imagine the work involved, each rock rooted out of the fields, hauled to the fence line, hoisted into place. When I mentioned the walls to our B&B landlady, she said, "Then you'll want to meet Mr. Townsend. He's patching a wall just down the road."

Next morning, as Tib and I followed a chest-high wall, we heard the unmistakable tap-tap of a mason's hammer on the other side. After a moment, a dust-covered cap appeared, then a pair of blue eyes, and then the torso of a wizened man covered with stone dust.

Mr. Townsend seemed pleased to be asked about his trade. "I've been building walls since I was a lad," he said. "Helped Dad clear the pastures." As a teenager he was apprenticed to a mason. Most walls were built by local farmers, Mr. Townsend said, though they usually needed help from real wall-men like himself. "Not everybody gets to work on walls all year round like I do," he said. "For a farmer, walls are winter work."

After a quarter of an hour, Mr. Townsend signaled that he had to get back to work by bending (straight-backed, I noticed) to pick up a large fieldstone. As he did so, he said something that has changed the way I look at the "stones" in my own work—interruptions, time pressure, an aging body.

"Our fields are full of rocks," he said, gesturing toward the pasture behind him. "But . . ."—and here Mr. Townsend settled the huge fieldstone into place—"the good Lord helps us turn these stones into something useful, doesn't He!"

Father, help me to see the obstacles in my life as building material.
—JOHN SHERRILL

We have different gifts, according to the grace given us....
—ROMANS 12:6 (NIV)

oday, Tib and I stopped to admire a garden very different from the wildflower bouquets we enjoyed yesterday. On the gray stones in front of us was a flat patchwork of subtle color—gold, gray, black, white, rust, chartreuse.

"Lichen!" I said to myself.

When I was a boy, we kids called lichen "rock fuzz." Later on, in college, I gained a lot of respect for this humble-looking life form. I learned that lichen is not a single organism but a mutually dependent relationship between two totally unrelated living things, fungus and algae. The fungus establishes the secure foothold that the algae require and hoards the needed moisture. The algae convert the sun's energy into food for them both. Together they colonized the barren rocks of the early earth, life's first beachhead on land, preparing the way for all that followed.

Interdependence. I looked at the wall before us, the hard, unyielding stones, and then at this hardy pioneer, linking very different needs and abilities to do the impossible. And I thought I had a glimpse of the body of Christ at work, each member depending on others with different contributions, each an image of the one Lord.

Father, help me to rejoice in our differences. Those most unlike me
may be the ones I need most.
—JOHN SHERRILL

MAY 16

"For I am the Lord your God who takes hold of your right hand and says to you, Do not fear; I will help you."

—ISAIAH 41:13 (NIV)

*L*ast spring, my wife, Rosie, flew to Memphis to visit our daughter Danita. It's a flight that normally takes an hour. On this particular day, however, it took close to three hours. There was a storm in the area, and the plane had to be rerouted twice to try and fly around it.

From the moment the plane took off, Rosie had the feeling that it was going to be an unusual flight, so she began to pray. As the plane repeatedly ran into turbulence, she started praying harder. Finally, as the pilot began trying to fly around the storm, Rosie began to have some really serious conversations with the Lord. The flight attendants had not been able to serve beverages for the first two hours. When the turbulence subsided, they began to serve. They had only served about six rows when the Fasten Seatbelts signs came on and the pilot instructed the flight attendants to be seated immediately.

"Within five minutes we hit something extremely hard," Rosie said, "and the glasses and beverages began to fly everywhere. People were really shaken up. I asked the Lord to take care of the family if I didn't make it. Then I felt the Lord telling me, *Look at your hands. What do you see?* My hands were pressed together, with the fingers interlocked tightly and the right thumb pressed down over the left. When I looked down, I saw that my thumbs formed a cross. Then I felt the Lord saying, *Whenever the turbulence gets so heavy that you think you can't go on, just look to the cross*."

When the plane finally landed, Rosie's hands were still clasped together, and her eyes were on that cross.

Jesus, in good times and hard times, let me look to Your Cross and lay all my cares on You.

—DOLPHUS WEARY

MAY 17

For now we see through a glass, darkly; but then face to face....
—I CORINTHIANS 13:12

*S*everal years ago my husband Paul's aunt Jeanne told us a lovely story about her father, Paul's grandfather, that I've always remembered. Aunt Jeanne had spent a lot of time with Grandpa in the last year of his life, especially after Grandma died. They read the Bible together, and, as Aunt Jeanne told us, he talked about how much he wanted to see Grandma again.

"I reminded him he was going to see Jesus, too," she told us, "and he looked at me in a puzzled way."

"You mean I'm going to see the dear Jesus Who died on the Cross for me?" he asked. Then Aunt Jeanne showed him one of several places in Scripture where Jesus makes that promise. "Oh yes," he said, smiling like a child who's made a wonderful discovery, "I want to see Jesus' face and be with Him forever."

"Grandpa had thought about heaven," Aunt Jeanne explained, "but he'd never really contemplated the most beautiful part of the promise—that one day he'd see Jesus face to face."

That's the miracle of the Ascension, God's gift to the disciples who actually saw Jesus rise up to heaven in a glorious cloud and His gift to us today. There can be no mistake: Jesus not only defeated death but sits beside God the Father in heaven. And His sacrifice makes it possible for us to enjoy life forever, not just with those we love, but also with Him.

On this Ascension Day, Lord, I rejoice in the opportunity
You have given me to be with You forever.
—GINA BRIDGEMAN

MAY 18

"Then I said, 'I have labored in vain, I have spent my strength for nothing and in vain; yet surely my just reward is with the Lord, and my work with my God.'"
—ISAIAH 49:4 (NKJV)

*W*hen should you give up on something that isn't working? For twenty years I have tried to grow asparagus for my wife, who is wild about it. I can get the ferns to come up, but then it dies.

I've read dozens of articles on growing asparagus, and they assure me that "growing asparagus is easy," which makes me feel dumber than dirt. Dozens of friends have given helpful advice, such as "Put salt on it," and "Never put salt on it."

"Danny," my wife consoles, "you don't have to do this. I can get all the asparagus I need at Ritter's vegetable stand. Give it up."

So why don't I just give it up? Maybe I hate to be defeated by things that are lower down on the food chain. Maybe it's my pride or my bullheadedness. In reality I think it's hope that keeps me going. Not just in gardening but in college teaching and in all my relationships. I keep praying for "impossible" things because deep down I think they just might happen. A few of them have.

I keep trying to overcome my bad habits—overeating, shyness, discouragement—because it would be so wonderful if I could do it. Just because I never have doesn't mean I never will. It doesn't matter if I give up on asparagus, but it does matter that I keep trying to overcome my temptations. My job is to try, and to leave the results to God, Who will give me my just rewards when the time is right.

Father, I believe You when You say that "All things are possible to him who believes" (MARK 9:23 NKJV). With Your help, I will keep trying impossible things.
—DANIEL SCHANTZ

MAY 19

Do not deceive with your lips.
—PROVERBS 24:28 (RSV)

J was about to go camping through northern California with two
former college friends and catch up on one another's lives. Sharise
was a high school teacher, soon to be a department chairman, and Anna was an
actuary with her own secretary. And I was working in a bookstore for little above
minimum wage. I liked my work, but it was not exactly a career I was eager to
share with my more successful friends.

So I began practicing how to present my job to them. *God, help me find a way
to . . . well, not lie exactly, but make it sound like I'm doing better than I am.* There
was a lull in the line at the registers, so I mentally practiced. *I'm in retail.* Nah,
true but too vague. *I'm in management.* (Well, I did manage the carts of books
to be shelved!)

Suddenly, I was interrupted by two customers. Behind the cash register
was a very expensive boxed Batman set that attracted a lot of attention from
collectors. So when the boy, about ten years old, asked what was in it, I handed
it over gingerly and warned, "Be careful. It's a collector's item: an action figure
and a graphic novel."

He opened the box and immediately his freckled face fell. "Oh," he said, "it's
just a doll and a comic book."

I had to laugh. The child had cut right to the chase. Call it what you will, it
was a doll and a comic book. And call me what you will, I was a bookseller. My
friends had liked me in college for myself, not for my grades or career plans. And
they would like me now, whether I was president of the company or president
of nothing!

*God, if there is something in my life I've been "fancifying," then for today, teach
me not to turn a comic book—or bookseller—into something that it's not.
Let me enjoy and be proud of who I am in Your eyes.*
—LINDA NEUKRUG

MAY 20

Your promise preserves my life.
—PSALM 119:50 (NIV)

My husband's mental illness, coupled with the stresses of a growing family, have plunged me into one crisis after another. Throughout the past eleven years, many friends and acquaintances have offered me welcome comfort. Practical help, like shoveling the driveway after a blizzard or repairing a wall. Social comfort, like a dinner invitation or an outing to the theater. Warm, fuzzy comfort, like a sincere word of praise or affirmation.

But no comfort has the enduring value of a Scripture verse shared either on the telephone or in person. Whenever someone shares a verse with me, I mark it in my Bible, and in the margin I write the name of the friend who offered it. Then when loneliness and anxiety engulf me, I grab my Bible and flip through its pages in search of the highlighted verses, marked with special names.

"So do not fear, for I am with you; do not be dismayed, for I am your God" (Isaiah 41:10 NIV); Lucille.

"The Lord...will satisfy your needs in a sun-scorched land" (Isaiah 58:11 NIV); Agnes.

"The Lord...will make...her wastelands like the garden of the Lord" (Isaiah 51:3 NIV); Olga.

Now as I reread each Scripture promise, I remember my friends Lucille, Agnes, Olga, and many others. Out of their own comfort from Scripture, they have offered me solace. Often they couple their words of blessing or promise with an "I'll pray for you." Suddenly, I feel surrounded by friends. (Are some of them praying for me right now?) Fellow pilgrims they are who have experienced God's presence on the journey. I do not travel this road alone. God is with me and so are a host of people of goodwill.

Father, I thank You for the solid comfort of Your Word and those who share it with me.
—HELEN GRACE LESCHEID

MAY 21

And this is the victory that overcometh the world....
—I JOHN 5:4

I read a magazine article one day about an organization called the "Not Terribly Good Club of Great Britain." It seems that a group of people who considered themselves failures in life decided to form the club for mutual moral support. In fact, some even took special pride in their negative status. "Not many people have failed as completely as I!" one member is quoted as saying complacently. Yes, the association was flourishing.

And then one day a Dutchman, Brother Andrew, joined them. After establishing his eligibility for membership, he explained that the real reason he wanted to belong was to be their chaplain. It was his desire to let all failures know that Jesus Christ, Whose mission apparently failed when He died on a cross, turned that defeat into the greatest victory of all time. "There's no such thing as failure for Christians!" he asserted.

Unfortunately for the club, many believed him. In fact, I understand that, following his statement, the membership fell off so drastically that the club no longer exists.

I will take this failure, Lord, and find a way to turn it into victory.
—DORIS HAASE

MAY 22

*What man of you, having an hundred sheep, if he lose one of them, doth not . . .
go after that which is lost, until he find it?*
—LUKE 15:4

*S*ome years back, my family gathered around the television watching the saga of Humphrey the humpback whale. He—actually a she— was the misguided whale who took a wrong turn and swam up a California river.

It was clear that if Humphrey didn't find her way back to the ocean she would die, and soon a bevy of workers were trying to turn the forty-five-ton whale around. They began tapping pipes beneath the water, trying to send her in the right direction. They continued until Humphrey turned and made her way downriver. When she finally broke into the bright, swirling waters of the Pacific, the workers cheered. Even in our South Carolina living room there were cheers. Humphrey was home!

I've never been physically lost like Humphrey, but there have been plenty of times when I've lost my sense of direction in life. I've taken wrong turns that carried me far from God and His plans for me. At times like that it's reassuring to know God always sends someone or something to find us and direct us back. There will be a friend who happens to say exactly the words you need to hear, a verse of Scripture dropped into your thoughts, a sudden insight from a book, even a casual comment by a stranger. All of these can be the "tappings beneath the water" that come to rescue us. For God has promised to leave the ninety-nine sheep and go after the one that is lost. He did it for Humphrey. He will do it for us.

*Lord, when I have strayed, open my eyes and ears to the gentle proddings of
Your Spirit leading me home.*
—SUE MONK KIDD

May 23

*For thou hast delivered my soul from death: wilt not thou
deliver my feet from falling...?*
—Psalm 56:13

At sixty-plus, my muscles don't seem to respond to messages from my brain as promptly as they used to. One day, strolling along the beach, I came to a two-foot-high step-up. Without thinking, I started to leap up, the way I had done many times before. The next moment, pain was shooting through my leg. My shin had struck the girder. I fell back on my haunches, then got up and hobbled off, embarrassed at my failure and hoping nobody had noticed.

That should have given me the message, but the same thing happened again as I was walking home from church. I kicked a fat acorn on the sidewalk and as I brought my foot down, my hip gave way and I went sprawling. A car stopped. "Need any help, fellow?" the man asked, and without waiting for an answer, he got out and helped me to my feet. "Thanks," I said, forcing a smile and feeling a little humiliated. "Just an arthritic hip acting up. I guess I've got to learn to accept my limitations."

He smiled back. "Well, that's something we've all got to learn, but if we didn't try to test those limitations once in a while, we wouldn't be human."

My smile grew real. "Thank you," I said. "Thanks a lot." Not for helping me to my feet, but for reminding me that everybody has limits. God gave them to us. But we know He'll understand if we test them once in a while—just to make sure.

*Lord, You didn't make me able to do everything, though I sometimes like
to think I can. So hold me up when I find out I can't.*
—Sam Justice

Love bears all things, believes all things, hopes all things, endures all things.
—I CORINTHIANS 13:7 (RSV)

*M*y friends Noreen and Will were devoted to their grandson Bobby, who suffered from multiple sclerosis from the time he was an infant. MS attacks the muscles, and Bobby spent most of his time in a wheelchair. He needed a lot of care, and Noreen and Will helped Bobby's parents look after him so that the boy could remain at home.

When Bobby died at the age of twelve, his family was devastated. Like all their other friends, I worried about them, wishing I could do something to help. But whenever any of us reached out to them, they turned away. All we could do was pray that God would heal the pain of their loss. Unfortunately, Noreen and Will seemed to be turning away from God, too, and they stopped coming to church. They'd been active in so many of our events that it was hard to go on without them, but we kept praying for them.

About a year passed, and one Sunday Noreen and Will showed up again. After the service they stood in the vestibule as we all gathered around them, tearful and smiling. Then Will held up his hand; he had something to say. He and Noreen were remodeling their house so they could open a day-care center for disabled and handicapped children. "It's something we know how to do," he said, "and it's something that needs to be done."

When I left the church and walked out into the bright sunlight, I closed my eyes and thanked God for answering our prayers for Noreen and Will. But God had done more than heal their pain. He had inspired them to offer their love for Bobby to as many other children as they could fit into their home. He had turned a terrible loss into a beautiful gift.

Thank You, Lord, for the many times You have brought
something good out of our suffering.
—PHYLLIS HOBE

"Not my will, but thine, be done."
—LUKE 22:42

I don't think the Easter lily we bought last year is going to bloom again this Easter," I said to my husband, Roy. Easter was two weeks away, and all of our children would be home. I had hoped the lily would flower in time to adorn our fireplace hearth. It was a family tradition to keep last year's Easter lily in hopes that it would blossom once again. This year didn't look very promising. I was not handling my disappointment well.

It wasn't just the stubborn Easter lily that concerned me. Our oldest daughter, Misty, was getting married in August to a young man she had only known a short while. Our daughter Kristen had arrived home from college with a drastic new hair color. Our seventeen-year-old son, Christopher, was far more interested in playing with his rock band than in school. Our youngest son's best friend had moved away, and Kevin didn't seem to be doing anything to make new friends for the summer.

It was two months after Easter before our lily finally blossomed, one flower at a time, until there were four beautiful blooms. "It's just like our four children, isn't it?" Roy mused, as we admired God's handiwork. "We just need to step back and allow them to develop in their own time, to be whomever God has meant them to be." My husband was right. Just as my Easter lily had bloomed when it was ready, my children would do the same.

God, give me the patience to do what I can and leave the rest to You.
—MELODY BONNETTE

O magnify the Lord with me, and let us exalt his name together.
—PSALM 34:3

Not long ago I ate too much for dinner and tossed and turned half the night. Once up, I cut myself shaving. At breakfast, I knocked over a cup of tea. Then I remembered I had to go to the bank—but the car wouldn't start. I kicked a tire, turned an ankle, and came in fuming.

My wife, Ginny, greeted me. "Having a bad morning, huh?"

"I shouldn't have gotten up," I snapped, limping to the table.

"Why don't you go upstairs, lie down, and spend some time praising the Lord?"

"Praising the Lord!" I said, incredulous. "Like for what?"

"All the beautiful things in life—including your wife."

Reluctantly, I limped upstairs to give it a try. I said, "Praise the Lord! Praise the Lord!" grimly at first, over and over. And as I did, almost in spite of myself, I began to relax. Yes, I began to see, there were many things to praise Him for: good health, wonderful children, an abundance of friends, my beautiful—and sensible—wife.

And I discovered something else, too—you can start praising God while in a bad mood, but once you start thinking about what you're saying, you just can't stay in one for long.

Lord, help us to remember that there is healing and
joy in daily praising Your name.
—SAM JUSTICE

MAY 27
PENTECOST

And suddenly a sound came from heaven like the rush of a mighty wind....
—ACTS 2:2 (RSV)

About thirty miles north of Nairobi, Kenya, is a small community called Kijabe, the Place of the Winds. It is perched on the escarpment wall overlooking the Great Rift Valley. When I lived in East Africa, one of my assignments was to write about the work at the mission hospital there for donors in the United States. The views from Kijabe are extraordinary, and I always enjoyed my visits there.

One afternoon the nursing director and I were trying to concentrate on a quiet task together when the wind became particularly gusty, blowing our papers around. "Wind can be so unsettling," I remarked as Norma got up to close the windows. "Yes, but I think maybe that's its job here on earth—to rearrange things," she replied. With the windows closed we were nearly oblivious to the wind. It howled around the buildings as we carried on with our task.

Later, thinking about what Norma had said, I remembered how the Holy Spirit came with the sound of the wind at Pentecost. The Spirit came to rearrange people's lives, changing their priorities and reordering history. For the people who were there, nothing was ever the same again.

Am I open to that Power in my life? Or do I close my soul up tight at the prospect of change? Am I willing to let God the Holy Spirit blow out the cobwebs and reorder my comfortable routines?

Holy Spirit, I want to keep open the windows of my heart and
let You rearrange my thinking and my doing.
—MARY JANE CLARK

*Better is the end of a thing than the beginning thereof: and
the patient in spirit is better than the proud in spirit.*
—ECCLESIASTES 7:8

$\mathcal{W}$hen my grandson Bob received his college degree, our family attended the graduation. After the usual round of congratulations and hugs from friends and family, we gathered at a restaurant for lunch. We had placed our orders when I said to Bob, "We are so proud to be here to see you receive your bachelor's degree."

"Then start planning for the time when I get my master's degree, Grandmom," he said.

"And you're going to start that next fall?" I asked.

"Yes, I am." His voice was almost hard with determination. "I'll have to work to pay for it, but I already have a job here at the college."

"That's great!" I exclaimed. "What will you be doing?"

He straightened his shoulders a bit and fixed his eyes on my face as he answered, "I'll be moving furniture, emptying trash, mopping floors, painting walls, and—"

I interrupted him to ask, "You'll be doing custodial work?"

"Yes. Are you ashamed of me, Grandmom?"

"Oh no!" I reached over to clasp his hand in mine. "I'm very proud of you. Not every young man your age would be willing to do that kind of work to get his education."

Bob moved into my outstretched arms and we hugged each other, both already looking forward to that next graduation day.

Dear Lord, bless those who work hard to make the most of the gift of life. Amen.
—DRUE DUKE

MAY 29

"These stones are to be a memorial to the people of Israel forever."
—JOSHUA 4:7 (NIV)

Although I've never served in the military, like most of my generation I was deeply affected by the Vietnam War. Many of us lost our political innocence because of that war, and most of us, including me, lost friends. So the Vietnam Veterans Memorial, the most visited site on the Mall since it opened, holds a special place in my heart. I visited it that first year, and I've returned every year since.

The memorial, a slash in the earth opened to receive the two arms of a wall that rise to meet in the middle, was conceived to inspire reflection and healing. On the wall are carved the names of the 58,226 men and women who died or remain missing in Vietnam.

Since it was constructed, the wall has inspired people to leave offerings of love and forgiveness at its base. Medals, helmets, dog tags, and bracelets are accompanied by countless photographs and letters. Each night park rangers collect and preserve the offerings that have become a record of love and healing. Seeing those mementos through the years has helped me to deal with the sense of futility and loss I felt for the names I knew on the wall.

As the years passed, I wondered how long people would continue to leave things at the memorial. One day last year, I watched a pregnant woman leave a sonogram photo at the wall. "He would have been her grandfather," she said to her companion. Then I knew, the remembering would last for generations.

Father, let me always remember that the wounds of conflict are healed
only by forgiveness and hope.
—ERIC FELLMAN

Let brotherly love continue.
—HEBREWS 13:1

O ur house is slowly becoming a library. I collect books faster than I can read them, and I never want to part with my "old friends." But this week I decided to select some books to give away.

As I gazed at my shelves, I saw an old Bible concordance. The book had been my father's, and I inherited it when Dad died thirty-four years ago. I have used it often to look up Bible verses I vaguely remembered but couldn't quite put my finger on. The cover of the old concordance is threadbare, and it has a broken spine. Computer software has now taken its place.

I took the book from its shelf to put in my giveaway box and opened it one last time. On the flyleaf I saw something I had never noticed before: "Marvin Shipp" was scrawled there in large letters. Marvin Shipp had been my father's college roommate. Below the name, an old letter was wedged into the binding. Marvin had written it to my father on January 1, 1942, when Marvin was a young army private being shipped off to combat in Europe. He wrote:

Al, I sure hope they don't drag you into this war. And, while I'm on the subject, things being what they are and all, if something should happen to me, then, of course, I want you to have my books and the rest of the stuff I left with you. It's kind of a grim thought, but we might as well face it.

Marvin Shipp was killed three years later in the Battle of the Bulge. It broke my father's heart. Now I realized why Dad had never thrown away this old book. And I knew that it would have a home with me forever.

I dusted off the old concordance and placed it in a more prominent place on my shelf. Then I stopped and gave thanks for a memory almost forgotten, a treasure nearly thrown away.

Dear God, thank You for friendships that are eternal and continue
to enrich us throughout the generations. Amen.
—SCOTT WALKER

He led them by a straight way, till they reached a city to dwell in.
—PSALM 107:7 (RSV)

*N*ew neighbors moved in this week. Very nice people, recently transplanted from Connecticut. I'm glad the house next door is once again full, but new neighbors not from Pittsburgh require a different approach. This city requires explanation. Pittsburgh is a surprisingly mystical place.

Pittsburgh's peculiarities put wrinkles in all trajectories. Cross an intersection and Seventh Avenue changes into Ninth Street. Fifth and Sixth avenues run parallel—until they meet. Street names mutate. To get from the north side to Emsworth, just follow one road: California Avenue–Lincoln Avenue–Church Avenue–Center Avenue. What do you mean you got lost?

And if you do get lost, asking for directions is asking for trouble. Ask how to get on the parkway, and the answer will be simple: "Go down to where the J&L Steel Mill used to be, right across from the old Lasek's." Roger, bub. Thanks for the help.

Truth is, I won't tell my new neighbors any of this. They seem on the ball, able to figure it out. But maybe I'll tell them stories of other neighbors, neighbors I sometimes knew only for a few minutes. The fan at the Pirates game who tracked me down when I lost my wallet. The cars that pulled over when I've had a flat. The people who helped out when a storm took down my maple tree.

Our grandparents taught us to work hard, to brush the mill soot off our shirts and put our shoulders to the wheel. And come the weekend, stop over, 'cause the Steelers are on and we've got cable.

Lord, thank You for my city, for neighbors, new and old, and the life we have together. And keep me mindful of Your city, not made with hands, eternal in the heavens.

—MARK COLLINS

June

JUNE 1

*A*lthough our granddaughter Jessica started tennis late, she has improved dramatically. Last year I got to see her compete as a high school junior. For the most part, Shirley and I were bystanders, cheering good shots and looking elsewhere when shots went awry. That is, until an incident late in the season.

Jessica was doing well, leading in the first set of a match with a fairly good opponent, when she turned her ankle while running down a cross-court volley. Although she didn't fall, she gingerly limped to the sidelines where her coach examined her injury. I watched from a distance as the two discussed what should happen next. Jessica obviously wanted to continue, and she did, although not at full strength. Gradually, her rival took the lead and eventually won the match.

Afterward we wandered over to where she sat in the grass with a couple of teammates. She was massaging her swollen ankle, but I could tell by her eyes that the real hurt was losing the match. Putting my arm around her neck, I leaned down and whispered that I was proud of her courage. I felt a couple of sobs under my arm, so I turned my attention to her ankle. "A little ice tonight and you'll be ready for your next match," I predicted, and she was.

But the incident reminded me of how powerless I sometimes felt as a parent. And that feeling revisited me with my granddaughter. What we want to do is make everything all right for our children and our children's children. We want to shoulder their pain, pave over the rough spots, and kiss away all the "boo-boos" and "ouches" of life. But, of course, we can't. The best we can do is show our kids we care, and point them to a heavenly Father Who is always there—even when parents and grandparents can't be. That's an important truth to impart to those we love.

*When I go off half-cocked, Lord, and overplay my role,
remind me once again Who's in control.*

—FRED BAUER

June 2

Let the brother of low degree rejoice in that he is exalted.

—James 1:9

This is how the furor began.

In the morning I'd talked on the telephone with my friend John and told him I had a dental appointment at eleven thirty and would come to his house for lunch about twelve thirty. What was not specified was the day that this was to take place. John assumed it was to be that same day. I thought we were on for the following day. I went off to the ball game with my old friend Harold, who'd come down from Connecticut.

Twelve thirty came and went. John waited. And waited. He telephoned my apartment; no answer. He wanted to call my dentist to see if I had kept the appointment, but he didn't know the dentist's name. He tried several other people, who didn't know either but were disturbed that I hadn't appeared. Could Van have had an accident, a possible recurrence of his stroke?

John called the superintendent of my building, who went up and let himself into my apartment with a passkey; only the dog was there. Now deeply distressed, John called Harold, with no success. Then he tried my two godchildren, who were in different parts of the country; then friends in Baltimore and New Mexico who might know the name of the dentist; and finally Guideposts, where I had worked for so long. They were quick to respond with an all-points alert. Brigitte and Elizabeth called hospitals, Edward the police station. Everyone was involved. Everyone had desperate thoughts. Celeste eventually went up to my apartment with the key I'd given her when she stayed with my dog Shep.

Six o'clock. Harold dropped me off, and I blithely approached the doorman, who greeted me effusively while saying that Celeste upstairs would explain. And she did, after the warmest hug I have ever received. The rest of the night was spent on the phone apologizing, but the thing that moved me then, and moves me now, was the heartfelt surge of relief that everyone expressed. There was no mistaking it, I was loved.

Father, help me never to forget those I frightened. I love them.

—Van Varner

JUNE 3

O satisfy us early with thy mercy; that we may rejoice and be glad all our days.
—PSALM 90:14

*T*he look of sheer joy on Mary's face said it all. It was as if no one in the history of the world had ever learned to walk before. Eyes glowing, arms held out for balance, she laughed and gurgled and staggered toward me, in love with life and her newfound ability.

Ah, that look! If I had a dozen babies, I'd still find each one's face in that first week of walking a miracle. Without a word, that look rejoices, *I can do it!* With ecstatic amazement, it proclaims, *I am wonderful!* Above all, it shouts, *God is so awesome and the world is good!* It is not a look you see on the face of most fourteen-year-olds. Or fifty-year-olds. Or me, for that matter.

Why not? It could—it should—be there.

> *Lord, today let me fling out my arms and run, giddy with joy,*
> *into Your loving embrace.*
> —JULIA ATTAWAY

June 4

You received the Spirit of sonship. And by him we cry, "Abba, Father."
—Romans 8:15 (NIV)

*W*e first met Ravit and her parents, Bennie and Erella, at my daughter's nursery school, where Ravit and our daughter Jessie quickly became best friends. Just arrived from Israel, they were looking for a place to live while Bennie did some postgraduate work at the university. The duplex across the street from us was available, so we helped them find furniture and settle in there.

Our families quickly became intertwined, sharing everything from child care to a washing machine, and hand-me-down clothes went both ways. They visited our church one Sunday morning and we went to their synagogue for a Bar Mitzvah. They came for Christmas dinners and Easter picnics; sometimes we all squeezed into their tiny kitchen for a Shabbat meal. When one of us was sick, Erella's wonderful chicken soup appeared on the scene.

Late one afternoon, I went over to Erella's to borrow a cup of sugar. Erella and I visited as she fixed supper; the girls played in the living room with Ravit's baby sister Hila. Suddenly, Hila sped across the carpet on hands and knees toward the screen door. She had seen her daddy through the window, walking home from work. Pulling herself up, she began pounding on the door, calling out excitedly, "Abba! Abba! Abba!" A moment later Bennie came through the door with a wide smile and scooped her up in his arms.

I immediately thought of Paul's reminder that we are God's children, that He is our Abba. We can run to Him with that same eagerness, with the confidence of a well-loved child. And He takes us in His arms, loving and accepting us just as we are.

Abba Father, may I come to You with eagerness and excitement, and with the childlike assurance that I am welcomed and loved.
—Mary Jane Clark

JUNE 5

*To every thing there is a season, and a time to every purpose under the heaven....
A time to weep, and a time to laugh; a time to mourn, and a time to dance.*

—ECCLESIASTES 3:1, 4

*M*y wife, Beth, and I were rushing to catch a plane to the Philippine Islands where I would be delivering a series of lectures. As I drove madly toward the airport, a torrential rain beat down on the windshield, and I prayed that traffic would not become congested.

Careening into the airport parking lot, I parked in the first available space. Grabbing our luggage, we sprinted to the ticket counter and then on to the gate. If we had arrived two minutes later, we would have missed our flight.

Five weeks later we returned. As we walked through the long-term parking area, I could not find my car. Looking intently at my parking ticket stub, I discovered my mistake: In my haste to make the flight, I had missed the long-term parking exit and had instead parked in the short-term lot. The short-term parking fee was seven dollars a day; my blunder had cost me two hundred and fifty-two dollars! I was fit to be tied.

As I drove slowly home, I fumed in silence, like a smoking volcano ready to explode. Suddenly, Beth started giggling and then burst into laughter. And before I knew it, I was laughing, too. Our sense of humor had caught up with our ridiculous plight. I could hear the voice of my mother repeating her favorite maxim: "Well, you can laugh or you can cry!"

Sometimes I have a choice as to whether my own mistakes will spoil a wonderful occasion and erase a happy memory. At that point, I really do have to count the cost. The memory of five wonderful weeks with Beth was worth far more than an expensive taste of humility. And laughter is better than anger any day.

*Lord, You changed water into wine. Transform my anger
into peals of laughter. Amen.*

—SCOTT WALKER

163

JUNE 6

*Deliver me from mine enemies, O my God: defend me from them
that rise up against me.*
—PSALM 59:1

There are verses of the Bible that I would rather skip, whole passages that I would like to believe simply don't apply to me and my modern-day circumstances. "These words probably meant something to believers hundreds of years ago," I tell myself, "but for me, they don't count." The verses I stumble over are the ones that ask for God's vengeance, like this from the fifty-ninth Psalm: "Consume them in wrath, consume them that they may not be."

"I don't have any enemies," I said to a friend. "Or at least not enemies on whom I would wish such harm." I like to consider myself a mild-mannered, easygoing person.

"Okay," my friend said, "maybe you don't know any people you'd wish vengeance upon, but what about spiritual enemies? Do you have any of them?"

"Sure," I said. "Things like sloth, envy, anger, pride. They drive me nuts."

"Spoken honestly," he said. "Then look at the Psalms as your chance to ask God to wreak havoc on them. The language is strong because that's just how we should speak to our enemies. Especially spiritual ones."

So I went back to the fifty-ninth psalm and looked back at passages like "Let them make a noise like a dog and go round about the city. Let them wander up and down for meat, and grudge if they be not satisfied." How about that for sloth? Why not that for pride? Strong words for some terrible foes—and just what they deserve. The psalmist knew exactly what he was doing. Some things we shouldn't be mild-mannered about.

Consume my spiritual enemies, Lord, that they may not be.
—RICK HAMLIN

JUNE 7

Let your eyes look directly forward, and your gaze be straight before you.
Take heed to the path of your feet, then all your ways will be sure.
—PROVERBS 4:25–26 (RSV)

*W*hen my husband and I visited Maui last year, we took a bike ride down the face of a volcano—thirty-eight miles of winding, hairpin turns. Before we began the rather intimidating journey, our leader talked to us about "visual reality."

"You will tend to go wherever you look," he said. "You must, of course, be cautious about glancing back over your shoulder to talk to your mate. But also be careful about looking at the spectacular landscape along our route." He pointed to the sides of the road, where lava rock fell away thousands of feet without the support of even a guard rail.

As we rode, I stole furtive glances over my shoulder once or twice to say something to my husband. I managed to take in much of the scenery. But, mainly, I focused on our leader. I kept his brightly striped bike helmet in my line of vision. As he careened around a curve, I imitated his lean and waited expectantly for him to come into view again: mile after mile, through lava rock, pine groves, pineapple fields, and, finally, to the edge of the ocean itself.

I had made it! And I'd done it by going exactly where I had been looking: in the direction my guide intended for me to go. It was a lesson I'd remember long after I left Hawaii.

You, Lord, are the Guide of my life. Help me keep my eyes fixed on You.
Become my "visual reality" all day, every day.

—MARY LOU CARNEY

So the descendants of Aaron were given Hebron (a city of refuge)....
—I CHRONICLES 6:57 (NIV)

J had been talking to the director of a ministry in Jackson, Mississippi, about coming down to take a look at some of the things they were doing for the outcasts of the community. Finally I gave him a call and set a date to tour the ministry's homes for homeless men and women. As we drove down the street where the ministry is located, I was encouraged to see how much work was being done. Old houses were being torn down and replaced with new ones and other houses were being remodeled.

At the end of our tour we walked into a small, hot room where thirty people had gathered for chapel. A man walked in who seemed disturbed and was talking loudly. The song leader quietly left his place up front and gently said some words to the disturbed man. He became quiet and the service went on. As the singing came to an end, the man said that he wanted to sing a song, and the ministry's director assured him, "You and I will sing a song together at the end of the service."

I had been asked to give a short message at the service, and after I finished the director and the disturbed man sang "Do Lord, Remember Me." They were way off key, but that didn't matter at all. Here, in the midst of a city filled—like so many—with poverty and indifference, was a real city of refuge for the poor and hurting.

Lord, thank You for cities of refuge that reach out to mend broken lives.
—DOLPHUS WEARY

JUNE 9

Mary... sat down at the feet of the Lord and listened.
—LUKE 10:39 (GNB)

I'm a compulsive helper. No sooner does a friend mention a problem than I have a solution.

Recently my good friend Kathy faced a particularly difficult time with a sick daughter, a looming mortgage payment, and an out-of-work husband. Of course, I was at the ready with doctor referrals, job applications, and offers of a loan. My efforts were stubbornly, if affectionately, ignored.

I was mulling over Kathy's problems during a walk yesterday when I noticed a boy and his younger sister riding bikes. They sped around their driveway. Suddenly, the little girl's bike turned over, and she fell with a thud. She looked mournfully at her brother, uncertainty and the beginning of a wail on her face. I started to rush over to see if she was hurt and, if not, encourage her to avoid unnecessary tears.

Her brother, however, knew what she really needed. He studied the woeful expression on her face for a split second before deliberately spilling his bike in the exact same way. They sat there, an arm's length apart, gazing at each other for a few moments. I had enough grace to stop in my tracks. She said something, too softly for me to overhear, and he nodded. Eventually, without another word, they got up and began to ride their bikes again.

That evening, I invited Kathy to visit a local park with me. "What for?" she asked warily, preparing for my usual deluge of helpful suggestions.

"Just to sit together," I replied. We sat together, not saying much, absorbing the scent and sight of just-blooming roses, and watched the sun set. I think it helped.

Lord, help me recognize when it's best just to step back and listen.
—MARCI ALBORGHETTI

JUNE 10

Walk in love....
—EPHESIANS 5:2

*I*t was my sister Keri's wedding day, and my job was to walk her down the aisle. It was hard to believe that my baby sister was getting married, much less to Ben, my best friend and college roommate. I could hardly get my mind around the idea.

Nothing would ever be the same. I pulled the crisp white collar of my formal shirt away from my neck as I waited for Keri to come down from her dressing room. I was standing up as straight as I could, my legs trembling slightly. I checked my tie in the mirror and adjusted my cummerbund.

All of a sudden, Keri was there. She was beautiful. I swallowed hard as I looked into her eyes. This was the little girl I had watched over as a child—playing in the creek, running through sprinklers, sledding down snowy white hills—and I was about to give her away.

Just before the sanctuary doors swung open Keri wrapped her arms around me and whispered, "Brock, thanks for everything you've done throughout our lives together. You'll always be my hero."

The rest of that walk was like a dream. I remember the hundreds of smiling people, Keri and I giggling as we made the slow approach to the front of the church and the look of appreciation on Ben's face as I gave him a wink. I remember my dad standing there, eyes brimming with tears, waiting to conduct the ceremony. But most of all, I remember how I felt as I lifted Keri's veil, kissed her on the cheek, and made my way back to the front pew where my mother waited.

God was in this place. I knew that He had put Keri and Ben together. I knew that many wonderful memories lay ahead of us. And I knew that the trip that I had just taken down that long church aisle had been a walk of pure love.

Father, help me learn to trust You completely and always to walk in Your love.
—BROCK KIDD

Talk no more so very proudly, let not arrogance come from your mouth....
—I SAMUEL 2:3 (RSV)

ome years ago I saw an ad on television for some sort of cosmetic product or shampoo. The ad began with a model saying, "Don't hate me because I'm beautiful." While I am not beautiful, I never had any inclination to hate her. I thank God—if not every day, then when it occurs to me—that I do not conform to the media's idea of beauty. Believe me, I have enough problems.

When I first came to Los Angeles, I had a roommate who was classically beautiful. She devoted at least half of her energy trying to ensure that she stayed that way, another quarter of it worrying about what it would be like if she lost that beauty, and the last quarter fretting that all men ever saw in her were her looks and that she would never be loved for herself.

I have been blessed with many things. If I were beautiful, too, I think I would have fallen into arrogance, thoughtlessness, and selfishness. But my looks have kept me, not humble, but humble enough. And I know for certain that I am loved for myself.

So I have to be grateful that God knew what He was doing when He decided to give me a roundish body, a narrow forehead, and pouchy eyes. He knew I'd need them to find my way from myself and closer to Him.

Thank You, God, for my imperfections that remind me of
Your care for me.
—RHODA BLECKER

JUNE 12

The swift of foot shall not ... deliver himself.
—AMOS 2:15 (NKJV)

*S*he looked at me as if I had just crawled out of a cave with a club in my hand. "You mean you still write with a typewriter?"

I smiled, thinking of all the writers who "still" use a typewriter, a pencil, or even a fountain pen. She shook her head. "But a computer is so much faster and easier." I'm sure she's right, but my computer tempts me to do the "quick fix" instead of the total rewrites that are necessary. After all, writing is not like microwaving a ham sandwich. It's more like sculpting in marble.

Writing is only one of many things that I can't seem to hurry. The beautiful garden outside my window tends to bloom when it's good and ready. "And don't forget marriage," my wife reminds me. "That takes time to create."

In an age that seems to worship the gods of "Speed" and "Convenience," it gets harder and harder for me to pace myself. I feel swept along by a riptide. I know, there is a time to pour on the steam and get a job done fast. But the older I get, the more I relish the process of writing, gardening, relating, and the less I'm interested in setting speed records.

My friendship with God has not been about speed or convenience but about wrestling with angels all night long. I am a block of marble and God is sculpting me, but I keep resisting His chisel. My character is taking shape slowly, with many setbacks, and I have no choice but to be patient with the Sculptor.

These days I often find myself rehearsing a little prayer I memorized in my teens.

Not so in haste, my heart. Have faith in God and wait. The feet that wait for God are soonest at the goal that is not gained by speed. So hold thee still, my heart, and wait His lead.
—DANIEL SCHANTZ

JUNE 13

Now my days are swifter than a post.... They are passed away as the swift ships:
as the eagle that hasteth to the prey.

—JOB 9:25–26

*J*s buying a 1985 Yamaha Riva 180cc motor scooter a sure sign of male middle age? You bet your bottom it is.

And your bottom would know. So would your spine and your brain and all your extremities, especially if they're straddling a tiny 330-pound frame rolling fifty miles per hour down US 30. Some sensations simply defy description. Even if too much blues guitar had rendered you hard of hearing, you would still know you were on a motorcycle. You would know it the same way Beethoven knew his Ninth Symphony, written while he was stone deaf—yet he heard all the notes, all the voices.

Why have I, a mild-mannered suburban male with 3.0 children, a lawn, and a mortgage payment, bought such a dangerous machine? Part of the answer lies in cliché: I want to feel the thrill of speed, the wind against my face, the throttle in my right hand. Yet I know the real reason I'm riding: To ride anything with two wheels on an open road is to deliver your fate into the hands of God.

While the rest of the world drives SUVs the size of Sherman tanks, I putt along unprotected, save for a fifty-dollar helmet. I am extremely careful and extremely aware of my tiny place in this world. Bikers hardly seem like a band of believers, but as soon as I pull up on the throttle through a tight curve near the exit ramp, leaning my body ever so slightly, keeping my head up, my eyes active, I'd say that I'm as close to God right now as I am to the pavement, and I know, in the words of the hymn, that "grace will lead me home."

Father, bring everyone on the road today safely to their destinations. And
give me a fresh sense of prudence to go with my old bike.

—MARK COLLINS

JUNE 14
FLAG DAY

Blessed is the nation whose God is the Lord; and the people whom
he hath chosen for his own inheritance.

—PSALM 33:12

*B*ring out the flags! On this day in 1777, our Congress adopted the Stars and Stripes as the national emblem of the United States. My heart still thrills when I visit a school and stand with the students to face the flag and say the Pledge of Allegiance, which ends with the words "one nation under God, indivisible, with liberty and justice for all."

It's interesting that the words *under God* were not added until 1954, sixty-two years after the original pledge was written. President Eisenhower said that the addition of those words represented "the transcendence of religious faith in America's heritage and future."

So today I think about America's future and the meaning of patriotic emblems and pledges, and particularly about what liberty means to me:

1. the liberty to worship as I choose,
2. the liberty to vote for the candidates of my choice,
3. the liberty to attend school and study different subjects,
4. the liberty to travel freely from state to state,
5. the liberty to assume responsibility as a citizen for the protection and preservation of all our freedoms, including freedom of speech and justice for all.

On this Flag Day, why not take a moment to list some of the things liberty means to you?

Almighty God, You stand above all nations. Today I pledge
my foremost allegiance to You.

—MADGE HARRAH

In an abundance of counselors there is safety.
—PROVERBS 11:14 (RSV)

ears ago I believed I heard God tell me to write a biography. I spent three years working on it before learning that the core of the story was untrue. How can we confirm the guidance we think we're hearing? My friend Charles Blair offered me one answer he found at a cost that makes my three misspent years seem cheap. With faith and determination Charles had built the largest church in Denver. Seven thousand people drove to hear him preach each Sunday. He had a daily radio program and went into a million and a half homes on TV each week. Then in the early 1970s he believed God was telling him to build a badly needed housing and medical complex for the elderly. "Trusting God" for the money, he borrowed huge sums, then borrowed more to pay interest on the first loan, and so on. At last, hopelessly in debt, Charles realized that he'd mistaken his own can-do spirit for God's directive. My husband and I flew out to be with him.

"Of course I knew," Charles told us, "that before any major decision, guidance must be submitted to a group of wise counselors. I'd done that." What he hadn't done was select advisers with different outlooks from his own. "I listened only to people who, like me, believed that with enough faith you could do anything."

For twenty-five years, Charles labored to pay off that staggering debt until the last dollar was repaid. Charles' ministry is back on track and his counselors include the cautious along with the bold, the practical as well as the visionary. His wisdom came too late for my book project. Like him, I'd checked my guidance only with people as excited about the subject as I was.

Nowadays, since suffering with Charles through his ordeal, I seek out personalities very different from my own to confirm or deny what I hear. "The body of Christ" has new meaning for me—different organs, different functions, as necessary to each other in our differences as the eye is to the hand.

What fuller understanding of You, Father, will someone give to me today?
—ELIZABETH SHERRILL

JUNE 16

O my Strength, I watch for you; you, O God, are my fortress, my loving God.
—PSALM 59:9–10 (NIV)

*M*ost of the time I'm the one who puts three-year-old John and five-year-old Elizabeth to bed. After prayers, I brush their teeth, give them a drink of water, tell them stories, and tuck them in. Actually, I tuck Elizabeth in. Then I pick up John and take him to the blue chair. We bought the blue chair for my dad when he lived with us. It's an overstuffed velour-covered recliner that now sits in our bedroom next to the window.

Cradling John in my arms, I sit down in the chair. In the light from the hallway, I watch him, eyes closing and breathing slowing, as he settles down. He's such a big boy now, I think, such a guy. In my mind's eye I can see him at sixteen months, lying on a hospital gurney as an anesthesiologist gets him ready for surgery. I close my eyes and pray: *Thank You for bringing him through the surgery, Lord. Keep him well, help him grow up strong.*

I open my eyes and look at my son. In repose, his face is sweet, innocent. A couple of hours ago, though, there was mischief in it as he teased his little sister. I put my head back and close my eyes again. *Keep his soul as healthy as his body, Lord. Don't let his mischief turn to meanness.*

Carefully, slowly, I get up, lifting my sleeping son. I carry him to his room, put him gently in his bed and give him a good-night kiss. I know I could easily get John to go to sleep by himself. But for as long as he lets me, I'll be happy to sit in the blue chair and hold my son in my arms.

Lord, thank You for the children who teach me to know the power of Your love.
—ANDREW ATTAWAY

Hear, ye children, the instruction of a father....
—PROVERBS 4:1

*M*y interview for a security clearance was going well. The interviewer and I liked each other. Then she asked, "Tell me about your father." Without thinking, I answered, "I never knew my father." The interviewer blushed and passed quickly to the next question.

Perhaps it was my hunger for warmth, attention, and companionship that triggered my blunt response. Mother and Father divorced before I was two. Mother remarried when I was seven. From time to time I wondered about my "real" father. Over the years I made no attempt to find him. Now I wrote to my mother to let her know about my angry feelings.

I received my security clearance; I also received a letter from Mother. "I can understand your anger, son," she wrote. "Try not to be too critical. Try to remember all the fine people who reached out to help you."

My thoughts raced back to the Reverend Gardiner M. Day, our minister, who gave me a job during the Great Depression; to Edward Welch, my high-school English teacher, who nurtured my talent for public speaking while teaching me the joys of reading and writing; to John B. Clark, my high-school principal, who helped me get into college with a much-needed scholarship; to Herbert Kenny, arts editor at *The Boston Globe*, who hired me to be a book reviewer; to Dave McKinney, the aerospace engineer who selected me to serve in the Project Gemini space program.

Suddenly, I was aware that I had many fathers, caring men who guided and encouraged me, each in his own way. So on this Father's Day, I give thanks to my Father in heaven, to the father I never knew, to my stepfather, and to all the fatherly men who have touched my life.

Heavenly Father, thank You for opening my eyes to see and to appreciate the gifts of my many fathers.
—OSCAR GREENE

JUNE 18

I will instruct thee and teach thee in the way which thou shalt go:
I will guide thee with mine eye.

—PSALM 32:8

*O*ne Saturday morning when my son Ryan was nearing his fourteenth birthday, I realized that although all of Ryan's friends had been learning to drive for some time, I hadn't started teaching him. So I got Ryan up and we took the car to a nearby park.

I talked to him about the mechanics of driving: how to steer, how to use the brakes and the different gears and the accelerator. When he seemed to be comfortable with the basics, I let him get behind the wheel and drive while I sat next to him. Whenever he made a mistake, he'd say, "I'm sorry, Dad. I'm sorry." I knew he was afraid and anxious to please me.

After a few lessons, Ryan's assurance grew, but I could see that my presence in the car was still making him nervous. Then one Saturday morning, when there was no one else in the park, I let him drive by himself. As he passed by me, I could see the big smile on his face. When we left the park, he couldn't seem to stop saying, "Thank you, Dad."

I grew up without a father, and I know how hard it was not to have a dad in my life. So whenever I have a Saturday free, I take Ryan to the park for a drive, and I praise God that He has blessed me with the time to be with my son.

Lord, help me to remember that every day I can be a blessing to others,
especially my children.

—DOLPHUS WEARY

JUNE 19

The labourer is worthy of his hire. . . .
—LUKE 10:7

*A*re you sure you can do it?" I asked my husband, John. "I'd feel a whole lot better if we called the tree service."

"No way! It'd cost a fortune, and besides, Ian can help me. I've already got it all figured out." I watched uneasily as he propped the ladder against the huge oak tree. The limb that needed to be trimmed overhung a bed of particularly prickly cacti. John double-twisted the rope around the branch to be cut, then threw the end down to Ian. "Now, when it starts to break, pull hard. Put your whole weight behind it."

I sat on a rock and held my breath. "Pull!" yelled John. Ian pulled. The branch broke with tremendous force and spun the ladder completely around. One corner of the top rung caught on a small stub on the tree.

John dangled by one hand from the ladder. "Help," he said in a strangled voice.

"I'm coming, Dad," said Ian as he pushed through the bushes. "What'll I do?"

"I don't know," croaked his dad. "If I move, I could jostle the ladder off the stub."

"Just drop, Dad," said Ian. "It's not that far down."

"I'll fall in the cactus," growled my husband.

"I'm getting the camera!" I said. "Don't come down till I get a picture." I raced into the house, but by the time I got back out, John had slowly inched his way to the safety of the ground. The fellows were furious. "All you could do was laugh!"

"Sorry, darling. But you didn't get hurt, and it was funny. Wish I'd gotten my picture."

We call the tree service now. As expensive as it sometimes is, as the Scripture says, "The laborer is worthy of his hire."

Thanks, Lord, for those with the expertise to do the jobs we can't.
—FAY ANGUS

JUNE 20

Thou hast put gladness in my heart....
—PSALM 4:7

*T*he start of summer was family time in our vacation cabin at Mammoth Lakes in California. For two glorious weeks, we became part of the history of the rustic log cabin built by settlers in 1908. All the furniture, beds included, was made of massive logs. We put our feet up on the iron rail that fronted a huge rock fireplace and sipped hot chocolate to the rhythmic creak of rough-hewn rockers. No phone, no television, just us and the children, and then just us. Now that my husband, John, was gone, it would be just me.

"It won't be 'just you,'" my son Ian insisted. "Let's all go. You can fish with the kids, Mom, and I'll teach them to tie hooks at the very same table where Dad taught me."

Apprehensive and sad, I went.

Driving up the highway into the Inyo National Forest was like entering a warm embrace. The snow-capped mountains and dancing aspen were still home away from home. As we stepped into the cabin and my son gave me a teary-eyed hug, I once again felt the comfort of John's arms around me.

We pulled out the photo album. The grandchildren giggled over stories—the dog falling through the iced-over lake, a lightning storm that zapped our power, the bear we met on the climb to the top of the falls. We cozied up in the same rockers and hiked the same trails, absorbed in the nostalgia of then. But it was now. Time to move on to new adventures.

Traditions kept. Traditions created. Then and now, both better than good.

For tears and sadness turned to joy and gladness, thank You, Lord.
—FAY ANGUS

JUNE 21

The desire of a man is his kindness....
—PROVERBS 19:22

*L*ike many people, I don't like to stand in line, especially when I'm in a hurry, so I do my food shopping at a market known for its fast checkers. You load your cart, pay your bill, and you're out of there! But one day the line was moving slowly, and when I looked ahead I saw that the checker was talking to a customer. I was annoyed. I wanted to go home, cook dinner, and get to a meeting, and this woman was holding me back.

As I inched forward and began to unload my cart, I could hear what she was saying. She greeted the customer ahead of me with a smile that looked genuine and said "Hello" as if she meant it. She mentioned the weather (it was a nice day) and said she was looking forward to a camping trip with her family that weekend. The customer ahead of me actually began to relax and responded with some remarks about her garden. Then they exchanged a few words about their children. It was all very pleasant, and it rubbed off on me. I felt the stress begin to lift from my shoulders. I even hoped the checker might say a few words to me.

She did. Her smile made me feel welcome, and when she mentioned her cat, I told her about mine. The whole conversation took only a few seconds, but it made a difference in my day. I remembered that I was more than someone who got things done. I was a human being. I mattered.

On the way to my car, I thanked God for reminding me that "small talk" is a pretty big part of our daily lives. Sure, it takes a few seconds of our precious time, but in our busy world, it accomplishes something essential: It connects us to each other—like a handshake or, better yet, a hug. And it's so easy to give.

Dear Lord, when time becomes so important to me that I start putting people last, help me to remember that You always find time for me. Amen.
—PHYLLIS HOBE

JUNE 22

Pour out your hearts to him, for God is our refuge.
—PSALM 62:8 (NIV)

I've always admired people who are disciplined in prayer. But despite my best intentions to set aside a time for earnest prayer each day, it doesn't always happen.

One day as I was driving home from town I thought, *This is a perfect time for praying.* I began to formulate a prayer, but it sounded wooden and phony. I made a few more attempts, but the words just wouldn't come. Finally, in desperation, I gave up. "Lord Jesus, I just can't pray today," I said. "Is it okay if I just look out the window for a while and say nothing?"

As I climbed Marshall Road, I drove past a pink splash of Japanese cherries in bloom. "I like that," I said out loud. "Thanks, Lord." At one house, a neatly landscaped yard was ablaze with red azalea bushes. My heart leaped with joy. "That's neat, Lord," I exclaimed. At a roadside garden, clumps of bright yellow and red tulips swayed gently in the wind. "You did a great job when You made tulips," I said. Almost home, I crested a hill and spread out before me lay Mount Baker, its rugged snowcapped peaks mellowed by a late afternoon sun. "Wow, God!" I whispered. "You must be incredibly great to create a scene like that."

And so it went all the way home. I wasn't praying, mind you, I was merely expressing my delight in the pristine beauty I saw and telling the Person I felt was responsible for it.

When the words won't come, Lord, open my eyes to the prayer-starters
You've put all around me.
—HELEN GRACE LESCHEID

June 23

He shall not fail nor be discouraged....
—Isaiah 42:4

*S*hortly before I graduated from college, I learned that my best friend and classmate wouldn't be graduating with me. Margaret had good grades in every subject except chemistry, and she had flunked her final exam. Science courses didn't come easily to her, but I knew how hard she had worked to master chemistry and my heart ached for her when she gave me the bad news.

"Guess what?" she said, holding back her tears. "They said I can't get my degree, but I can go to the class dinner if I want to." The class dinner was a fun event, the highlight of the senior year, and without thinking I said, "Then you're going?" "Of course not!" Margaret said, and now she was crying. "What have I got to celebrate?" She turned and ran down the hall.

I didn't see Margaret for several days, and when I called her she always made an excuse to avoid getting together. I went to the class dinner determined to smile so I wouldn't spoil anyone else's good time. Then I saw someone standing by the front door, waving to me. It was Margaret!

"I thought you'd never get here," she said, grinning and pulling me toward the door. When she saw the look on my face, she said, "I decided that I'm not going to let one course turn me into a failure. I don't think that's what God has in mind for me."

"What are you going to do?" I asked.

"I'll take the course again," she said. "As many times as I have to."

She meant what she said. Then she got a master's degree and went on to teach children with learning disabilities. Margaret taught me a lot about persistence. It's not just our stubbornness that makes us keep trying. It's our faith that failure isn't what God has in mind for us.

When I run into obstacles, dear Lord, help me to look for ways around them.
—Phyllis Hobe

JUNE 24

So that your trust may be in the Lord, I teach you today....
—PROVERBS 22:19 (NIV)

*W*hen an unexpected career change hit me this year, I found myself frozen with doubt as the challenge of finding another job loomed before me. There was the financial burden of having two kids in college and another headed that way. Then there was the daunting prospect of diving into the cold waters of the job market.

After an early morning men's meeting one Wednesday, I stood in our church parking lot, pouring out all of my doubts to my friend Len. Suddenly, he blurted out, "Well, will you look at that?" I turned around, but I couldn't see anything special. The sky was clear and the sun was peeking above the trees on the ridge behind us. "Look at what?" I asked.

"Why, it's amazing," he replied with a grin. "Eric Fellman has lost his job and the sun is still coming up!"

My astonishment was just turning into anger when Len continued. "Eric, how long have you and Joy been married?"

"Almost twenty-one years," I replied. "Why?"

"How many days have you gone hungry in twenty-one years?"

"None."

"How many days homeless?"

"None."

"So, if God has taken care of you for twenty-one years, why do you think He is suddenly going to stop now? Has He stopped bringing up the sun or sending the rain or anything else you can notice?"

"No."

"So quit whining and get on with it." With that Len climbed into his vehicle and drove away. I climbed into my car, looked at the rising sun, and got on with it.

Lord, let me know the power of Your promises today, and
help me to trust the wisdom of Your leading.
—ERIC FELLMAN

JUNE 25

Be not afraid, only believe.
—MARK 5:36

*L*ast summer while in New York City, my family and I made a pilgrimage to the top of the Empire State Building. Up and up and up we went—1,250 feet to the observatory on the 102nd floor. At the top we gazed through the windows where a piece of white cloud drifted by. It was said sometimes visitors could see it raining below them while they were in the sunshine. I peered down. Below, the city seemed minuscule.

"Look!" cried my son. I hurried to his window expecting to see a spectacular sight. Instead he pointed to an ordinary bee perched on the window ledge. "How did it get way up here?" he asked incredulously. I gazed in awe at the tiny creature, at the tissue-thin wings that had somehow flown more than a quarter of a mile straight up into the winds.

Back in the elevator we were still talking about the bee on the window ledge, pondering how it could fly so high. "Maybe it just kept saying 'I think I can. I think I can,'" teased the elevator operator.

We all laughed then, but today when I face some especially difficult problem or seemingly impossible task, I recall the bee at the top of the Empire State Building. And I am reminded that with faith in God and belief in ourselves, we can overcome anything. We can fly as high as we think we can.

Help me fix my eyes on You and keep climbing.
—SUE MONK KIDD

JUNE 26

I took them up in my arms.... I led them ... with the bands of love....
—HOSEA 11:3–4 (RSV)

J met Cathy at a women's retreat that I'd been asked to lead. She was a young mother who'd lost her husband to cancer a few months before. She tried to appear cheerful, but pain cloaked her like a shadow, quietly visible.

One morning I noticed her sitting beneath one of the oaks, her arms folded about her shoulders as if she were trying to hold herself. I went and sat beside her. "I found this," she said. In her hand was a bird feather, the top dangling limply from a snapped center. "It's broken!" she added, her voice quivering. Somehow I knew she wasn't talking about the feather so much as her own heart. I reached for her hand, praying for a way to comfort her.

Later I found myself thinking about a sign I kept on my desk inscribed with these words by Hildegard of Bingen: "God hugs you. You are encircled by the arms of the mystery of God." And I thought about Cathy beneath the tree holding a broken feather, desperately trying to hug herself.

That evening I asked the women to gather in a circle. I turned to the woman on my right and repeated Hildegard's words, then circled my arms around her and gave her a hug. "This is God's embrace," I said. "Pass it around." I watched as one after another, each woman looked into the next one's eyes, spoke Hildegard's lovely words, then followed with a warm hug. Beside Cathy was a large grandmotherly woman.

When she passed on the embrace, Cathy fell against her, sobbing, almost disappearing inside her arms. The older woman held her a long while, rocking her tenderly back and forth, while the rest of us looked on in awed silence. Later Cathy wrote to me saying that experience was the beginning of healing for her. "Those arms were God's arms," she wrote.

God, there are so many broken hearts in Your world and sometimes my arms are the only arms You have.
—SUE MONK KIDD

JUNE 27

He will turn again, he will have compassion upon us . . . and thou wilt cast all their sins into the depths of the sea.
—MICAH 7:19

I am on the beach in Avalon, New Jersey, trying to tune in my new hand-cranked radio. It's a gorgeous day, the kind you pray for when you're going on vacation. My kids are in the surf—a distracting little fact for a man trying to tune a radio.

"Daddy, c'mon in," Faith says.

"In a minute," I call to her. I find that if I hold my finger to the dial I can hear bits of Bonnie Raitt.

"Dad, are you coming?" Hope calls.

"In a minute, okay?" I call back, sounding cross. Bonnie comes and goes, replaced by the news, fading in and out, like a shorthand telegram: Middle East . . . Jerusalem . . . trouble. . . .

"Daddy . . . " Grace starts.

"In a minute, I said!"

And that, ladies and gentlemen, sums up my relationship with the Almighty. I can't seem to tune in God. I have been given vast gifts—wonderful, curious children, a job that allows vacations, and this earth, "our island home," as *The Book of Common Prayer* says. And my reply to these divine gifts is consternation. Instead of enjoying what's in front of me, I try to find God the way I try to find a radio station, wondering how to make sense of the voices coming in from thin air. Meanwhile, the inquisitive, playful voices of my own children—my own hymns from heaven—go unheeded.

I'm sure there's more to this metaphor—something about gratitude, I'll bet, and something about spiritual recognition along the lines of the disciples on the road to Emmaus, unable to recognize Jesus—but you'll have to excuse me. I'm wanted elsewhere—no doubt for a frantic game of Dunk Daddy, who very much needs to be re-baptized in this ancient, eternal, endless sea.

Lord, on the days when my spirit can only hear static, help me hold on to the clear signals of Your presence.
—MARK COLLINS

185

JUNE 28

Till he fill thy mouth with laughing, and thy lips with rejoicing.
—JOB 8:21

J had carefully completed a form to do some volunteer work and now I sat facing a woman for my lengthy interview. I felt I answered all her questions well. Then one caught me off guard. She asked, "What do you do for fun, Mrs. West?" I stared at the woman for a few moments. Nothing came to mind.

Finally we went on to another topic, but her question hung over me even after I got home. It's not easy to break out of an old mold. I knew I was too serious, too condemning, too judgmental of others and of myself. Life had become much too grim, and thanks to the woman's question, I would try to change all that.

I didn't learn to "have fun" overnight, of course. But I did start in small ways. I went out back and tossed a Frisbee with my collie. Even he seemed stunned at the new me, but soon we were running together, and I was laughing. I hadn't been to the movies in over a year, but I invited my married daughter and her little girl to see one with me. We went out for dinner first and then pigged out on popcorn at the movies. Sitting there in the dark, I realized I was smiling, enjoying the film. Why, I was actually having fun!

Now I'm asking God to show me how to laugh more, to smile, to kid, even tell silly jokes once in a while. Most of all, I want to stop being so grim.

And now I ask you: What do *you* do for fun?

Father, You created us for pleasure, too. Help me find small ways that I can begin to laugh, to have fun, to enjoy my life.
—MARION BOND WEST

JUNE 29

This is the rest wherewith ye may cause the weary to rest....
—ISAIAH 28:12

*J*t had been one of those days! With so much to do before house guests arrived, I got out of bed in the morning, running. Now it was the middle of the hot summer afternoon and I was sweeping the sidewalk, mentally enumerating the remaining chores to be done before dark. From his sandbox next door, my two-year-old neighbor Tyler came running. After his usual, "Whatcha doing?" he said, "Let's swing in your swing."

"I'm too busy today," I told him.

Disappointment spread over his face. I glanced toward the swing hanging in the breezeway and saw it move gently in the light breeze. It *did* look inviting. "All right," I told him. "Just for a few minutes." He raced up the front steps and waited for me to lift him into the swing beside me. He didn't talk, just snuggled against me as my toe made the swing glide to and fro. A butterfly fluttered past my face. Two bees hummed among the flowers, and a slight breeze stroked my tired body. Tension and anxiety began to slip away. Soon I was humming softly. I became aware of the fragrance of the flowers, the brilliance of the day, the wonder of the small boy beside me, all creations of a loving God.

On those days when you become entangled in a maze of activities and overwhelmed by all that you are called upon to do, go and find a quiet spot where you can get away for a while. Relax, think about Him, and let His unending strength and peace refresh you.

Thank You, Father, for this moment in Your presence. Fill me now with
Your peace and refreshment. Amen.
—DRUE DUKE

When thou passest through the waters, I will be with thee....
—Isaiah 43:2

*S*ometimes, when life gets rough, I need a towline to keep me from sinking. Over the years, certain Bible passages have been towlines that have held me up in turbulent waters. Here are a few with strong fibers I can hold onto when

I'm tired—"I wait on the Lord to renew my strength" (Isaiah 40:31);

I'm lonely—"He will never leave me, nor forsake me" (Hebrews 13:5);

I have financial worries—"My God shall supply all my need" (Philippians 4:19);

I'm depressed—"The Lord my God will enlighten my darkness" (Psalm 18:28);

I'm tempted—"God will not let me be tempted beyond my strength" (I Corinthians 10:13);

I'm feeling guilty—"Renew a right spirit within me" (Psalm 51:10);

I'm tense—"Peace I leave with you" (John 14:27);

Someone has wronged me—"'If God be for me, who can be against?" (Romans 8:31);

I have too much to do—"He performs that which is appointed for me" (Job 23:14).

Maybe you'd like to add your favorite towlines to the list and keep them handy for those times when the sea of your life gets rough.

In my hour of need, Lord, I will reach for the Holy Scriptures,
with their strong, saving towlines.
—Marilyn Morgan King

July

JULY 1

This is the day which the Lord has made; let us rejoice and be glad in it.
—PSALM 118:24 (RSV)

hna Fiske was my mother's closest friend. A brilliant woman, a pioneer in the education of learning-disabled children, Ahna also had a lovely singing voice. With Mother accompanying her on the piano, she often gave concerts in hospitals and nursing homes.

So it seemed particularly poignant when Ahna, in her eighties, entered a nursing home herself. Mother warned me when I went to visit her old friend in a pleasant facility in Sudbury, Massachusetts, that Ahna would not know me. Sure enough, that accomplished woman had lost all of the past, even events only minutes old. Over and over—always graciously, but each time as though greeting a total stranger—Ahna welcomed me into her room as though I'd only then arrived.

Otherwise her observations were as keen as ever. She was clearly aware that her memory no longer served her, for she kept asking, "Have I just told you that?" Just as clearly, she was determined not to let forgetfulness spoil her zest for life. As I stood up to go, she apologized for not remembering the name I'd repeated a dozen times.

"I can't recall much of anything these days," she said. "I just enjoy the moment I'm in and don't worry about the other ones."

I walked down the chlorine-scented corridor with a wisdom more than human ringing through Ahna's words. *Don't live in the past. Don't live in the future. Right now, this present moment, is My loving gift to you.*

Father, let me find You in the fleeting moments of this day.
—ELIZABETH SHERRILL

Now faith is the substance of things hoped for, the evidence of things not seen.
—HEBREWS 11:1

As I drove along a rural road in New Mexico on a hot summer day, I wrestled with the problem of what to do about my parents and Larry's mother, all of them terminally ill back in Missouri. They wanted to live out their last days in their own homes, yet they were becoming increasingly helpless, and good home health care was hard to find in the small towns where they lived. They resisted the idea of coming to live with us or going into a nursing home, but Larry and I, with our own family and jobs, couldn't keep flying back and forth to Missouri to care for them. I felt lost and confused as I tried to come up with the best solution. If only I could look into the future and see what lay ahead, maybe I'd know what to do.

In desperation I prayed, "Lord, please, give me an answer!"

A couple of miles ahead the road slanted up a hill and vanished, dissolving into the sky. The trees on either side of the road shimmered and danced on air, while a lake suddenly appeared, drowning the valley in front of me.

I knew, of course, that I was viewing a mirage, but I wondered what a child who had never before seen a mirage might think as we drove toward apparent disaster. In my mind I started explaining about mirages and how things aren't always what they seem.

"Sometimes," I said to my make-believe child, "you have to keep going on faith even when you can't see the end of the road."

And I laughed out loud.

"Okay, Lord, I get the message," I said. "All I can do is keep on keeping on, trusting that You will pave the way."

Father, today I will set aside my fear for the future as I move forward, placing my faith in Your guidance and vision.
—MADGE HARRAH

JULY 3

But the Spirit itself maketh intercession for us....
—ROMANS 8:26

A police siren sounded just as my friend Pastor Elsie Crickard and the bell choir finished playing at Pleasant Valley United Methodist Church. A few seconds later there was another siren, this one even closer.

Fearing that a parishioner might have fallen in the parking lot, Elsie asked an usher to check, then called for prayer. "The Lord wouldn't want us to continue the Order of Service when someone is in need right outside our door," she said. "Let's pray for the person, the need, and for guidance on how we can help."

The usher returned just after the "Amen." "It's a car fire," he told Elsie. "Your family car just burned up."

After they viewed the remains, Elsie thanked the congregation for their prayers. "I thought I was praying for someone else, yet I was really joining the prayers you prayed for me!"

Two weeks later Elsie took me for a ride in a lovely lilac sedan. "This is a wonderful car!" she said. "I'm convinced that the prayers of my congregation gave my husband and me a peace that helped us find a reliable car at a price we could almost afford."

I'm convinced, too! I thank God for the people of Pleasant Valley who prayed when the siren sounded and for everyone who prays for people and needs unknown to them. Most of all, I thank God for the Holy Spirit Who prays for us and with us when we can't find the words.

Thank You, Holy Spirit, for the power of intercessory prayer in the lives of those who are prayed for—and those who pray.
—PENNEY SCHWAB

JULY 4
INDEPENDENCE DAY

*He hath sent me to bind up the brokenhearted, to proclaim liberty to the captives,
and the opening of the prison to them that are bound.*

—ISAIAH 61:1

*M*y wife, Joy, and I took a whirlwind trip to India to participate
in a conference and visit some friends. We spent several days
in places where it seemed that nothing worked. I was more than ready to get
back to hot water, cold soda, and my cell phone.

Finally, on the plane, we settled into our seats and waited for takeoff. And
waited. And waited. After almost an hour, the pilot told us, "We have an unusual
problem. Security has discovered a man in a maintenance uniform hiding in
the baggage compartment. All your luggage must be unloaded and reinspected
while they question the man."

Fears of hijacking or worse ran through my mind. In a little while the pilot
reported, "It looks like everything will be okay, folks. Our maintenance man was
trying to smuggle himself into the United States. He has been begging security
not to send him home, but to let him go to America and freedom."

As we took off, I couldn't get the unknown stowaway out of my mind. He
was willing to endure twelve hours in a cold baggage compartment and risk
imprisonment to come to America. He wasn't, like me, anticipating the creature
comforts of our consumer society; he longed for freedom.

In the last couple of years I have visited many countries, and everywhere
people want to know about America, to know if I can help them get there.
Do I really understand the great gift of freedom, divinely given and so
easily forgotten?

On this Independence Day, I have decided to say a prayer for those who long
for the great gift I almost take for granted. Won't you join me?

*Lord, You sent Your Son to "set the captives free." Help me never to take my
freedom for granted and to pray for oppressed people everywhere.*

—ERIC FELLMAN

JULY 5

God setteth the solitary in families....
—PSALM 68:6

*T*here is something very reassuring about a summer's twilight walk around the neighborhood. Lights are being turned on, families are getting ready for dinner, and before the drapes are drawn, I can see people bustling about. With windows open, sounds and scents drift through the evening cool. Music, laughter, a baby's cry, voices calling to each other, and then the tantalizing aroma of someone's dinner.

"Ummm," I tell my husband, whose long-legged stride I try to match, "roast chicken there!" Or, "Barbecue—fabulous! Stop. Smell. That's about all we'll get of it tonight!"

"Rats!" he says. "Salad again for us?"

I nod my head. We've walked around our neighborhood for almost forty years. We know each house as though it were our own. Some are repainting, remodeling, replanting the walkways, with people moving in and out, and some, like ours, remain much the same.

O little homes, set forth on every hand,
You little walled-in worlds of joy and fears,
Built on the common place of smiles and tears,
You are the strength and sinew of the land.
(Author unknown)

As we walk, I pray for the families in the homes on our route. We've all been through earthquakes, fires, and floods. We've shared the joy of our celebrations and the sadness of our bereavements in a continuum of life that makes each one of us an integral part of the whole. We are indeed the strength and sinew of our land.

Be with me in this place I call home, dear Lord. Keep my family and the families around me in Your love, and help us to reach out to one another.
—FAY ANGUS

JULY 6

For this reason he had to be made like his brothers in every way....
—HEBREWS 2:17 (NIV)

*P*erhaps it wasn't so, but I couldn't help thinking people were staring as I wheeled my mother into the crowded fast-food restaurant after church that Sunday. It was Mom's first outing since she had been released from the rehabilitation hospital following a serious stroke. She was slumped in her wheelchair, her hands quivered, and a black patch covered her drooping eye. To cover my embarrassment, I busied myself settling Mom at the table while Dad ordered.

In the wheelchair bag I found a nice purple-checked bib with lace edging that Aunt Josie had made. As I tied it on Mom, I sighed. Even the lace couldn't disguise the fact that the bib was as big as a bath towel, big enough to cover Mom's torso and fold down into her lap to catch the large amounts of food she spilled.

Dad came over with a tray of food, sat down, and quietly said the blessing. Then he rummaged through the wheelchair bag and got out a second bib. This one was a faded, ratty-looking terry cloth affair, with just a hint of blue left from the constant washing at the rehab hospital. Dad draped the bib over his suit, vest, and tie, tied it around his neck, and then took a bite of his hamburger.

My tense shoulders relaxed at once. In a busy fast-food restaurant full of onlookers, my father had just shown me that the best cure for self-consciousness is a self-forgetful act of love.

Dear Lord, help me do something loving today that will have people staring—and smiling.
—KAREN BARBER

JULY 7

But the Lord has been my stronghold, and my God the rock of my refuge.
—PSALM 94:22 (NAS)

*D*on Garner and I have been good friends since we met twenty-five years ago in seminary. While I have been a pastor, Don has been an Old Testament professor. Don is a gifted biblical scholar and has a love for archaeology and the ancient Jewish world.

This summer while on an archaeological dig in the Middle East, Don received word that his twenty-year-old son Aaron had been killed in an automobile accident. Stunned by grief, Don faced a grueling forty-eight-hour trip home—by himself, but never alone.

I telephoned Don as soon as he got home. As the phone rang, I struggled with what I should say. Then I heard Don's voice, and I knew the words didn't matter. What mattered was the sound of a familiar voice, a human touch across the vast expanse of miles and distance.

As Don described his journey, he said a curious thing. "Scott, you and I have studied the Bible for years. We've taught it and preached it. But I've got to tell you, I don't think I really knew what it's all about until now. And what I've discovered is that this thing we call faith is real. It will hold you up and get you through."

I know from my own experience that Don is right. You can read all the books about theology, quote Scripture from memory, preach lofty sermons, and teach great Sunday school lessons, but until you chart your own personal pilgrimage through pain, you cannot fully fathom that God is with you.

Some years ago while struggling with the pain of my father's death, I scribbled these words by the Scottish preacher James Stewart in the back of my Bible: "It is when you have sunk right down to rock bottom that you suddenly find you have struck the Rock of Ages."

Father, thank You for the times when You have taught me
that faith is real. Amen.
—SCOTT WALKER

July 8

Look not only to your own interests, but also to the interests of others.
—Philippians 2:4 (NIV)

*I*f you've ever visited the island of Maui, chances are you've driven the Road to Hana. Almost every tourist does! My husband and I made the fifty-four-mile trip in a rented convertible. As we slowed for the curves (there are six hundred of them!), we could hear the whooshing roar of waterfalls crashing into lush undergrowth. And the scenery was spectacular! But the thing that impressed me most about that trip was the bridges.

Fifty-two bridges. And all of them one-lane. At the entrance to every one was a YIELD sign—on both sides. Both approaching cars were supposed to yield! No one had the right of way. So what happened? Politeness. Chivalry. Charity. And an occasional laugh as both parties kept motioning for the other one to cross first.

No one has the right of way. It made for a good drive through paradise. It might be a good way to live my life, too. Suppose I surrender my right to that prime parking space (even if I saw it first)? Or how about I take the piece of pie that got squashed in the cutting process? And why shouldn't I be the one to have the middle seat (elbows in, please!) on my next business flight?

I may find that when I don't insist on my own way, I help create paradise no matter where I am.

Forgive me, Father, for the times I insist on having my own way at the expense of others. Humble me that I might know the joy of yielding.
—Mary Lou Carney

JULY 9

For God loveth a cheerful giver.
—II CORINTHIANS 9:7

*L*ate one afternoon a white pickup truck pulled into our drive. In it was Mario, a new neighbor. We'd met him shortly after he and his wife moved in. Mario jumped out of the truck, and we exchanged greetings. "I just wanted to give you my card and let you know I have a business painting and staining houses. I'd be glad to give you some references if you need anything done," he said, glancing at our porch and deck, both of which desperately needed work. In fact, just that morning I'd been dreading that I was going to have to find someone.

Before I committed myself, I wanted to check out his work. It was top quality, so I called him back for an estimate. The figure he gave me was way too low, and in addition, he volunteered to repair our fence for nothing. "Mario," I said as we stood in the driveway, "I'm always looking for a bargain. But this is really too low."

He shuffled around, hands in his pockets, looking back toward his house. Finally he said, "Well, I'll tell you. Usually I'd charge two hundred dollars more. But a few days after we moved in, our driveway was blocked by a tree, and your husband loaned my wife a car so she could get to work. Remember?" I did remember.

"But it wasn't worth all that, Mario," I said. "You could have rented a car for less."

"Yes," he said, his face flushing, "but it gives me great happiness to pay back with interest!"

Lord, when I pay back favors, help me to remember Mario's attitude—and Yours.
—SHARI SMYTH

JULY 10

I woke up feeling troubled. It was Sunday morning, July 14, 1996, and Hurricane Bertha was gone. Her punishing winds had diminished to a tropical storm by the time she limped into Medford, Massachusetts. Her visit brought four inches of much-needed rain. Although we had suffered no damage and the day was sunny and bright, I still worried. On Saturday, Hurricane Bertha had ripped through Wilmington, North Carolina, where my recently widowed friend Margaret lived. I'd tried to call her but got no answer.

On Sunday I ushered at church. Things moved smoothly, yet I was still worried about Margaret. Then, as I was helping with the collection, I heard the congregation softly singing.

Breathe on me, Breath of God
Fill me with life anew,
That I may love what Thou dost love,
And do what Thou wouldst do.

The words were soothing. After the service, I rushed home and called Margaret. Still no answer. Then I remembered receiving a letter from a friend of Margaret's who lived in Massachusetts. I called, and she said, "Margaret is just fine!" Suddenly I was fine, too. I had finally gotten through to someone.

Later, a letter from Margaret arrived. "We are well," she said. "Had trees down and debris, but no damage to the house."

With my mind fixed on Bertha's ferocious winds, worry had troubled my heart even at church, and I couldn't think clearly how to reach Margaret. I had forgotten that the gentle breath of God's Holy Spirit is always with us to sustain and uphold us, and to fill us with life. We'll be just fine . . . we just have to remember how to get through to Him.

Father of Comfort, never let my worries break my connection to You.
—OSCAR GREENE

JULY 11

Unless the Lord builds the house, those who build it labor in vain....
—PSALM 127:1 (RSV)

*L*ike our new home, Robert's and my marriage is built on a mountain. That mountain is strong and tall and absolutely dependable. Its name is Shared Prayer, and it's a solid place we enter together every evening. This daily practice started the evening Robert first visited me, and it has continued into our marriage.

We've discovered that it's much easier to be faithful to our daily prayer commitment if we set aside a special time and place for it. It's so important to us that in our new home we've provided ourselves with a small room that we use only for prayer.

We planned that room from our hearts. It's furnished with a small table, covered with a white cloth, above which hangs the needlepoint cross that was given to me by a *Daily Guideposts* reader. The room has an oak floor, a softly glowing amber light with a dimmer, and two kneeling cushions. It's the place where we come together before God, sometimes praying aloud, sometimes singing, often just sitting together in silent prayer, and always concluding with a warm hug. It's this daily prayer time, as much as anything in our lives, that creates the deepest bond between us.

We haven't always had the luxury of a separate room for our home sanctuary, but we've found that it's possible to have a "place apart" for prayer even in a crowded home. For many years, my sacred space was simply my green prayer chair, with my Bible and a notebook on the table next to it. All that you need is a quiet corner of any room, faithfulness to your prayer commitment, and a heart that longs for communion with God.

Tonight, Lord, when the busy day winds down and the last lights flicker out, may couples, families, and friends stand together on the mountain called Shared Prayer, in houses all over the world.
—MARILYN MORGAN KING

JULY 12

Let your conversation be as it becometh the gospel of Christ....
—PHILIPPIANS 1:27

I was flying back home from a business trip, trying to watch the in-flight movie, but the elderly man next to me kept interrupting the movie to ask a smattering of unrelated questions. I took off my headphones to answer him, but in order not to miss anything, I put them back on immediately afterward. Each time, however, I felt a little more guilty. I had been trying to be more open to people, and now I was intentionally doing the opposite.

Finally, I gave my seatmate my undivided attention. He was from Nebraska, traveling with a tour group of seniors. The next day was his wife's birthday. In 1948 he was supposed to go to New York, but he never made it. He was quite sure that Orville and Wilbur Wright would faint if they saw what had become of their grand invention.

As the southern tip of Manhattan appeared outside our window, I pointed out as many sites as I could. "Golly!" he said with amazement. "And what might that building be over there?"

"That's the Empire State Building, sir."

"Oh my," he said, "there it finally is."

The plane landed, and when it came time for him to get up to leave, my new friend turned and offered me his hand. "Nice to meet you, young man. I'm sorry I interrupted your show."

As he made his way down the aisle, his wife moved toward me and said, almost in a whisper, so that no one else could hear, "Years ago, while they were in the service, stationed in Virginia, he and his buddies got passes to go to New York City. His buddies got into some sort of trouble and they weren't allowed to go. He was so disappointed. You just gave him the tour he never had."

Then she whispered, "He's not doing too well."

I looked ahead and watched his labored walk and thought to myself, *Lord, without even knowing it, I just gave a dying man a gift.* And I almost missed the chance.

Lord, thank You for the blessings given and gained in simple conversation.
—DAVE FRANCO

July 13

"You are the world's light—a city on a hill, glowing in the night for all to see."
—MATTHEW 5:14 (TLB)

*T*he Old Point Loma Lighthouse sits high atop a bluff overlooking the Pacific Ocean and San Diego Bay. I can see it clearly across the water, miles away from our summer vacation spot on Coronado Island. I feel irresistibly drawn to it, as well as to another lighthouse I've visited, Marblehead Lighthouse on Lake Erie, in the Ohio town where my husband's parents live.

I've never really understood my fascination with these beautiful nineteenth-century structures. Is it the connection to the past, to the solitary lighthouse keepers who lit the oil lamps nightly to guide far-off sailing ships? Something more struck me when I visited both landmarks last summer.

I gazed at the Old Point Loma Lighthouse silhouetted against the sky, and thought of safety, security, a beacon in the dark that offers guidance and comfort. A few weeks later, when our family visited the Marblehead Lighthouse, I climbed the dozens of steps to the top and looked out at the boats dotting the water. It occurred to me that each of these views points to God's expectations for different times in my life. Looking toward the lighthouse reminded me of when I was a new mother, constantly seeking help and advice from others more knowledgeable, reaching out for a beacon to guide me. Now that I'm older, the view is different. Others look to me for leadership, and I feel God's urging to take on new tasks. I've always found a beacon to guide me when I've needed it, in helpful friends and loving family, and in God Himself. The lighthouse is always in view. Now it's my turn to be the light.

God, strengthen me to shine a guiding light for others as
You have always done for me.
—GINA BRIDGEMAN

JULY 14

And thou shalt love the Lord thy God with all thy heart, and with all thy soul, and with all thy mind, and with all thy strength....

—MARK 12:30

$\mathcal{E}$very Wednesday at 6:45 AM, a group of parishioners gathers in the Resurrection Chapel of St. Mark's Church in Mount Kisco, New York, to celebrate the Eucharist. The exquisite Gothic chapel has Tiffany windows, fresh flowers, a dedicated spiritual purpose. The prayers of generations are in the walls.

Immediately after the service, I go to Cardiac Rehab. What a contrast! Rehab's atmosphere is totally secular. Chrome machines, fluorescent lights, the morning news on television. And in this setting, men and women row and climb and run and pedal until their workout suits are drenched in sweat.

One Wednesday as I was leaving St. Mark's for Rehab, I commented on this contrast to my friend Mary Lynn Windsor, one of the 6:45 regulars. The Resurrection Chapel was holy ground, I said, but Rehab certainly was not.

"Oh, I don't know," Mary Lynn said. "Doesn't Jesus tell us to love God with all our heart and soul and mind and strength? At Rehab you're loving God with all your strength."

What a difference that remark made to me as I walked through the door of Rehab! Yes, my nostrils still smarted with the smell of disinfectant and my eyes narrowed against the glare, but I knew now that, incredible as it seems, I was stepping onto holy ground.

Always and everywhere, Father, You are there.

—JOHN SHERRILL

JULY 15

The crooked shall be made straight, and the rough places plain.
—ISAIAH 40:4

*I*f you've ever watched a square dance, you know that a square of dancers must listen to the caller. If the dancers don't listen, the square is broken and becomes eight people milling about. And if each of the eight dancers tries to restore order on his or her own, the broken square looks like a bargain basement full of pre-Christmas shoppers looking for a good buy. It's only when the dancers stop and follow the caller's directions that order is restored and the dance continues.

It wasn't long after my wife and I became square dancers that I decided square dancing was a lot like life. A broken life, like a broken square, becomes frenetic and disorganized when I try to correct the problem by myself. It's only when I listen for the Lord's directions that order is restored in my life.

The more I dance, the more I learn that if I want to enjoy square dancing, I have to listen to the caller. The more I live, the more I learn that if I want to enjoy living, I have to listen to the Lord.

Lord, when my life seems to be getting out of hand, open my ears
to hear Your call.
—RICHARD HAGERMAN

"Will a man rob God? Yet you are robbing Me! But you say,
'How have we robbed You?' In tithes and offerings."
—MALACHI 3:8 (NAS)

*I*t was more money than I'd ever held in my hand, and I'd found it folded to the size of a postage stamp underneath the big maple tree in front of our house on Madison Avenue. Ten dollars! By the time I ran to Mother with it, I'd spent it a dozen times in my mind: Barbie clothes, Nehi grape sodas and Mallo cups, Nancy Drew mysteries.

But Mother put a fast end to my dreaming and instead of shopping, I was tacking a sign to the maple tree to ask if anyone had lost anything in our neighborhood. After a long week of no inquiries, Mother agreed that I could keep the money.

Sort of. "This is as good a time as any to learn about tithing, Roberta," she said. "The first dollar belongs to God. When you tithe with a willing heart, I think you'll be amazed at how far the rest of your money goes."

Why is it that every time something good happens, some adult comes up with a plan to ruin it? I groused. But that Sunday as I dropped a dollar bill in the collection plate, I felt joyful, a part of something bigger that I didn't quite understand.

And it was amazing. The department store downtown announced a sale on Barbie clothes. Then a lady at church asked Mother if her girls liked to read Nancy Drew. Nine dollars stretched further than ten would have.

In my teen years, as I earned money babysitting and selling cosmetics, Mother continued to stress the principle of tithing, of offering God the first portion of my earnings, not what's left over. By the time I graduated from nursing school and had a real job, tithing had become a part of who I was.

My mother is gone now, but that lesson from childhood is with me still. "Give God the first dollar, the first part of your day," I hear her say. "And watch Him take care of things." And you know what? He's done just that.

Thank You, Lord, for stretching my skimpy resources
beyond my wildest imaginings.
—ROBERTA MESSNER

JULY 17

The fear of the Lord is the beginning of wisdom....
—PSALM 111:10

My mother was out back hanging up the wash, so I was all alone in the house, playing war with some lead soldiers in my parents' upstairs bedroom. I had an old brass tray that I used as a gong and a battered tablespoon to strike the tray at the start and the end of each battle.

Suddenly I thought I heard a strange noise. A monster was coming out of its hidden lair in the closet or the attic or the basement! My heart beat so loud I knew the monster would hear it and come to devour me or, worse, carry me away—like some winged older brother—to torture and torment me forever.

In terror, I began to sing and beat the gong. I cried a river of tears and sang at the top of my voice for an eternity of long seconds. I could almost see the shadows of the fangs and beak of the monster projected in the designs of the flowered wallpaper in front of me.

Then the distant *bang*—the back screen door slamming, the signal that my cavalry was going to charge over the hillside against the dragon.

"Mother!" I screamed. I knew the monster could hear me, too, so I beat the gong twice as hard. I heard running footsteps on the stairs. *Dear God, let it be my mother!*

The door burst open. My mother looked bigger than my dragon/beast, and she sent it scurrying back into its dark lair as she pressed me to her bosom and let me sob. Suddenly a new dread filled me with terror. "What if you died, Mother? What if God took you away? Who would save me then?"

She smiled and held me close. Then she walked through the doorway of my fear and brought me the story of Jesus and His love.

Lord, thank You for reaching out to us in the arms of those who have
helped us through the terrors of growing up. Amen.
—KEITH MILLER

JULY 18

*When [Peter] saw the wind, he was afraid and, beginning to sink, cried out,
"Lord, save me!" Immediately Jesus reached out his hand and caught him....*
—MATTHEW 14:30–31 (NIV)

*S*ome years ago, I took my family to visit Hershey Park, the amusement park in Hershey, Pennsylvania. Our older sons Ryan and Joel went off in search of the most challenging rides, while my wife, Kathy, and I took ten-year-old Kyle to sample the gentler ones, like the merry-go-round.

But Kyle was unhappy. "These rides aren't exciting enough," he said. "Let's try that one over there."

It was called The Rotor, and it was a cylinder of sorts. Inside, it looked like an empty soup can with padded walls. We stood in a circle against the walls as a voice came over the loudspeaker and said, "Welcome to The Rotor. This will be a ride you'll never, ever forget."

Suddenly, we began to spin around. *No big deal*, I thought. Then we began to spin a little faster. Pretty soon we were spinning yet faster. My shoulders were thrust up against the wall and I couldn't move. The voice came back over the loudspeaker and said, "Now experience The Rotor!" All at once, the floor dropped completely out from under us and we hung suspended.

I began to try to think of some faith-building Scripture, but all I could think of was the simple prayer of Peter as he sank into the sea: "Lord, save me!"

At last the floor came back up, and the ride began to slow down. My stomach was churning, my legs were like jelly, and my thoughts were in total confusion. Weak and wobbling, Kathy and I managed to walk out and find a place to sit down. Kyle ran out, overflowing with enthusiasm. "That was great, Dad!" he said.

If you should ever go to Hershey Park for an outing on some summer afternoon, beware of the "exciting" rides. But if you want to test your faith, step aboard one.

*Lord, when the bottom falls out of life, help me to pray, believe in You,
and keep a positive attitude.*
—TED NACE

July 19

"Tell them how great things the Lord hath done for thee...."
—Mark 5:19

*M*y friend Cheri and I do walk-talks together five mornings a week. It provides us both with the regular exercise we need and a chance to share whatever is going on in our lives. Almost every time, our shared processing of life events brings insight, and we both leave feeling a little wiser than before. But early last week, I was in one of those everything's-going-wrong moods, so Cheri let me talk. I ended up listing all my problems and complaining about them.

I follow our walks with my morning prayer time, so when I got home, I sat in my blue prayer chair by the window and opened a little book titled *Safe within Your Love* by Hannah W. Smith. My reading ended with this prayer:

My Father, help me to notice what I say to others about the challenges spread before me. Do I tell them, "I have such great problems"? Or do I say, despite my problems, "I know a great God"?

Suddenly, all of those problems that my mind had magnified clicked into proper perspective as I offered them to my all-powerful heavenly Father. After prayer time, I called Cheri and apologized for my problem-listing monologue. Then I said, "It's been awhile since we've talked about our relationship with God. Let's put that on the agenda for tomorrow!" It's been the subject of our walk-talks all week, and we're both feeling enriched.

Loving Father, let my problems be reminders that now is the perfect time to tell a friend, "I know a great God."
—Marilyn Morgan King

July 20

Each one had a harp and they were holding golden bowls full of incense,
which are the prayers of the saints.
—Revelation 5:8 (niv)

*R*ecently my cousin Mary Sue phoned to tell me, "Mother died last night."

I was devastated. Aunt Sue was no ordinary aunt. She was a woman of prayer who prayed for me by name every single night. Years ago an elderly neighbor—"Old Brother Joe" everyone called him—had done the same for me. But Joe, too, had died. Then, two years ago, another blow: Mom's death. I still tell myself, *I'll ask Mom to pray with me about that,* before suddenly remembering I no longer can.

With both Old Brother Joe and Mom gone, only Aunt Sue was left to pray for me faithfully and daily. Now Mary Sue's call. I panicked. "What am I going to do?" I wailed over the phone, more concerned with my own plight than with hers.

Surprisingly, it was Mary Sue who comforted me instead of the other way around. "I believe prayers go on and on," she answered. "They never die." At first I thought her words were too good to be true—until I remembered Revelation 5:8.

Aunt Sue lived to be a hundred and three, Mom past ninety-seven, Joe into his late eighties. If all the prayers of those three are in golden bowls, think how many they must fill! I, too, must have started filling bowls years ago when I first began praying for my sons, my grandchildren, and my other relatives and friends. Yes, and even a great-grandchild now on the way.

Heavenly Father, how wonderful that prayers, old or new, are still at work.
—Isabel Wolseley

JULY 21

"I am the light of the world. Whoever follows me will never walk in darkness, but will have the light of life."

—JOHN 8:12 (NIV)

*H*er porch, overgrown with vines, sagged and creaked as I walked across it and stepped into a dark Victorian parlor crammed with heavy furniture. I was eighteen and had accepted a summer job taking care of Mrs. Martin, an elderly woman from our church. Although I'd never met her, she was rumored to be "difficult."

Mrs. Martin's daughter-in-law ushered me into the front bedroom. Mrs. Martin was propped up in her bed, arms clamped across her bosom, mouth drawn tight as the drapes. She didn't like the sun pouring in, I learned in the next few days, among other things.

Three days later, I was chained to one of Mrs. Martin's awful moods when the doorbell rang. There stood Deacon Moore, beaming like a lighthouse. Across the years, he had lost a wife and son in an accident, and there'd been other tragedies as well. But at eighty-four, he carried himself young. I brought Deacon Moore through to the front bedroom, where Mrs. Martin, robe buttoned to her throat, hunkered in semidarkness. "How are you today, Mrs. Martin?" he began.

When she stopped her litany of complaints, he held up his hand. "Mrs. Martin, when life hands you a hardship, you can focus on the awfulness or you can focus on God, Who allowed it. Either way, you'll come through it. Because we do, you know. But one way, you'll be imprinted with the hardship, the other, with God."

I spent the summer trying to focus on God, and I came through. And perhaps that was one of the reasons I was put there. Because across thirty-five years, that light from Deacon Moore has gotten me through darker storms than Mrs. Martin.

Lord, for myself and for those coming after me, may I blaze a trail of light that leads to You.

—SHARI SMYTH

He heareth the cry of the afflicted.
—Job 34:28

My dad's doctor had told me that Alzheimer's disease might change Dad's personality, and now it was happening. Dad had always been a kind, generous, helpful man, but now he was becoming suspicious and angry. The staff at the nursing home understood and were patient with his outbursts, but I couldn't accept the change in his behavior. He just wasn't the man I had known. Dad was especially resentful toward his new roommate, Alvin.

One day I brought a little box of candy with me. It was a brand my dad used to buy for my mother, and I hoped it would remind him of happier times. As soon as he saw it, he smiled, and for a few minutes he reminisced about the old days. Then he removed the wrapping and opened the box. There were six different kinds of chocolate-covered candies in it, and I recognized one as my dad's favorite. He reached for it—and stopped.

Alvin was in his wheelchair on the other side of the room, head bent and silent; Dad suddenly wheeled himself over to him. I didn't know what he was going to do, so I followed along behind him. Dad parked his chair in front of Alvin's and held out the box of candy. "Alvin!" he said, rather sharply, and Alvin's head came up.

"Would you like a piece of candy?" Dad said in the gentlest way. It seemed to take Alvin forever to reach for the box, and his fingers were clumsy. Dad picked out his favorite piece and put it in Alvin's open hand. A tired smile came over Alvin's face as he put the candy in his mouth. "Thank you," he mumbled.

"Here, have another one," Dad said, holding out the box. This time Alvin picked up a candy by himself, and Dad's eyes were bright with encouragement. "He's a nice guy," he said, turning to me. "He just needs a little help."

Quietly I thanked God for showing me that the man I always knew and loved was still there. I think he was also assuring me that no illness on this earth can destroy the goodness in a person.

Thank You, Lord Jesus, for the comfort and love You give me
when others seem far away.
—Phyllis Hobe

JULY 23

My soul thirsteth for God, for the living God....
—PSALM 42:2

*L*et's go sit by a stream somewhere," my husband, Lynn, suggested late one Saturday afternoon. I'd been working for hours on a project, trying to squeeze the right words out of the thoughts in my head. I wanted to be done, but I felt too weary and depleted to finish. That's why Lynn suggested the "time-out" by the stream. Since we both grew up in Colorado, we've come to rely on the sound and sight of a rushing mountain stream for rejuvenation.

So we grabbed a couple of sweatshirts, turned on the telephone answering machine, hopped in the car, and stopped at a take-out place to get a bag of Mexican food for a picnic dinner. Then off we went, in search of a stream. We headed up a nearby canyon where the rushing water runs alongside the road, and pulled into one of the first parking areas with no cars. We found a picnic table right by the water and spread out our fast-food feast. After eating, we simply sat and listened and drank in the sound and sight of that rushing water.

By the time the shadows began to disappear into the gathering dusk, I felt renewed. What is it about a mountain stream that replenishes me when I feel depleted? It reminds me that God is the endless source of the love that flows into my life and touches all the dry places in my thirsty soul. It washes away the sludge of stuff that clogs my brain and slows my thinking.

God's creation is filled with other reminders of Himself that replenish people in dry times. For some, it's the ocean or a sunrise or the formation of a flock of birds flying in the sky. As we headed back down the mountain, I knew I'd be able to finish my project with renewed strength.

Father, I'm so thankful You have tucked reminders of Yourself into Your creation.
Let me take a "time-out" to soak them all in.
—CAROL KUYKENDALL

July 24

He hath delivered my soul in peace from the battle that was against me:
for there were many with me.

—Psalm 55:18

*W*e had a family gathering last summer at a beach house with our five children, their families, plus in-laws and cousins—a total of twenty. I had looked forward to it for months because I seldom get to see some of them. But after a few days of youngsters shouting and crying, older ones tramping in and out noisily at all hours, and tempers flaring—the way they often do when too many people are crowded together, no matter how much they love one another—my nerves began to frazzle. Soon I found myself counting the days until they would go and quiet would return, and I felt ashamed of myself for feeling that way.

One morning, to get away, I drove to a secluded beach and sat there for a long while watching the surf break gently on the shore, gazing out at the vast tranquil expanse of the sea and the ships on the horizon. Gulls were swooping down for bits of food and occasionally broke into loud squabbles over a choice morsel . . . just like my noisy relatives, I thought, and began to laugh.

I thought of the beauty God had created throughout His universe. Even families—my family, too, for though they might be noisy and fractious, our love for each other was part of the beauty of life. Right then and there, I gave thanks for them and, with a full heart, got up and returned to the beach house. This moment of quiet and communion with God had renewed me and brought the things that were really important back into perspective. In the future I would remember—not where to turn but to Whom I must turn when chaos and confusion reign.

Lord, let us draw aside and come into Your Presence so that we can gain a fuller
measure of Your peace before returning to the noise and clamor of the world.

—Sam Justice

July 25

But my God shall supply all your need....
—Philippians 4:19

The French have a proverb: *Si jeunesse savait, si viellesse pouvait,* which means, roughly, "If only youth had wisdom, if only age had strength." I thought of this one day last summer when I found my little boat swinging wide in deep water because the wind had changed and the tide had come in. "No problem," I said to myself, "I'll swim out, jump in, pull up the anchor, and row to shore."

This was a maneuver I had not attempted for three or four decades. In the old days I would swim out, grasp the gunwale, give a quick heave with arms and shoulders, and land more or less gracefully in the boat. So I swam out, grasped the side of the boat, and gave a confident little heave. Nothing happened. I gave a much larger heave. Still nothing; I seemed to be glued into the water, and a dark realization entered my mind. It wasn't Father Neptune who had me by the feet, it was Father Time. The lithe youth of half a century ago was gone, and here was this ancient character, thirty pounds heavier, in his place.

People were watching with amusement from the bank. Was I going to have to beat a humiliating retreat? Then the old French proverb came to mind. If age didn't have power, it was supposed to have wisdom. "Think!" I said sternly to myself. So I thought for a while. Finally I went around to the bow, grasped the anchor rope, tied a loop in it about the size of a stirrup, put my foot in the loop, and stepped grandly into the boat.

And the moral? Well, I guess it's that when the good Lord takes away one attribute, He supplies us with another—if we're wise enough to use it.

No matter what my difficulty, Lord, let me draw upon the many resources You supply both within and around me.
—Arthur Gordon

JULY 26

He leadeth me beside the still waters.
—PSALM 23:2

ometimes people with Alzheimer's become agitated without any apparent reason. When it happens to my father, the staff at the nursing home usually can calm him down with reassuring words. But one day the head nurse called me and asked if I could come over to see him right away. "He's very upset," she said, "and maybe you can help."

When I arrived at Dad's room, he was wheeling his chair back and forth and he kept looking behind him as if he thought someone or something threatening was there. I had never seen his eyes so haunted. "We don't dare leave him alone," the nurse said. "He keeps trying to get up and we're afraid he'll fall."

I put my arms around him and said, "Hi, Dad, it's me." I could see he didn't know me—sometimes that happened. *Lord,* I prayed, *I don't know what to do. Help me!* If the professionals couldn't do anything for him, how could I? Then I remembered that whenever I'm upset—really upset—I read the twenty-third Psalm. It's like medicine for my soul.

There was a Bible in Dad's night table, and I opened it to the Psalms. I held it in one hand and put my other arm around Dad's shoulder. "The Lord is my shepherd," I began, holding the Bible in front of him so he could see the words. By the time I got to "I will fear no evil," I felt Dad's shoulders relax and he breathed more slowly. The nurse nodded and smiled. When I finished, Dad looked at me and knew me. "Again," he said.

We went through the psalm two more times, and he was calm. So was I. The twenty-third Psalm had restored our souls.

Thank You, Lord, for the comfort of Your words.
—PHYLLIS HOBE

The Lord gave, and the Lord hath taken away; blessed be the name of the Lord.
—JOB 1:21

*W*hen I stepped into the large, nearly windowless sanctuary of our church last Sunday, I encountered unexpected darkness. "The power's out," an usher whispered. I stood in the doorway expecting to hear him say that the service was canceled, but instead he directed me to a pew in the dim inner twilight.

How can church go on without electricity? There won't be any organ music, I thought. Just then, two men wheeled in a piano, and the sanctuary filled with music. *I'll never hear the minister without a microphone,* I fretted. The minister stood in the pulpit and apologized for the lack of electricity in a clear, loud voice. I heard every word. *The choir won't be able to see a thing up there in that darkness,* I decided. At anthem time, the choir filed down from the dark loft and arranged themselves on the chancel steps, where sunlight drifted into the sanctuary from the side door.

As we stood and repeated the Apostles' Creed from memory, I felt a sudden burst of understanding. *My fellow churchgoers haven't let what's missing keep them from worshiping. The electricity may have been subtracted from the service, but it has only emphasized the deeper things that run on their own power. God's presence is here all the more powerfully, not despite the darkness, but because of it.* I had always assumed that God makes things new by adding something. Now I understood that things can also be transformed by subtraction.

During the offertory, the choir sang "All Hail the Power of Jesus' Name." I heard a loud *whoosh* as the heater fan and the lights pulsed once, twice, and then stayed on for good. Perhaps I wasn't the only one a little disappointed.

*Lord, as the subtracting goes on in my life, help me to add up the ways
it transforms me into someone wonderfully new.*
—KAREN BARBER

JULY 28

I am the bread of life....
—JOHN 6:35

*L*ast summer while I was taking drawing lessons, my friend Betty learned she had cancer. The day before she went to the hospital for surgery, her spirit seemed nearly depleted. "What am I going to do?" she said, thinking about the demanding weeks ahead of her. "How will I find the strength?"

That evening I found myself doodling on my drawing board, thinking of Betty. Soon I was sketching a loaf of bread. A simple, homemade loaf. Then I put it aside and went to bed. But during the night I had the most curious dream. Betty was sitting at a table before a loaf of bread, eating a single piece.

The next morning when I came upon my drawing, an idea began to stir in my thoughts. I reached for my Bible and found the verse, "Behold, I will rain bread from heaven for you" (Exodus 16:4), remembering how day by day God sent nourishment from heaven while His people wandered in the wilderness. There was always just enough for each day. They simply had to trust Him for tomorrow's.

I penciled the verse beneath the sketch of bread and carried it to Betty's hospital room. It was to remind us both—when we walk in difficult places, God sends the strength and nourishment to face what comes our way, not all at once, but day by day.

I will trust You, Father, for the ability to face whatever this day brings.
—SUE MONK KIDD

JULY 29

I will trust, and not be afraid....
—ISAIAH 12:2

*J*uly 29,1970, ended our son's forty-day leave. Within hours he would board a plane for Nha Trang, Vietnam. I stood at the bedroom door as he put on his army uniform. Our son—only three weeks after he became engaged to Marie—was off to war. I blinked back tears. Butch forced a smile with, "Dad, take care of my girls," meaning his mother and Marie. I nodded, unable to speak.

The phone rang. Ruby answered, then beckoned to me. "That was the surgeon at the hospital," she whispered. "It's about that lump in my breast. They won't know if it's cancer until after the biopsy. Should we tell Butch?" I shook my head. Our son left and my wife went into the hospital. Despair swept over me as I imagined the worst: Butch returning in a box and Ruby losing a downhill battle with cancer.

I went outside and stared at our giant oak. Soon the leaves would turn fiery gold. When the oak was bathed in color, the leaves would tumble, and the tree would be bare. Yet spring would bring new life. To most trees, but not all. When their time came, trees died, the same as people. I knew what I must do—trust in the Lord...trust all my seasons to Him.

The tumor turned out to be benign. One year later our son returned, with new lines etched in his face and terrible experiences etched in his mind. But he was alive. He was home again. I had trusted our Father and He had blessed us with another spring.

Father, teach us to bear our griefs with fortitude, just as we accept our joys without question. But most of all, teach us always to trust our circumstances to You. Amen.

—OSCAR GREENE

JULY 30

My flesh and my heart faileth: but God is the strength of my heart,
and my portion forever.
—PSALM 73:26

atherine and Joe had been married more than thirty years. They had no children and their lives were centered around each other. Then Joe died and Catherine was desolate. "I can manage the day," she said. "I stay busy outside. But, oh, when I have to go in the house without him, the loneliness. . . . "

Last week in her garden as the day was ending, she looked toward the house with dread. "Lord God, have mercy on me," she whispered. "I am so alone." At that moment, a large orange and black butterfly swooped past her face and perched lightly on her shoulder. It opened and closed its lovely wings as it rested quietly there. "I stood very still," she told me. "I didn't want to frighten it. Then a strange thing happened: my own fear and dread seemed to drain out of me. A great calmness came over me such as I hadn't known since Joe died. I took one step forward slowly, then another. The butterfly rode partway and then flew from my shoulder and landed on the screen door."

Her eyes, which had been sad for so long, began to twinkle. "I suddenly knew I was not alone. God is with me all the time, even in the house. I believe He sent His messenger, the butterfly, to remind me."

I still go to visit with Catherine each chance I get, but I've stopped worrying about her. She has learned the truth of His promise, "I will not leave you comfortless: I will come to you" (John 14:18).

Lord, let me feel Your comforting Presence in my loneliest hour,
then make me bright with Your joy.
—DRUE DUKE

JULY 31

They looked unto him, and were lightened....
—PSALM 34:5

*D*o you have a favorite "comfort" food? You know, something warm and soothing that tastes just right when you're tired and achy? Some favorites mentioned in an article I recently read were chicken soup, bread pudding, tea and toast with a soft-boiled egg, hot cocoa, warm applesauce, oatmeal, and macaroni and cheese. My favorite is sugar-sprinkled buttered toast covered with warm milk.

One day, a few years ago, I was lying on the family room sofa clutching a box of tissues, suffering from a bad case of allergies. "Here's a hot cup of tea for you, Mom," said my daughter Lauren. "Maybe it will help you feel better." Taking a few tentative sips, I started thinking about that cup of tea. It was such a simple thing, but it warmed my insides and helped relieve my headache. *It's just like so many of God's words,* I thought. How many times had my favorite psalm comforted me when I was worried or depressed! Like "comfort" food to my soul, it soothed and consoled me.

Here are some of my favorite "comfort" verses, which, like that hot cup of tea, usually help perk me up. Often I'll write them on index cards and tape them to the refrigerator or prop them on my desk.

He shall cover you with His feathers, and under His wings you will find refuge (Psalm 91:4, RSV).
Now may the Lord of peace Himself give you peace always in every way (II Thessalonians 3:16, NKJV).
The eternal God is thy refuge, and underneath are the everlasting arms (Deuteronomy 33:27).
The Lord is near to all who call upon him (Psalm 145:18, RSV).

Eternal Comforter, I need Your peace and solace today. Amen.
—ELLEN SECREST

August

AUGUST 1

Then the Lord opened the servant's eyes, and he looked and saw
the hills full of horses and chariots of fire....
—II KINGS 6:17 (NIV)

*H*e sat on a stool beneath the stone overpass just north of the zoo in New York's Central Park, a favorite spot with street musicians because the arch makes a natural sounding board. I'd often paused there to listen to a trumpet or a guitar or an accordion. This young man, however, was playing an instrument I didn't recognize, a kind of long-necked, two-stringed violin held on his knees. The bow, positioned between the two strings, produced a haunting nasal melody, ephemeral and melancholy.

I stopped, enthralled and puzzled. I could see only one man, one instrument, yet the echoing space swelled with a great chorus of sound—flutes, gongs, plucked strings, drums. Stepping closer, I saw a small tape player at his feet. An entire orchestra was creating the music, the young man adding his single melodic line. I read the placard propped against the tape player:

HELLO! HERE IS THE NATIONAL PEOPLE'S ORCHESTRA OF BEIJING (AND ME).

In smaller print the placard explained that the young musician, from China, was a student at Columbia Medical School, supporting himself with these street performances. It had taken courage, I thought, to come alone to a strange land far from home—the kind of courage, in fact, needed on every journey of faith.

God reached out to me beneath a bridge in Central Park to remind me that on my journey I never need to feel alone. When the road ahead is dark and threatening, I can tell my fears:

HELLO! HERE ARE ANGELS AND ARCHANGELS AND ALL THE HOST OF HEAVEN (AND ME).

Father, remind me on my journey today that mine is the name in parentheses.
—ELIZABETH SHERRILL

AUGUST 2

Be still, and know that I am God....
—PSALM 46:10

As I was walking to the office one morning—a luxury I treasure after years of commuting—I passed a young woman going in the opposite direction. I watched her with fascination. She was struggling to pull a cigarette out of a pack while holding a phone between her shoulder and her ear, all while crossing a busy Manhattan avenue. I held my breath, hoping that she wouldn't become involved in a fourth simultaneous activity by being hit by a car.

She crossed safely and was soon out of sight, but I began to think about the activities of my own hours and days. Anyone who has raised a family, held a job, and kept house at the same time knows how to do many things at once. But while I have no cell phone and don't smoke, I began to see that "multitasking," as the techies call it, had become almost an addiction in my life. Setting the table while watching the news while opening the mail may not be as hazardous as crossing the street talking on the phone, but by the time I sit down to dinner the rhythm is set. Eat fast. Clean up. Move on. But to where?

I decided to learn to sit still and be quiet for five whole minutes each morning before leaving my apartment. It wasn't at all easy, but I clung to that wonderful and reassuring phrase from Psalm 46: "Be still, and know that I am God." I'm not perfect, and I still fidget and tend to cram in too many things, but I'm better, and those five minutes have had an extraordinary influence on my day. If I listen carefully, mysteriously and clearly, I realize what will really count in the day ahead. And that never means picking up the dry cleaning or planning errands for my lunch hour.

God, let me learn to listen to You at least once a day without interruption.
—BRIGITTE WEEKS

AUGUST 3

And all the days of Methuselah were nine hundred sixty and nine years....
—GENESIS 5:27

*W*hen my eighty-seventh birthday rolled inexorably around, I reminded myself hopefully that I was just a youngster compared to the ancient biblical character Methuselah. But one of the grandchildren had another idea when she sent me a birthday card. "Congratulations on your special day, Granddad," she wrote on it, "but what about all your yesterdays? I don't think they should be left out. So here are thirty-one thousand, seven hundred, and forty-three more congratulations just to take care of them!"

More than thirty-one thousand yesterdays! Whether or not she included leap years I don't know, but that's an astonishing number of sunrises and sunsets. This year, when Thanksgiving Day comes around, I'm going to remind myself that each yesterday was a gift from the Creator of all things...and be truly thankful!

Father, when You send another day, teach us not to take it for granted
but make it count in the pattern of our lives.
—ARTHUR GORDON

AUGUST 4

Yet I will rejoice in the Lord, I will joy in the God of my salvation.
—HABAKKUK 3:18

The older I get, the more I am trying to learn, or relearn, how to relax. My wife, Rosie, and I have found the perfect place: Laity Lodge, a Christian retreat and conference center in the west Texas hills, two and a half hours north of San Antonio.

On our first day at the lodge we were introduced to the many activities available to us, including swimming, horseback riding, art, tennis, and—unexpectedly—signing, the finger language used by many hearing-impaired people. My first choice was tennis, but on second thought, I decided to give signing a chance. I thought it would be worthwhile even if I went to only one session and learned the alphabet.

At the first class the teacher told us that we would stand together as a group at the final service and use our hands to "sing" a song with the piano accompanying us. My first thought was *No way! I'm not going to embarrass myself.* But she patiently encouraged us to let go of our inhibitions, relax, and allow God to use us.

As we finished the first day of practice, I was still awkward. My hands and fingers were not moving with the best rhythm. I was still self-conscious, imagining how silly I thought I'd look, trying to make the proper signs in time with the music. Then I remembered just what I would be doing—participating as best I could in a worship service to praise the Lord.

That Sunday morning, we stood before the group of worshipers signing the song "I Surrender All." As I moved my hands, I lifted my spirit in praise, and my heart was filled with joy and thanksgiving.

Lord, help me to follow You joyfully despite my fears.
—DOLPHUS WEARY

August 5

God . . . causes the growth.

—I Corinthians 3:7 (NAS)

*J*felt very little joy that Easter morning. Just a few days before, the doctor had told me my only sister had terminal cancer and I was grieving for her. Not only that, but so far she had shown little interest in God's offers of hope and peace. What could I possibly do to help her?

Preoccupied with my thoughts, I wandered into the kitchen. On the windowsill was a hibiscus plant that had been given to me as an expression of sympathy when my mother passed away. I had been diligently nurturing it along ever since, and in God's perfect timing, a large coral blossom shaped like a trumpet greeted me that Easter morning. It was both a glorious message of resurrection hope and a beautiful reminder of my mother's faith.

As I stood there admiring the bloom, God seemed to say, *For several months now you have been concerned about the soil and the sunshine and the water for this plant, and that is good. But remember, the budding and the blossoming are My business. You do the possible. I will do the impossible. You tend to your sister's physical needs with loving patience and diligent care, but leave the flowering of her soul to me.*

At that moment, the anxiety I had been experiencing disappeared. I simply resolved to reach out to my sister with love that was "rooted and grounded" in God (Ephesians 3:17 NAS).

As I write this a few months later, I can see some tiny buds of belief beginning to swell. They give me hope that my sister will eventually blossom out in faith—resurrection faith.

Lord, as I watch a soul slowly open like a flower in the light of Your presence,
I can only say with Paul, "How . . . unfathomable [are Your] ways"
(Romans 11:33 NAS).

—Alma Barkman

AUGUST 6

At thy right hand there are pleasures for evermore.
—PSALM 16:11

I was on hold on a pay phone at Exit 87 outside Jackson, Tennessee.

A few minutes earlier, my husband, David, and I had been riding happily down the interstate, talking about all the places we hoped to travel to someday. David was at the wheel of an eighteen-foot rental truck loaded down with stuff for our daughter Keri's graduate-school apartment in Memphis.

The blowout came quickly: a pop, then a low hiss. We were lucky to make it to the exit.

I had called the rental agency's toll-free number for assistance, while David trekked off to look for help. Now, on the other end of the phone line, a recording droned on: "And for fifteen dollars you can get an extra copy of your rental contract sent..."

I spotted a moth in the gravel by the phone. Its wings were white with black spots. The spots formed a lovely pattern, the same on both wings. Its legs were cobalt blue. The moth seemed to be having a bit of trouble. I looked around and my eyes fell on a tree that seemed to offer a nice shelter for the moth's recovery. I laid down the phone long enough to scoop up the moth with the original rental contract (which we got for free when we rented the truck) and transported it to the tree. Back at the phone, the voice of a real, live person told me a road service representative would be along to fix the tire in fifteen minutes.

A few minutes before, I had set my sights on traveling out into the blue horizons of someday—completely oblivious to the view along the way. Now, I watched the moth fly over to a patch of dew-drenched grass, hover for a moment, then fly away.

On hold, on a pay phone, on a nondescript exit of the interstate, I had learned a timely lesson: Someday is now.

Father, You plant the potential for pleasure all along the road of life.
Give me the wisdom to enjoy all that is close at hand.
—PAM KIDD

August 7

I will restore health unto thee, and I will heal thee of thy wounds, saith the Lord.
—Jeremiah 30:17

*T*he news from home had me worried. Dad was in the hospital with a torn Achilles tendon. After surgery he wouldn't be able to walk for six weeks. I could picture him trapped upstairs in the bedroom and Mom shuttling up and down, bringing him his meals, mail, newspaper. If I were closer to home, at least I could run errands for her or help Dad with his physical therapy. But they were in California, some two thousand miles away, so I had to content myself with phone calls and letters. What else could I do?

Then my friend Gary had a seizure. He lives in an apartment across the street. The doctors weren't sure what the cause was, but they didn't want him going to work on his own. "Rick," he asked me one evening on the phone, "could you accompany me on the subway in the morning? My doctor doesn't want me to be alone, in case I have another seizure."

"Sure," I said. "No problem."

The next day I met Gary outside his building and we walked to the station together. "I know you like to pray in the mornings," he said, "so go ahead. I have something to read." On the train I took out my Bible and he took out his newspaper. When I closed my eyes, I had a lot on my mind. *Lord, be with Mom and Dad back home. I wish I could be there.* Then it occurred to me that God had given me something good to do right here. Be with Gary as the doctors helped him.

Later when I talked to Mom, she told me about all the people who had been giving them a hand. "I'm sorry I can't be with you," I said.

"That's all right," she said. "I know there are things you need to be doing there." Someday I'd tell her the half of it.

Let me serve You, Lord, wherever I am.
—Rick Hamlin

AUGUST 8

You have planted them, and they have taken root; they grow and bear fruit....
—JEREMIAH 12:2 (NIV)

*A*nd these," our Hawaiian guide said with a flourish of his hand and a wide smile, "are pineapples!" Gentle laughter rippled through the bus. Every tourist knew that! But then he proceeded to tell us something we didn't know: Pineapples will grow bigger if they're given room. "Could be very big!" the guide continued. "But they are deliberately grown small so they will pack into cans that fit on your grocery store shelves."

As we drove on through the huge fields of sweet-smelling fruit, I felt a twinge of sadness that they were forced to fit into a predetermined space. *Glad it's not like that with people*, I thought. Or was it? What about the people "growing" near me—co-workers, family members, fellow churchgoers, friends. Was I allowing them to reach their potential? Giving them space to try their ideas, express their opinions? Was I allowing them room to make mistakes, to take risks that would enable them to grow?

The bus lumbered toward its next attraction, but I looked back at those pineapples. "Grow," I whispered softly. It was what I planned to do—and help others to do, too.

Use me, Father, to cultivate all that is fine and noble in others.
And don't let me cramp their growth in the process!
—MARY LOU CARNEY

AUGUST 9

When the morning stars sang together, and all the sons of God shouted for joy?
—JOB 38:7

*A*ll I have to do is walk out into the evening and look up into the sky and the memory returns. I was five years old. My dad stood over my bed, gently shaking me awake. "Come with me, Brock. I have a surprise for you."

He carried me out into the yard where my mom had spread a big quilt. I realized that it was way past my bedtime. Why had my parents awakened me, and why were we outside in the warm summer night?

"God is going to give us a special show," my father whispered to me.

For the next few hours we lay side by side on the quilt. We watched the shooting stars flare across the sky one after the other, sometimes two at once.

I had a unique feeling that night, one that to this day I find hard to describe. I was receiving a gift, a revelation of God's wonder. This gift was given, I felt, exclusively to me and my parents by the Lord God Himself.

This show, the Perseid meteor shower, returns to the summer sky every year in August, and I have seen it many times since. I have seen it from a canoe on a rural lake in Alabama and from the roof of my college fraternity house in Knoxville, Tennessee. I have even seen it over the Grand Canyon. But no meteor shower will ever match the one my parents awakened me to see from an old quilt in the backyard that summer night.

Lord, let the star's song be heard and let us all shout for joy!
—BROCK KIDD

Though I walk in the midst of trouble, thou wilt revive me…
thy right hand shall save me.
—PSALM 138:7

We've had our share of extraordinary pets, but when it comes to determination and sheer instinct for survival, Gussie tops the list.

My husband was the first to spot her. "What on earth?" he mused as he peered out the kitchen window. "Is that a small gray rock moving out there?" Both our daughter and I looked. Then, quick as lightning, our daughter was out the door and racing across the lawn. She came back in holding a baby possum.

We filled a basin with warm water, then made a solution of antiseptic mixed with shampoo. As I gently sloshed the little creature through the water, hundreds of fleas rinsed off her. We changed the water and did it again. And again, until she was completely clean. She didn't seem to mind, perhaps because she was barely alive. Dehydrated, she kept sucking on an eye dropper filled with liquid nutrition. Then, wrapped in a soft washcloth, she fell asleep in our daughter's hand.

"Because it's August, we'll call her Gussie," decided our daughter. "Do you suppose we could keep her?"

I frowned, not comfortable with the prospect of a possum in the house. "Better check with the Humane Society. Possums are wild creatures, and they could be dangerous pets."

Our daughter was put in touch with the Opossum Society, which rescues little creatures such as Gussie. Soon we were deep in the world of possum rescue, a world that has reached into our hearts and enriched our lives as we have learned the gentle ways of these small wild creatures.

"The secret was she kept moving, or I wouldn't have seen her," my husband observed, obviously impressed.

"That little creature didn't give up!" I agreed. "She's given me an example I'll never forget."

Dear Lord, when I'm consumed by worries and troubles, help me to trust that
Your gentle hand will reach out to rescue me, Your mercy heal my wounds,
and Your love revives me and holds me forever against Your heart.
—FAY ANGUS

Be strong and of a good courage; be not afraid, neither be thou dismayed:
for the Lord thy God is with thee whithersoever thou goest.
—JOSHUA 1:9

*A*fter the recessional every Sunday, our minister stands in the back of the sanctuary and in his rich preacher's voice delivers a stirring benediction: "God is with you. Therefore, go out into the world and fear nothing."

The words fill me with courage. Yes! I can do anything! At least until I hit the glare of the noonday sun in the parking lot. Fear nothing? Not the confrontation I must have with a friend? Not the talk on storytelling I'm supposed to give? Not the overloaded schedule I can't possibly keep? *How, Lord?*

My mind goes back to a long-ago summer day. I'm about ten, a scrawny child standing on a platform twenty-five feet above our local swimming hole. The courage to jump has drained out of me; the bottoms of my feet seem cemented to the hot wood. Behind me, a line of impatient kids is yelling at me to jump. Finally, an older boy steps close and whispers, "The first time you have to jump scared." I close my eyes, release my sweaty grip, and fall. My stomach dives to my ankles; I feel the cold shock of the water. It swallows me, and down I go until I feel slimy plants and mud against my bare legs. Then I begin to rise upward. I emerge from the water spitting victory.

Now, as I pull out of the church parking lot, I hear the pastor's challenge as it was meant to be heard: The "go" comes first. The "fear nothing" comes after.

Lord, thank You for meeting me as I step out into my fear.
—SHARI SMYTH

AUGUST 12

"All nations will call you blessed, for you will be a land sparkling with happiness...."
—MALACHI 3:12 (TLB)

*T*here's something magical about this place. On a rented bike, I glide along the waterfront of South Haven, Michigan, a small resort town on the eastern shore of Lake Michigan. I held a ministry internship here thirty-nine years ago, but the town is not the same unspoiled paradise. Now it's a tourist magnet. The once placid harbor is packed with sailboats.

And yet something about this town sparkles.

At the bicycle shop the bearded salesman is so entertaining that I urge him to start his own sitcom. He laughs. "Thanks, and don't worry about getting this bike back right on time. Enjoy yourself out there."

When an ATM machine balks on me, the bank teller actually crawls inside the machine and fixes it. "There," she says sweetly, "now you can enjoy the rest of your vacation without money worries."

When I accidentally leave my toolbox at the motel, I go back for it, but it's gone. Oh great, two hundred dollars' worth of tools just vanished! But when I tell the manager, he sends out a search party. A young groundskeeper, wearing an "I Love Jesus" T-shirt, finds the box in the laundry room, and he hands it to me, glowing with joy at his success. "I know how it is," he says. "You can buy new tools, but they don't have the same feel as your own tools."

Now I remember why I'm drawn back to South Haven in the summers. It's not just the cool breezes and blue waters. It's that small-town spirit of joyful service.

May the happiness of the Savior shine through me and touch those I meet today.
—DANIEL SCHANTZ

AUGUST 13

And Agrippa said to Paul, "In a short time you think to make me a Christian!"
—ACTS 26:28 (RSV)

*I*n the days of the Model-A Ford, outdoor advertising signs had much longer messages than today. The reason is simple enough: When people were driving down the road at forty miles an hour, they could read a lot more words than at sixty or more. Speed, I'm told, doomed my all-time favorite outdoor ads, those five-sign rhymes posted by Burma Shave. Readers of a certain age will recall those entertaining fence-post sayings. I'm not sure I can quote it exactly, but one of the rhymes quipped:

> He saw her beauty
> And made a bum's rush
> She saw his stubble
> And gave him the brush.

What brought this all to mind was a series of recent outdoor ads attributed to God. An anonymous Florida resident commissioned a Fort Lauderdale agency to create some billboards that would call people's attention to spiritual matters in a provocative way. What started out to be a local campaign turned national. At last count, thanks to the Outdoor Advertising Agency of America, the pithy sayings have appeared on more than ten thousand billboards. Among my favorites: "Loved the wedding. Invite me to the marriage." "Let's meet at my house Sunday before the game." "What part of 'Thou Shalt Not . . .' didn't you understand?" "Do you have any idea where you're going?"

Isn't it amazing what can be communicated in a few words? Our mistake sometimes is thinking that we need to set aside a whole hour to reach God, when in fact we can talk to Him on the move, in short takes, day or night. Something like a billboard.

> *Lord, when I'm stressed and my day is peaceless,*
> *Help me live a prayer that's ceaseless.*
> —FRED BAUER

AUGUST 14

The pride of thine heart hath deceived thee....
—OBADIAH 3

*A*s I scrubbed the spines off the dozens of green-and-white-marbled pickling cucumbers in my kitchen sink, I was pleased with my first attempt at gardening. Bulbs of garlic and pungent dill waited on the draining board. This morning my seventyish rancher friend Margaret Norman was teaching me how to put up dill pickles. I longed for them to be as tasty as hers and had often joked that I would always choose a jar of her dills over any of the stunning silver, turquoise, and jade jewelry she made.

"Now first, honey, you steam the jars." I felt myself tensing. I wanted to boil them.

"Try to pack 'em like this." I listened politely but felt I had a better idea.

"Then you mix up the brine, boil it, and seal 'em." I'd had enough.

"But, Margaret, I read that you're supposed to boil the jars."

Margaret had had enough, too. "Okay, kid," she sighed, "I can see you've got your own ideas. Go ahead and do it your way, and tell me how they come out." She hung up her potholder and walked out the kitchen door.

Too busy to feel upset, I continued working in the steamy kitchen. Later I admired my beautiful pickles, a filigree of dill and pearly garlic at the bottom of each translucent jar. Several weeks later, I was ready to taste my handiwork. Yuck! No vinegar! My beautiful pickles were nothing more than boiled cucumbers in jars of water.

I sheepishly confessed to Margaret. She smiled gently. "Well, honey, I knew you weren't about to listen to me. I had to let you learn on your own." She patted my hand and gave me a jar of dills from her root cellar.

To this day, I can't make dill pickles like Margaret, but I do know a little better how to listen.

Lord, give me the sense to recognize my pride and friends patient enough to teach me in spite of it.
—GAIL THORELL SCHILLING

A bruised reed he will not break, and a smoldering wick he will not snuff out.
In faithfulness he will bring forth justice....

—ISAIAH 42:3 (NIV)

or a couple of years I volunteered three days a week at our tiny church office, where they have given me the title Director of Communications. This meant that I wrote and edited the monthly newsletter and updated the weekly bulletin. It also meant that I heard many of the joys and sorrows of the church family.

One week, many of our families seemed to be struggling. Financial loss, severe illness, a breaking marriage, a miscarriage, a death in the family—the list went on and on. I knew that behind each of the prayer requests lay people who were hurting, struggling to let their faith grow in adversity and uncertainty.

I was absentmindedly typing the prayer list for Sunday's bulletin as I concentrated on praying for the various people and their needs. When I looked up at the computer screen to check my work, I found I had typed the phrase "each member" as "each ember."

The image of an "ember," something burning low, brought to my mind the "smoldering wicks" of Isaiah 42. As I corrected my mistake, I smiled and thanked God that His promise was sure: Not one of these "embers" would be snuffed out. He would sustain them and bring forth a good result in His own perfect way and time.

Lord, bless and sustain those whose faith candle burns low today.

—ROBERTA ROGERS

"As I was with Moses, so I will be with you...."
—JOSHUA 1:5 (NIV)

onight I had a "Moses Moment," one of those times when I tell God, "I can't.... I don't want to.... I won't!" It struck me about 6:00 PM as I began the final preparations to teach a 7:30 PM Bible study at our church. Weeks earlier, when I agreed to fill in for this one-night stand, it had sounded like a fine idea. But now I was filled with dread and fears of inadequacy. "I'm not a Bible study teacher, Lord. Surely there will be people there who know more about this passage than I do. I'm tired. My stomach is filled with flutter feelings. I can't...."

I call it a "Moses Moment" because Moses voiced similar fears when God told him to go somewhere and speak. "Who am I that I should go? What if they don't believe me or listen to me? O Lord, please send someone else to do it. I can't...."

Then I remembered the gist of what God told Moses: "Go, and when you get to the place where you feel afraid, I will be with you. I will give you what you need."

In spite of my flutter feelings, I forced myself to read over the text and study my notes. Then off I went to teach the class. Two hours later, as I drove home, I felt pretty sheepish because none of my fears had materialized. I led the class through the study of the Scripture passage. And my feelings of dread disappeared as soon as the class started.

I also felt pretty sheepish because I've endured many "Moses Moments" in my life when I dread the challenge before me. I should know that my flutter feelings are merely part of the preparation. Enduring them helps me trust God's promise that when He calls me to do a task, He'll provide what I need. Always.

Lord, when I face another "Moses Moment" and say, "I can't,"
remind me of Your promise that together, "We can."
—CAROL KUYKENDALL

"It is more blessed to give than to receive."
—ACTS 20:35

Twenty-five years ago I was a newly married man. Three days after our wedding, Beth and I moved from our childhood homes in Georgia to attend seminary in Louisville, Kentucky. We opened a joint checking account and deposited all of our financial resources: a grand total of 110 dollars. As seminary classes began, we both frantically looked for jobs. Our checking account dwindled to nothing after our second trip to the grocery store.

Two weeks later I trudged dejectedly to the campus post office, worried about the mounting bills I was receiving. In my mailbox I found an envelope from my home church. In the envelope was a check for a thousand dollars and a note from some people who loved and supported me. As I stood there in stunned amazement, I began to cry. I was learning the joy and the grace of receiving a gift.

Tonight, twenty-five years later, I am writing a check to send to a young woman attending Yale Divinity School. She was a member of our church during her undergraduate days at Baylor University, and Beth and I are very fond of her. This is her first experience of living away from Texas, and her finances are extended to the breaking point. Now Beth and I have the opportunity to give, just as we had the opportunity to receive.

The Bible is right when it says that "it is more blessed to give than to receive." I always thought this verse meant that it is better to give than to receive. What I'm discovering now is that it means it's more joyful. Nothing has made me happier this year than to send this money to someone I love. And nothing has made me more grateful than to realize that the God Who takes care of my needs also enables me to meet the needs of others.

Dear God, thank You for allowing me both to give and to receive. Amen.
—SCOTT WALKER

AUGUST 18

Cause me to hear thy lovingkindness in the morning; for in thee do I trust....
—PSALM 143:8

I've been a bit out of sorts the past couple of days from lack of sleep. It's not that I can't get to sleep but that I wake early in the morning, no matter how late I get to bed.

This morning, for example, I found myself wide awake at about four thirty, following a late night. After lying in bed for an hour, tossing and turning and hoping to go back to sleep, I finally decided to get up. I thought of reading or writing in my journal or answering mail, but none of those things had a strong appeal for me at 5:30 AM. So instead, I chose a CD of lovely, ethereal music, put on the headphones so I wouldn't wake my husband, and kicked back in the recliner that faces the east living room window.

The silence of the starry sky felt like the expectant hush that comes over a theater when the lights have dimmed, just before the curtain rises. I felt a sense of great anticipation as the sky turned, ever so gradually, from diamonds on black velvet to an etching of evergreens on parchment, then to a soft, candle-glow gold as the morning sun rose over Mount Dewey. Something inside of me knelt, and I found my soul at prayer. Could it be that God had been waking me in the early morning so I could experience the wonder of His presence in the light of the dawning day? I believe so! And there was a bonus. My husband said he noticed right away that I was in good spirits!

On those days when I find myself unable to sleep in the early morning hours, I hope I can remember that Someone is waiting for me—Someone with a gift beyond words.

Creator of all that is, how many times must You call before I answer?
When I waken early, let me recognize Your call and rise to meet You
at the edge of the dawn.
—MARILYN MORGAN KING

August 19

Ask the Lord for rain ... and he will answer with lightning and showers.
Every field will become a lush pasture.
—ZECHARIAH 10:1 (TLB)

*I*t had been an extremely hot summer with practically no rainfall. Backyard gardens lay parched, and daily the produce offerings of grocery stores and markets grew smaller and smaller.

At the morning worship service on Sunday, the pastor said, "I'm sorry that the church is not cool today. We have some paper fans in the pews, but not enough for everyone. So if you find one, please share it with those near you."

He cut the service short that morning and asked the congregation to join him in prayer. It was a beautiful prayer, thanking God for His many blessings. He finished with these words, "And please, Lord, send us rain. Rain, now, would really be a shower of blessings."

That night I was tempted to skip church, but my conscience wouldn't let me. So I was there when, just as we had begun to sing the first hymn, the pastor raised his right hand high in the air. "Listen!" he exclaimed loudly.

The organist stopped playing, and we all heard the wonderful music of rain pounding on the roof and beating against the windows of the church. You can imagine the happiness, the gratitude, and the praise expressed throughout the rest of the service.

As my friend Lita and I were leaving, a little girl joined us at the doorway, which was blocked by the downpour. In her hand, she carried a small red umbrella, the only one I saw anywhere in the church. "I see you brought your umbrella," Lita said to her.

"Of course," she replied with a big smile. "I knew I'd need it. We prayed this morning for rain."

Oh, Father, grant me the faith of a little child. Amen.
—DRUE DUKE

Lo, children are an heritage of the Lord....
—PSALM 127:3

I'm sitting in my yard early on a summer morning, sipping coffee with a fresh newspaper and sleepy sons draped one over the other on my lap. As I hear the new young crows croaking and bleating at their parents, I have to grin, even as I want to snarl at them to stop their incessant blubbering.

I've heard that same relentless moaning and whining from my own children, and I have lurched around the house at night goggle-eyed and gibbering just like the crow mothers and fathers blearily hopping along the fence in front of me, complaining quietly to themselves in crowspeak. I mutter insults at the noisy young crows, in utter sympathy with their exhausted parents.

All creatures are thrown headlong into raising their young without the slightest training or semblance of an organized system. It's astonishingly exhausting, and it never ends, as far as I can tell, until you do, and it's the greatest thing that ever happened to me. Despite the lines cut into my face by those bleary nights, and the worry lines cut around the tired lines, there are also laugh lines that otherwise wouldn't be there. And I'm not tired enough to think that this exhaustion and this joy and these children aren't extraordinary miracles from the Maker of all things, moaning new crows included.

Dear Lord, You have given me riches beyond imagination or measurement, for which I am speechless in gratitude. Could You maybe do me one more favor and let the children learn how to sleep through the night?
—BRIAN DOYLE

AUGUST 21

*"Who am I, O Lord God, and what is my house, that
thou hast brought me thus far?"*
—II SAMUEL 7:18 (RSV)

*W*hen I look at my kitchen, I don't see the spotless counters, the crumb-free toaster, the scrubbed stovetop. I don't notice the sparkling sink, the smudgeless dishwasher, the streak-free refrigerator. I don't observe the clean floor tiles, the carefully stacked cookbooks, the immaculate pottery. And, I'm ashamed to say, I barely note the metal sculpture depicting Jesus at the Last Supper. What I see is one doorless cabinet. The gaping cabinet. The cabinet with the dishes, glasses, serving bowls, and measuring cup sitting there in plain sight. My plain sight.

I'm obsessed with this open cabinet. The hinges broke months ago, no hardware store seems to have them, and I can't locate the original builder to find out where to order them. And since we're renting, it doesn't make sense to replace all the other cabinets, which work just fine. And so I daily mull over alternatives.

What about draping a curtain over the cabinet? A decorative towel? Could I somehow lean the door against the opening? Perhaps I should just empty out the entire cabinet and simply stare at the bare space?

Today my friend Lori came over to visit. She had never seen our place before and was full of compliments. I was chewing on the inside of my mouth when I showed her the kitchen. "It's perfect," she exclaimed enthusiastically.

"Perfect?" I groaned. "Yeah, sure, if you ignore the gaping cabinet!"

"Mmm," she said, glancing at it briefly, "I hadn't even noticed it. But this Last Supper sculpture is really great!"

It's a good thing God is more like Lori than like me.

*Lord, thank You for the grace that forgives my faults and
renews me in Your likeness.*
—MARCI ALBORGHETTI

August 22

The Lord will guide you always....
—Isaiah 58:11 (NIV)

*T*he most amazing experience my wife, Joy, and I had last year was visiting the mountain gorillas in Rwanda's Virunga National Park. Because of the fragility of the gorilla population and the danger involved, only two families of gorillas are visited, and only eight visitors are allowed to see each family each day. As we began the hike to their habitat, we were handed twenty-eight rules for visiting the gorillas. Here are my favorites:

- All visitors should stay together in a tight group. Please stay behind the guide at all times.
- Keep your voice down at all times. If you are stung by nettles or ants, please try not to cry out!
- If a gorilla charges you, please follow the guide's example. Crouch down slowly and wait for the animal to pass. Do not attempt to take a picture at this time, and do not run away.
- Do not attempt to touch the gorillas.

When we reached the family of eleven, led by a three-hundred-pound silverback male, I was trying hard to remember all the rules. Do they really think I'm going to crouch down and not scream if that big fella charges? Joy, who knows no fear, was enthralled by the baby, who didn't know the rules and tried to touch her. I was about to panic when the guide reached through the bamboo undergrowth and gently pulled Joy behind him.

I watched the two guides closely as they kept themselves between us and danger. It was a wonderful picture of the way Jesus leads me through life if I let Him. He leads me up the mountain, knows the location and nature of the dangers, stays between me and them, and then always leads me safely home.

Jesus, thank You for being the shepherd and guide for all Your followers. Help me learn to stay behind You and follow Your example in all we do.

—Eric Fellman

August 23

The light that shines through the darkness—
and the darkness can never extinguish it.

—John 1:5 (TLB)

*T*he lure of the Blue Ridge Mountain breezes was just too tempting, so instead of heading for bed as midnight approached, I let myself out onto the long gray deck and sank into a plastic Adirondack chair. Slowly my eyes adjusted and the stars above me became clear and clearer. For often-hazy August, the sky was unusually dark and the stars unusually bright. I sighed in pure pleasure: After years of living in dense Maryland woods, the open sky here in Virginia is a new joy for me.

Like a child discovering the stars for the first time, I began to play with ideas: Gee, what if all that is really a great black velvet drape and the stars are pinholes where heaven shines through!

Suddenly, out of the corner of my eye, I became aware of a flickering. Somewhere beyond the black mound of Massanutten Mountain was a thunderstorm. I watched the flashes and flickers silhouetting the ridge for quite a while but heard no thunder. Strange, I watched the TV forecast at eleven o'clock and there were no storms.

Curious, I crossed the deck, entered my office, and called up the Virginia weather radar on my computer. There was only one storm anywhere in the three-state area, a large red-orange blob covering Cape Charles—the point where Chesapeake Bay meets the sea at Hampton Roads—a five-hour drive away from us. The night was so clear that the darkness could not hold back the lightning. It bridged the ridges and lit up my deck 170 miles away.

As I called Bill to come see the silent display, I thought of how many times the Lord's light had bridged the dark valleys in my life to bring His peace and His presence. Watching lightning moving out to sea—beyond two mountain ranges, the long Piedmont and the Tidewater—I knew I was seeing a parable in action: Darkness cannot extinguish light.

Lord, bring Your light over the ridges and into the valleys of my life.

—Roberta Rogers

August 24

"I tell you the truth, anyone who will not receive the kingdom of God like a little child will never enter it."

—Luke 18:17 (NIV)

A few years ago, I traveled to Greensboro, Alabama, to help rebuild the Rising Star Baptist Church, which had burned to the ground. I'm a builder. When I stepped onto the red clay of the building site, I felt that I had entered the kingdom of God.

Everyone on my volunteer crew was unskilled but highly motivated. By the end of the week, I could trust each worker to mark and cut lumber accurately. Each worker, that is, except Ian.

Members of the church, including parents with their children, came by the building site each day to help with the work. Ian peeled off his nail belt the moment he saw the kids and went over to play with them. Some of my other workers grumbled about Ian's work habits. I couldn't blame them. I planned to talk to Ian on Sunday evening about how he was affecting the morale of the crew.

On Sunday afternoon, the congregation of Rising Star served us a huge meal at the building site. I looked forward to fielding questions about the dimensions and design of the new church. I was also prepared to point out how hard everyone had worked all week—everyone except Ian.

The church members were kind to me and my crew, but they had no questions for any of us—any of us, that is, except Ian. All afternoon, parents thanked him for being so good to their kids.

I still planned to talk to Ian that evening. After all, I too needed to thank him—for reminding me about the real kingdom of God. My crew and I thought we were in Greensboro to rebuild a church. None of us thought we could rebuild the broken hearts of its people. None of us, that is, except Ian.

Thank You, God, for giving me something to contribute to building Your kingdom.

—Tim Williams

August 25

For whatever was written in earlier times was written for our instruction....
—Romans 15:4 (NAS)

*B*ack in 1975, our family vacationed in Daytona Beach, Florida. I stretched out by the pool, anticipating a few days of total relaxation with no responsibilities.

Our thirteen-year-old daughter, Jennifer, suddenly whispered, "Mama, look at that girl!" I sat up, adjusted my sunglasses, and saw a beautiful young woman in a skimpy bathing suit serving drinks to some folks at the pool.

I quickly shut my eyes, got comfortable again, and announced, "We're on vacation. She's not my problem." But when I saw a small airplane overhead trailing an advertising sign, I suddenly sat up again. The sign seemed to say, *Marion, tell that girl I love her.*

Thirty stubborn minutes later, I put on my robe and marched over to the bar. "Look," I said to the young barmaid, "I know you're not interested in what I have to say, but God seems to want me to tell you that He loves you." As I turned to go, I felt a slight tug on my arm. Behind her heavy blue eye shadow, the girl fought back tears. "Are you sure, lady?" she said. "Me? He loves me?"

Esther and I struck up a friendship. When she wasn't working, we spent hours talking about God. As we sat on the beach, I showed her my Bible, all marked up with the discoveries I'd made in the four years I'd been a Christian.

On our last day at the beach, I invited Esther to our room while I packed. I gave her a cup of orange juice, a ten-dollar bill, and a big hug. Then God seemed to say, *Now give her your Bible, Marion.*

A long minute passed. Finally I managed to stammer, "Here. I...I...want you...to have this."

As our family headed back to Georgia, we got a final glimpse of Esther. She sat at the bar bent over her Bible, sharing it with two customers.

Today, Father, I suddenly remember the song I sang in vacation Bible school: "The B-I-B-L-E, yes, that's the book for me."
—Marion Bond West

For he will give his angels charge of you to guard you in all your ways.
—PSALM 91:11 (RSV)

My backpack was heavy. Despite the fog and early morning chill, I was hot—and I still had another mile to walk to the Edinburgh train station. Suddenly, out of the fog, looking like he'd just stepped out of a Sir Walter Scott novel, a man approached. I grew apprehensive.

"Good morn'. Can I help ye out, ma'am?" he asked.

"No, thank you."

"I don't mind. Ye look a wee burdened."

"I'm certain. Thank you!"

He shrugged. "I'll mosey on then."

The next morning, in a completely different part of town, I was holding a heavy bag and waiting for a city bus. Suddenly, out of the mist, the same stranger.

"'Ello, ma'am. Can I help ye today?"

I shook my head.

He leaned against the wall beside me. My apprehension increased. Not a single bus for half an hour! I prayed, *Now is a good time for a bus to come along, God!* In answer to my prayer, my fear vanished, and though I'm not a person who hears God talk, I heard: *He's here to help you.*

The man stood by. We talked a little. Mostly it was quiet, an odd time of calm such as I've never experienced before or since. Finally, "A bus be along the noon, ma'am," and he vanished into the fog.

I was not surprised when, less than a minute later, a bus wheezed out of the mist.

"No buses Sunday mornins, lass," the driver hollered. "I'm special run! But ye hop on! 'Tis not safe here!"

People to whom I tell the story often wonder if I'd met an angel. One thing I know, whoever he was, he was of God, sent to help and protect me.

Dear Lord, help me always to accept Your help and protection
in whatever form it comes.
—BRENDA WILBEE

AUGUST 27

The Lord is close to the brokenhearted and saves those who are crushed in spirit.
—PSALM 34:18 (NIV)

*D*inner was almost over, and the waiter was rustling around the table signaling that it was growing late. Long day. I was tired, tired of chattering, tired of trying to pretend that everything was fine. I felt as if my mind were full of black, nauseating mud.

"You're not well, are you?" said the old friend across the table. I opened my mouth to turn aside the remark with a plea of fatigue or work stress, and suddenly the tears cascaded down my face without a sound. Few things are more embarrassing than crying in a public place. I bowed my head. Thank goodness the restaurant was romantically dim.

"You should call your doctor," said my friend in a matter-of-fact voice.

"I did," I whispered. "She's on vacation for ten days, and there was some emergency number to call. I just couldn't." The depression had been deepening for several weeks, just as the darkness falls on a summer night. It was too late by now to see my way.

"I'll call him, right now," my friend said. I was astounded by her offer, unable to answer. She disappeared to the pay phone at the back of the restaurant.

"Let's go," she said on her return. "He's calling you at home in half an hour." And he did. One quarter, one friend, and I could begin my walk toward the light.

Thank You, Lord, for true and courageous friends who change our lives.
—BRIGITTE WEEKS

"Every one who believes in him receives forgiveness of sins through his name."
—ACTS 10:43 (RSV)

*A*s I watch the waves dance one after another to the shore, I wonder why I am so drawn to the sea. Is it simply the beauty of the sparkling blue-green water, powerful and unchanging like God Himself? My thoughts are suddenly interrupted by my son Ross, who, after bodysurfing for more than an hour, has just ridden a big wave all the way into shore and runs to tell me about it.

"You know what I love about the ocean, Mom?" he says, shaking saltwater off his face. "The waves keep coming. If you miss one, you just have to wait. There's always another one."

His innocent assessment falls into place in my mind like the last piece of a puzzle. *There's always another one.* The ebb and flow of the waves is an echo of God's own voice, calling me back to Him. Only recently I'd let go of some destructive feelings, anger at a friend over long-ago hurts that I wouldn't forgive and resentment over her successes. Holding on to those feelings separated me from God, and in my stubbornness I passed up opportunities to be forgiven. Yet like the gentle pull of the tide, I always felt God bidding me to return to Him. And when I was finally ready, so was He—ready to send another cleansing wave of forgiveness to wash away the pain.

Gazing at God's great ocean now, I think I understand its power to comfort me. The steady flow of the sea is a reminder that while in my weakness I may miss many chances God offers me to come to Him, He will see that there's always another wave of His love and grace to carry me in to shore.

Lord, wash Your love and forgiveness over me and bring me closer to You.
—GINA BRIDGEMAN

He has made everything beautiful in its time....
—ECCLESIASTES 3:11 (NIV)

his morning I dressed in the dark so as not to disturb my wife Julee, who was sleeping in after a late-night singing gig. Imagine my dismay when I arrived at work and discovered a small, ugly stain on my fresh shirt, a stain my neighborhood laundry had vowed to banish. It was virtually unnoticeable, I'm sure, but I immediately imagined that no one who came in contact with me could possibly ignore my blighted appearance.

It was a lovely Manhattan day. I was walking from lunch across West 32nd Street with a friend when I detected people staring at me. Yes, I was certain someone pointed. Then I noticed my companion grinning. "You'll never believe this," she said.

"What?" I was growing tense.

"There's a big, beautiful butterfly riding on your shoulder."

Out of the corner of my eye I made out a pulsating smear of color. "Careful," she whispered, "you might scare it off."

But it wasn't going anywhere, at least not anywhere I wasn't going. All the way across 32nd Street, west to east, the butterfly perched on my shoulder like a cool flame, and everywhere people stared and pointed and smiled.

"How did you teach him to do that?" one astonished kid asked.

The butterfly stayed with me for a good fifteen minutes, the entire way back to my office building, before fleeing the arctic air conditioning of the lobby. "That was amazing!" my friend said. Amazing, certainly.

But not as amazing as God, Who gives me a nudge when I'm thinking foolishly and shows me that He made people far more interested in beauty than in ugliness.

Thank You, Lord, for stains and butterflies and sunny days—for everything.
—EDWARD GRINNAN

August 30

And having done all, to stand.
—Ephesians 6:13

*I*t was our seven-year-old grandson Ryan's first year in 4-H Club and first county fair. He proudly showed me his reserve champion rabbit and purple-ribbon no-bake cookies. Then we went to look at Moonie, his calf. "We'll be in showmanship first," Ryan told me. "I have to lead Moonie around the show ring and make him stand in line with the other calves."

When the announcer called, "All junior beef showmen into the ring!" I breathed a quick prayer while our son Patrick gave Ryan final instructions: "No matter what happens, hold tight to Moonie's halter and stand still unless the judge tells you to move."

Ryan dragged a reluctant Moonie into the ring. During the second trip around the ring, one of the steers jerked away from his owner. He knocked down two 4-H'ers and spooked three calves before the ringman caught him and tied him to the fence. Through it all, Ryan and Moonie never moved a muscle.

"Weren't you afraid when that big steer got loose?" I asked after the competition was over.

"Not really," Ryan told me. "I was too busy trying to do what Dad said: 'Hold tight to Moonie, and stand still unless the judge says move.'"

Hold tight and stand still. It was good advice for me, too. The mission agency where I work recently experienced some setbacks and I'd reacted with a frantic burst of activity, pursuing projects and sources of funding that weren't really compatible with our work. Maybe the way to move forward was to do what Ryan did: Hold tight to the task and direction God has already given, and wait for His guidance.

Jesus Lord, forgive me when I think Your work depends on my efforts.
Give me the grace to move forward by standing still. Amen.
—Penney Schwab

The Lord is my strength and my shield; my heart trusted in him,
and I am helped....
—PSALM 28:7

*R*evered devotional writer Lettie Cowman tells this story in *Springs in the Valley*, sequel to her better known *Streams in the Desert*:

In the deep jungles of Africa, a traveler was making a long trek. Porters had been engaged from a tribe to carry the loads. The first day they marched rapidly and went far. The travelers had high hopes of a speedy journey. But the second morning these jungle tribesmen refused to move. For some strange reason they just sat and rested. On inquiry as to the reason for this behavior, the traveler was informed that they had gone too fast the first day, and that they were now waiting for their souls to catch up with their bodies.

I was reminded of that story when I rolled out of bed this morning, limp as a weeping willow. For the last week I had been on an exhausting business trip and today, finally, I was back home. I had more catching up to do than energy to do it. So before plunging into the papers that covered my desk, I poured myself a second cup of tea, opened my Bible to the Book of Psalms, and immersed myself in God's Word, His forever promises for forgetful pilgrims such as I. In a few moments I felt the first stirrings of restoration, and before I knew it my fragmented mind and weary bones seemed whole again. My soul, I guess you could say, had caught up with my body.

When we try to put too many tasks into too few hours, Lord, slow us down so we can hear Your voice and draw upon Your strength.
—FRED BAUER

September

*Then Jesus told his disciples a parable to show them that they should always
pray and not give up.*
—LUKE 18:1 (NIV)

I covered my ears at the yapping. It was Junior, the gangly brown boxer dog across the street. I adored him and welcomed his friendly visits to my porch, his pug face pushing into my lap. But when he was locked in his pen, his bark had a pitch that could shatter glass, not to mention a peaceful summer morning in the yard.

I knew what ailed him: He wanted to go inside. So today, instead of railing and wishing him laryngitis, I tried a new approach—I rooted for him. "Atta boy, Junior," I called, sitting on my steps. "Anytime now. Don't give up."

It seemed to go on forever. But finally, the door opened across the street. "I'm coming, I'm coming," said Junior's master, striding to the pen. When he unlatched the gate, Junior bounded out, jumping up on him, licking his face, and wagging his stub of a tail as if to say, "I knew you were in there and that you'd answer if I didn't give up."

In the sweet peace following Junior's victory, I thought how easily I give up on God when I'm asking for something and the only answer is a closed door. Where is my patience? My persistence? My faith that my Father hears and will answer in due time—His time?

Lord, thank You for turning a morning's annoyance into a lesson on prayer.
—SHARI SMYTH

"He will do everything I want him to do."
—ACTS 13:22 (NIV)

*Y*ears ago, when Chinook salmon still returned to breed in Idaho's streams, I stood in a wilderness place called Dagger Falls and watched the mighty fish circle in a deep pool ten feet below a vertical rock bank beside the falls. They were tired. They had left the Pacific Ocean three months before to battle the raging currents of the Columbia, Snake, and Salmon rivers to reach this point. Now they were dying.

Every so often a fish would accelerate around the pool, then leap up into the water, spilling over the ten-foot-high wall. I shuddered when a fish flailed and fell onto the pool's surface with a crack louder than the noise of the rushing water. I cheered when a fish ignored the pain of the fall and leaped again and again until it reached the top edge of the rock wall, then flipped and flapped until its tail disappeared into the river.

They have restless hearts, I thought. They're willing to do everything God wants them to do—return home and bring life to another generation.

Their example gave me a restless heart. And when I returned home, God led me to teach Bible classes to twelve- and thirteen-year-olds. There were times I was tired. I had three active daughters and a busy dental practice. I struggled—and sometimes failed—to make the classes interesting. But it seemed that I was doing what God wanted me to do. And, years later, when one of my former students thanked me for helping him to find Jesus Christ, I knew I had helped bring life to a new generation.

Lord, give me the will to do Your will in bringing the young to new life in You.
—RICHARD HAGERMAN

*And whatever you do, in word or deed, do everything in the name of
the Lord Jesus, giving thanks to God the Father through him.*
—COLOSSIANS 3:17 (RSV)

I once heard a group of people introducing themselves to a distinguished minister. In the group was a successful architect, a real estate developer, a college professor, an engineer, a doctor, and his wife. When the lone woman in the circle extended her hand, she reported, "I'm just a housewife."

"And so was Susanna Wesley," the minister responded. It was a splendid rejoinder. Susanna Wesley, wife of Samuel, famous English clergyman, was the mother of twenty-two children—including John, founder of the Methodist Church, and Charles, composer of six thousand Christian hymns. She committed her entire life to the home. One of the most charming stories about Susanna is that in addition to doing all the washing, cooking, sewing, and cleaning for her large family, she still found time to give one hour a week exclusively to each one of her children. That's devotion.

A philosopher once advised that it is important "to live your life as if it counted, otherwise it won't." Some people speak disparagingly of their calling—on this day when our country pays tribute to all who labor, it is important to see our work not as a curse to be endured, but an opportunity and blessing from God, for there is dignity, hope, honor, satisfaction, and reward in work...but only for those who believe that by doing their job well, they can make a difference. Proverbs 23:7 says it best: "For as we think in our hearts so are we."

*Father, remind me: There be only one secret to work's delight:
All worth doing is worth doing right.*
—FRED BAUER

I am the rose of Sharon....
—SONG OF SOLOMON 2:1

I was walking briskly out of the shopping mall, trying to remember where I had parked my car, when a young girl with bobbed blonde hair came up to me, smiling. "Here," she said, handing me a beautiful long-stemmed rose, "I want you to have this."

"How lovely," I said, and before I could thank her she had spun around and was off.

"The strangest, nicest thing happened to me, honey," I told my husband when I got home. "Look, a complete stranger gave me this gorgeous rose."

"Why?"

"I don't know. She just gave it to me, then was gone before I could even thank her."

"Hmmm, well, just enjoy it."

Enjoy it I did, for several days as I watched its deep crimson leaves slowly unfurl, and I prayed for many blessings for that sweet young girl.

It was months later, when I was sharing the joy of it with a friend, that I learned the reason for the rose. She explained that the florists in our area had started a new tradition. Late in the summer they chose a special day on which to give away a dozen free roses to anyone who would care to come in and get them. One catch: The roses had to be given away.

Next year, as soon as the florists choose their day, I'm running down to get a dozen of their give-away-roses to pass along. But I don't have to wait to do something nice for someone. I don't have roses blooming, but I do have glorious purple iris. Today I'll take some to the market, and maybe a lady will go home and say, "The strangest, nicest thing happened to me, honey. Look, a complete stranger gave me this gorgeous iris."

There's nothing quite like flowers to remind me of Your beauty and goodness, dear Lord. I praise You as the rose of Sharon, filling my life with the fragrance of Your presence.
—FAY ANGUS

SEPTEMBER 5

Lift up now thine eyes, and look from the place where thou art....
—GENESIS 13:14

*Y*ou can see Camelback Mountain from all around Phoenix, Arizona (a bit of it even from my backyard), and it really does look like a camel lying on its stomach. But seeing its most interesting feature is a tougher trick. There's a chunk of rock near the camel's forehead that looks like a prayerful figure trudging up the mountain clothed in a dark brown robe.

Because of the surrounding rock formations, you can see the Praying Monk only from certain angles. Driving my son Ross home from school, I catch sight of the monk as I approach from the west, but within a few blocks he disappears as I face the camel head-on. More than once I've heard Ross's frustration as he's tried to show the monk to out-of-town visitors. "Wait," he'll say, "you have to be in just the right spot to see him." And as promised, the monk suddenly pops into view.

Just the right spot to see him. Lately I've been thinking that's a clue to what can go wrong in my spiritual life. When my days are hectic, with prayer and devotional time cut short or even cut out, I start to feel disconnected from God. I'm simply not in the right place to see God clearly. God's always there, as steady as the familiar Praying Monk, but I'm driving down the road too busy with life's distractions to notice.

It's probably not a coincidence that this rock formation is a praying monk. When I spy the monk in prayer, he's a perfect reminder of what I must do when my priorities slip. I need to slow down, pull off the road if necessary, and make time for the things that bring me closer to God, especially peaceful time alone to talk with Him. I need to get myself back in just the right spot to see God unmistakably before me every day.

Lord, help me put all distractions aside, to see and hear and be with only You.
—GINA BRIDGEMAN

SEPTEMBER 6

This also comes from the Lord of hosts; he is wonderful in counsel,
and excellent in wisdom.

—ISAIAH 28:29 (RSV)

*E*very Saturday afternoon for the past two years, I've gone to an hour-long class to study Torah (the five Books of Moses) with a rabbi. Recently, I had to attend a conference on Saturday. I felt bad about missing the class, but the conference was very important to my career.

At one of the conference sessions that Saturday morning, the panelists asked for questions from the audience. One of the questioners introduced himself as a rabbi who had stayed overnight at the hotel to attend the conference (to avoid traveling on the Sabbath). After the panel session I greeted him and we talked about the questions he'd asked and the panelists' answers. We compared notes and discovered that we each had a free hour, so we sat in the hotel lobby and continued our discussion.

As the hour drew to a close, the rabbi said, "You know, I was feeling really guilty about coming here instead of going to my normal Torah study group, but you've made me feel as if I've done my Sabbath study anyway. Thank you."

I was caught open-mouthed, because I'd been just about to say the same thing to him. Instead I said, "I guess God just wanted to make sure we didn't miss our classes, so He put us in the same place at the same time."

He nodded. "It looks that way in hindsight," he said, "but then I suppose human beings are in charge of hindsight, and God is in charge of foresight."

Lord, thank You for the moments when I can catch a glimpse of
Your plan for my life.

—RHODA BLECKER

SEPTEMBER 7

I will not fear what flesh can do unto me.
—PSALM 56:4

"Pam, I just got a call from the hospital," my husband, David, was saying as he walked ashen-faced into the kitchen. "They have Aunt Kate in the emergency room and her doctor says this is it. She can't go back to her apartment. He's talking about a nursing home."

The next morning I began the six-hour drive that would take me to Kate. I had first made this trip as a new bride, twenty-eight years earlier. David had seemed so proud as he introduced me to his aunt Kate, a tall, genteel matron who played cutthroat bridge and enjoyed working under the hood of her 1968 Mustang.

Years passed, and our visits became islands of comfort for me. Perched on one of her ancient needlepoint chairs, I would drink coffee from an old Wedgwood cup and float in Kate's unqualified acceptance of life as it was. She adored my children, my husband, even me! She was my safe place.

Now I found Kate leashed to a hospital bed by an oxygen machine. "Pam," she said as I leaned over her, "don't look so distressed. This can't be helped. So the only thing to do is make the best of it."

In the next days I emptied her apartment, distributing her treasures to friends and loved ones as she directed. Kate and I talked matter-of-factly of heaven. Then, just as matter-of-factly, she picked up her little plastic radio, held it to her ear, and switched on the baseball game. "Don't you think it's time you were getting home?"

I had seen Kate's home—and her hope—as something tangible, something she could lose. Yet, being old, alone, and homeless hadn't even scratched the surface of this woman's spirit. Fear not—Kate showed me what those words mean by living them.

Father, help me to live knee-deep in today, trusting always
that You are my true home.
—PAM KIDD

SEPTEMBER 8

And I will bring the blind by a way that they knew not....
—Isaiah 42:16

*S*ome years ago I used to take my German shepherd for long walks in Philadelphia's Fairmount Park. I'd park my car and take one of the trails that went far up into the hills where I could walk Kate off-leash. After a while I got to know the trails by heart.

One day a friend of mine came along with us, and the two of us were so busy talking that we didn't notice where we were. Finally, Pat looked at her watch and said, "Gosh, I have to get back and make dinner! Which way do we go?" That's when I realized we were lost.

We were surrounded by woods and couldn't see far ahead of us. After trying several times to retrace our steps, we lost all sense of direction. "Wait a minute," I said. "If anyone knows the way back, it's Kate."

I looked at Kate, and in a commanding voice said, "Kate, take us home!"

Kate brushed past us to lead the way. But after a little while both Pat and I knew it wasn't the way we had come. Kate had taken us off the trail and was leading us up and down some pretty steep hills. She was full of confidence and kept looking back at us as if to reassure us. But the farther we went, the more nervous we got.

Then, suddenly, we came out of the woods and into a huge meadow. At the end of the meadow we looked down a slope and saw the parking lot far below us. "We're home!" I shouted and threw my arms around Kate. So did Pat.

"She knew where she was going all the time," Pat said. "It just wasn't the same way we came."

"No," I agreed, "it was a better way."

Since then I've always tried to remember that when I ask God for guidance—and I do it often—I have to trust Him to know which way is best for me. Even if I haven't gone that way before.

Lead me, dear Jesus, because Your way is always better than mine. Amen.
—Phyllis Hobe

SEPTEMBER 9

The Lord's mercies . . . are new every morning. . . .
—LAMENTATIONS 3:22–23

*W*ater Tower Place in Chicago has seven floors of shops, selling everything from electric back-scratchers to four-poster beds. One of my favorite stores is FAO Sweets—a smorgasbord of tasty treats, all displayed in huge, see-through bins. One of the clerks is always stationed by the door, handing small, empty plastic bags to everyone who enters this sweet-tooth paradise.

"Here you go, ma'am," he said to me as I stepped inside the door.

"Does everyone who comes in here fill these bags?" I asked, laughing.

The young man smiled back. "Well, we expect them to!"

The next morning, I stuffed the small bag of candy into my briefcase as I headed out the door for work. *Bless me today, Lord*, I prayed on automatic pilot. Suddenly, I saw the face of that young clerk. Was I expecting God to bless me as confidently as the clerk had expected me to buy candy? Or did I thwart God with negative attitudes and grumbling? With expressions as sour as lemon drops?

I still like to visit that candy store. But I know that the real sweetness in life comes from being open to God's everyday blessings: a warm muffin, a child to hug, an unexpected phone call from a friend, a "well done!" from my boss, a chance to help in our local blood drive. And a gumdrop at the end of the day!

You, Father, are the Giver of every good thing. Let me hunger for the sweetness of Your presence in my life—every day!
—MARY LOU CARNEY

SEPTEMBER 10

Study to be quiet, and to do your own business, and to work....
—I THESSALONIANS 4:11

I work in advertising and my work knocks around in my brain even when I'm not at the office. When I have a TV commercial to write, I try to come up with new ideas any time I get the chance.

Late one night my baby daughter, Noelle, needed someone to hold her to help her calm down. So I picked her up from her crib and held her close. Her crying stopped. Instead of putting her back in her crib, I lay down with her on our bed and kept a hand on her so she could feel me near. It worked perfectly. While I waited until her sleep was deep enough to move her back to the crib, I thought about the commercial I was trying to write.

After about five minutes, Noelle's hand, which had been above her head, moved down the sheets and rested just in front of my face, her index finger falling gently across my lips. It was as if God was saying through my sleeping baby, "Shhh . . . don't miss this moment."

I looked at Noelle, silhouetted by the lights of New York City just outside our window. And I listened to her soft breathing, the only sound in the room. Her little eyelids were closed and her stomach slowly eased up and down in a soothing rhythm. She was such a beautiful gift to her mother and me. Yes, this was indeed a moment. Dad. Daughter. And silence. Without her hand in front of my mouth, I would have surely missed it.

I closed my eyes and thanked God for the reminder. And kissed Noelle's tiny finger.

Lord, help me to put away the work of the day and take time to enjoy Your gifts.
—DAVE FRANCO

SEPTEMBER 11

Surely goodness and mercy shall follow me all the days of my life....
—PSALM 23:6

*I*t's the most enduring image I have of life in New York City in those days right after 9/11. The weather, it must be remembered, was gorgeous. Clear, bright, and sunny, while smoke rose from a pit downtown. The streets near our offices on 34th Street were almost empty, making it possible for fire engines, ambulances, and emergency vehicles to rush to and from a site newly christened Ground Zero.

Posters were being put up on streetlamps with images of the missing. Little shrines of candles and flowers were assembled in parks and squares. But most of us went to our jobs, trying to do our work. At lunchtime I headed out to pick up a sandwich and I noticed a stern-looking policeman on the corner of 33rd and Madison. That's how our police officers usually look, brusque and businesslike.

Just then a woman, clearly distraught, bumped into him. At any other time they would have backed away from each other in horror. Instead, the policeman gently put his arms on her shoulders and looked into her eyes saying, "Are you all right?" After a minute she nodded: "Yes, I'll be all right." And she went on her way.

It was a reminder to me that the brusque New Yorkers I live with have caring souls. Much of the time you don't know it. People are in a hurry, going about their business. But at that terrible moment we looked into each other's eyes and discovered how much goodness was there.

I shall not forget, Lord, all the goodness You have put in Your people.
—RICK HAMLIN

There was a man named Zacchaeus who was a chief tax collector, and he was rich. And he sought to see who Jesus was, but could not because of the crowd, for he was short of stature. So he ran ahead and climbed up into a sycamore tree to see Him....
—LUKE 19:2–4 (NKJV)

Nature often points the way to God. The river valleys of central Missouri are guarded by magnificent sycamore trees whose marble-white trunks are lightly burnished with pewter. As big as baseball gloves, the sycamore's leaves catch the slightest breeze and applaud their Maker. Like giant fingers, the trees' roots clutch the limestone and loam riverbank, looking for nourishment. These white-robed beauties lift their limbs to God as if praying for mercy. They remind me that all of creation longs to be delivered from the troubles of the earth.

Like Zacchaeus, I, too, long to reach higher to see Jesus because I am short. Short on joy. Short on patience and energy, short on hope and enthusiasm, and sometimes short on holiness.

Neither Zacchaeus nor I can change our stature, but I can put myself where I have a better chance of glimpsing God. On Sundays that means going to church for organized prayer and praise. Last night, it meant getting up at 3:00 AM to witness a glorious meteor shower. When I'm fixing a faucet for my mother-in-law or counseling a student or making breakfast for my wife, at such times I feel God's arm around me.

Everywhere there are sycamore trees to help me, when I look for them: people in need, a quiet park where I can pray, a special sunset I can applaud.

Lord lift me up and let me stand,
By faith on heaven's tableland,
A higher plane than I have found;
Lord, plant my feet on higher ground.
("Higher Ground" by Johnson Oatman Jr.)
—DANIEL SCHANTZ

September 13

Greater love hath no man than this....
—John 15:13

*O*ink, oink" was the familiar message on the phone. It was September 13 again, and Joe Caldwell had called me to "celebrate" the Bay of Pigs. Not the CIA's disastrous invasion of Cuba, but the anniversary of the off-Broadway opening of his play Cockeyed Kite. Both happened in 1961. Both events had similar fates.

Why, you might ask, has he taken me to dinner every thirteenth of September since then? Because one evening, he was despondent when one coproducer dropped out and Bill Nichols, the other producer, had said he couldn't manage alone. That's when I, with the confidence of youth as well as a firm belief in Joe as a playwright, blurted out, "I'll be your coproducer."

Bold words. I didn't have more than a couple of cents to my name. Still, I had said I'd coproduce, and I had to start learning how. From then on I tackled everyone I knew, slightly or well, and a host of people I didn't know, for a share, half a share, even small partial shares in the production. I squeezed enough money out, somehow. And there were other matters, like casting and dealing with the director, and the play itself, which centered on a thirteen-year-old boy with a weak heart who managed to accomplish one meaningful thing before dying. It never entered my mind that I, too, was performing one meaningful act—giving the play a chance at life before it met its own destined fate.

So the critics turned their thumbs down. Joe was discouraged, but it turned out that the published play has had performances (not many) all over, and that publishing it led directly to the novels that attest to his brilliant talent. The thing that both embarrasses and pleases me is Joe's unending gratitude. It is, above all else, an example of his sincere love, something that I feel every thirteenth of September.

Father, let me be the kind of man that Joe is.
—Van Varner

September 14

Teach and admonish one another in all wisdom....
—Colossians 3:16 (RSV)

I always felt that I had an assignment to fight the fiery dragons—the deep pains and problems of life—wherever I was, at home and school, in marriage and business. I had to fight other people's dragons as well as my own, because I'd survived so many dragons in my own life.

When I became a Christian, I was told that it was God's job to kill the dragons. I was to submit my whole life to Him and learn how to listen to Him, love His people, and do His will. And that advice worked for a while. But then, apparently out of nowhere, my life filled up with the raging dragons of overcommitment, pride, angry blaming, unkept promises, isolation, and loneliness.

I have a dear Christian friend who used to be as frantic and compulsive as I am. But now she looks peaceful and serene—even though she still lives a very busy life and helps others. Finally I asked her, "As busy as you are, how do you manage to be so serene and peaceful?"

"Well, one day I just got tired of fighting dragons," she said. "I'd had enough of the chaotic overload, and"—she looked very thoughtful and then said simply—"I just quit feeding the lizards."

"What do you mean?"

"Well, one day I quit dwelling on those small lizards of doubt and fear that develop into huge and fearful dragons for me if I don't deal with them when they first show up. I quit nursing the overcommitment, jealousy, and resentment in my life as soon as I saw them beginning. And after a few months of not feeding the lizards, there simply weren't any dragons left to battle!"

Lord, I'm so grateful You told me through my friend that if I confess my problems sooner, You will slay the terrifying dragons in my life and I won't have to run from them anymore. Amen.

—Keith Miller

SEPTEMBER 15

Do not interpretations belong to God?...
—GENESIS 40:8

I was cat-sitting for my friend Mabel Tendler, who has two and a half cats. Well, they're really two indoor cats and an outdoor orange cat who picks up food from several kind neighbors, including Mabel. "Make sure to feed him," she had reminded me. "I don't want the poor thing to go hungry. Here's his special dish." No sooner did I fill the bowl and set it down than I got a hungry customer. I heard the noise of dry food being crunched and I turned to see a big Doberman wolfing down the entire bowl of food.

"Hey!" I shouted. "That's not yours! Leave that alone!" He gave me a big-doggy leer and ran off with the orange plastic bowl clenched firmly between his teeth.

The orange cat never showed up the whole week I was there. And Mabel's special bowl was gone and I was responsible! I agonized all week. Would she cry? Would she yell? My mind conjured up Technicolor versions of how upset she'd be that I hadn't carried out her instructions correctly.

Well, Mabel came home, I confessed—and she laughed! "Oh, that happens all the time. Look in the left corner of the yard and you'll see where Dingo left the bowl."

"But what about the orange cat?" I asked. "The poor thing must have gone hungry."

"I think the orange cat mooches off about six neighbors besides me."

"Oh," was all I said, and then I had to laugh, too—at the doom-and-gloom scenario I'd created in my own mind.

God, is there some "cat dish" in my life I've been blowing up out of all proportion? Let me live calmly today and not in a frightening—and imaginary—future.

—LINDA NEUKRUG

SEPTEMBER 16

Give, and it shall be given unto you; good measure, pressed down,
and shaken together, and running over....
—LUKE 6:38

I woke up this morning feeling that all I wanted to do was to stay in bed and cry. I really had no reason to feel sad: I love my life, my husband and my children, this little village we live in, our spiritual community. In fact, I had no excuse at all for feeling tearful and wanting to stay in bed.

Today is Sunday. Robert and I attend church on weekdays so that we can stay with Belva, our hospice patient, on Sundays and give her husband an opportunity to go to church. It was a great effort for me to drag myself out of bed, get dressed, fix breakfast, and drive the five miles to Belva's house. But when we walked in the door, something unusual happened: Belva smiled and said "Hello"—quite an amazing thing for this end-stage Alzheimer's patient, who is usually mute and sleeps most of the time.

After her husband left, I began feeding Belva. She eagerly opened her mouth to receive each bite of cereal and spoonful of juice. And when she had her breakfast, she looked right at me and smiled again! I felt my heart open and my early-morning sadness left as mysteriously as it had come.

Sometimes I wonder which of us is nourished most by this Sunday morning ritual, Belva or me. But I do know that it's quite impossible to help someone else without having my own soul fed in the process.

When I'm feeling down, Holy One, please lead me to someone I can help,
so I may know the grace of both giving and receiving.
—MARILYN MORGAN KING

SEPTEMBER 17

On this wise ye shall bless the children of Israel, saying unto them,
The Lord bless thee, and keep thee.
—NUMBERS 6:23–24

*A*ll summer long we had been talking and praying about where our son Ryan would go to high school. He had been going to private schools since his first preschool at age three, but now he pleaded with us to let him attend a public high school. He had a number of reasons for wanting to go, some good (a wider range of courses to choose from, better sports and activity programs, a more diverse student body) and some not so good (he'd never had the privilege of riding a school bus). After carefully considering the pluses and minuses, my wife, Rosie, and I decided to listen to Ryan. But I was still uneasy.

On the morning of the first day of school, I went into Ryan's room full of concerns about this new chapter in his life. He and I prayed that he would be successful, both academically and personally, that he would make good friends, and that he would grow in character and in his walk with the Lord. I opened my heart and fears to God, acknowledging that I couldn't go to the school and protect him from all that he would encounter. By the time Ryan left, I was able to relax. Although a new environment, new challenges, and new temptations awaited him, he was in God's hands.

Ryan came home excited about his first day in public school. He talked about the bus ride, the other students, his new teachers, and what a good day it had been. I guess as a father, I'll always be anxious about my children, but each day I'm learning a little more about how to let go and trust God.

Lord, thank You for the blessing of Ryan's first day in high school.
Help me to deepen my prayer for him and my trust in You.
—DOLPHUS WEARY

For we are members of his body, of his flesh, and of his bones.
—EPHESIANS 5:30

Over the years, I've worshipped in many different kinds of churches: formal and informal, conservative and liberal, emotional and reserved, warm and very cold. I was in a chilly church once where the ushers wore gloves—in the summer—but I was never in a church like the one reputed to be so cold that the ushers wore ice skates. Beyond worship style, however, I have another criterion for evaluating a church: How serious are its members about reaching out beyond their church's doors?

The Pennsylvania church that my wife, Shirley, and I attend during the summer has impressed us with its missions, one of which is a shoe bank for families on a tight budget. Many of us take a pair of shoes for granted, but if the head of the house is out of work or ill or earning the minimum wage, finding money for shoes for four or five kids can be overwhelming. That's where our church comes in. With the help of a local store, the church purchases new sneakers at discount and dispenses them free to needy youngsters.

Recently, Shirley and I helped one Saturday just before the start of school. For better than three hours, we, along with several others, scurried around nonstop on our hands and knees, fitting kids with shoes. All told, we passed out more than 125 pairs. Our reward was the beaming smiles of grateful boys and girls. One little towheaded boy with bright sky-blue eyes was so overjoyed with his new sneakers that he gave me a big hug before skipping out of the room.

When the last of the crowd had departed and the workers sat down exhausted, I brushed the dirt off the knees of my tan chinos. "They look as if you've been working in a coal mine," Shirley observed with a grin.

"No, I've been praying," I answered. And in a way, I had.

Teach us, God, to make our lives a prayer,
So that our acts reflect You everywhere.
—FRED BAUER

*There is nothing better for a man than . . . that he should make
his soul enjoy good in his labour. . . .*
—ECCLESIASTES 2:24

*D*own the hill from our house lies a stretch of track that carries trains from Nashville to Memphis. Since our move here three years ago, my husband, David, and I have come to love the sound of the trains that pass at intervals throughout the day and night. Each comes with its own distinct sound, a personality lent by the engineer who sounds the whistle. We've named my favorite "Soul Man." He nurses the whistle like a man coaxing the blues from a horn on Beale Street. David favors "Puff Daddy," an engineer who pulls the whistle in quick, short shouts that sing a happy song as he moves down the track.

But beyond the poetry and the pure enjoyment of living near the rails, David and I have gleaned another lesson from our engineers: There's nothing better than to find something to enjoy in whatever work you happen to be doing. Cooking a meal, washing clothes, cleaning a house matter to those we serve in this way. Waiting tables in a restaurant, cleaning rooms in a hotel, pressing clothes in a laundry matter just as much. Take any job, and chances are that the bottom line will be one person serving the needs of another. As a child and adolescent therapist, our daughter Keri is helping others to have better lives. Despite some of the preconceived notions of what a financial adviser does, it's clear that our son Brock is working to help people achieve financial security and have better lives, too.

Dig down through the layers of your job until you get to the ultimate truth that what you do matters. Then find the glory in your job. Blow your whistle, toot your horn, enjoy the good in your labor. There's nothing better than this!

*Father, let me see my work as worthwhile and let me enjoy
the good that my work generates.*
—PAM KIDD

SEPTEMBER 20

A man that hath friends must show himself friendly: and there is
a friend that sticketh closer than a brother.

—PROVERBS 18:24

*I*t was a lazy Saturday morning, and I had stopped at a doughnut shop for coffee and a sweet roll. Relishing a day without schedule or agenda, I leaned back in my chair and breathed the sweet aroma of fresh pastries and brewing coffee. It was good to be alive.

That was when I heard an elderly woman's voice laugh and cackle, "Well, Maude, I can even remember when I could chew gum." Suppressing a chuckle, I turned to see four elderly ladies sitting at a corner table, giggling and carrying on like schoolgirls.

The waitress came to take my order, saw me quietly laughing, and said, "They come here every morning, sure as the sun rises. Drink a gallon of coffee together and have a good time. They're a sight!"

As I sipped my coffee and listened to their chatter, I reflected that friendship and laughter are gifts to be cherished, the best fruits of a lifetime. The surest investment for future happiness is not in money but in relationships.

Dear God, thank You for special folks who refresh my soul and make me glad.
May I cherish and nurture my friendships this day. Amen.

—SCOTT WALKER

"I will set in the desert the cypress tree and the pine and the box tree together, that they may see and know . . . that the hand of the Lord has done this. . . ."
—ISAIAH 41:19–20 (NKJV)

My Irish bride of forty years has soft, busy eyes, framed with delicate freckles. Yet without the blessing of eyeglasses she could not tell me from a tree. Severe astigmatism is complicated with so many retinal "floaters" that her eyes are like little goldfish bowls full of fish. "I wish I could see better," she says a hundred times a week, but I know few people who see as well as she does. She is like a detective in one of her beloved mystery novels and seldom misses a clue. There's more to vision than good eyes, and she knows the secret.

We can be out for a Sunday drive, passing by a drab soybean farm, and Sharon will keep up a constant prattle of appreciation. "Oh, look at all the billy goats! Isn't that interesting?" It's her favorite expression.

Our teenaged daughters used to mock her fascination with simple things. Natalie: "Oh, look at the pretty yellow centerlines on the road!" Teresa: "My, my, isn't that a pine tree? What a find!"

"All right, you guys," I'd fire back. "You should be more like your mother instead of so cynical and hard to please."

I have good eyes, but my mind drifts into never-never-land and I miss a lot. Oh sure, I see the eighteen-wheeler that crashed and burned in the ditch and the crop duster that landed on the highway in front of me, but I missed the old man out picking wildflowers with his granddaughter.

From Sharon I have learned that vision is less about having good eyes and more about being interested in the beautiful world around me.

Isn't she interesting?

Lord, I wish I could see better.
—DANIEL SCHANTZ

And the fruit of righteousness is sown in peace of them that make peace.
—JAMES 3:18

ere's the story of a September morning not too long ago. Daylight was misty until the sun burned off the fog and awoke Americans everywhere, including sleepy New Yorkers. But the sky was soon rent by explosions and smoke and seemingly endless agony. By the end of the day, 3,500 people lay dead, and not just New Yorkers. Thousands more were wounded, many of them mortally, and thousands more were missing.

Five days later the president saw an opportunity in this tragedy, a chance to bring the nation together. He spoke boldly of freedom and the cost of freedom, of the value inherent in the country's founding, and how Americans would not be in bondage to their fear. In fact, he said, no American would be in bondage, period.

And so it was on September 22, 1862, that Abraham Lincoln signed the Emancipation Proclamation, freeing Southern slaves from the most horrid of human institutions.

The Union "victory"—if, indeed, it was a victory—that had emboldened Lincoln was the battle at Antietam Creek in Maryland. The 51st New York fought that day—September 17, 1862—as did Georgians and Texans, blue Americans vs. gray Americans from everywhere. It was the single bloodiest day in our history, one of the largest losses of life in a one-day conflict on American soil ever—until another, more recent September day.

I tell this story for one reason. Somehow we all survived. Somehow we outlasted a war of brother against brother, and we will outlast the next horror. We will survive our own insanity until the bright day we are all called home. And I believe, childlike, that heaven really is in the sky, and that we'll look down on earth and see what astronauts see: that our little space island isn't blue vs. gray, but blue and gray, with room for the entire family.

Lord, may Your kingdom come, Your will be done, on earth as it is in heaven.
—MARK COLLINS

How excellent is thy lovingkindness, O God! therefore the children of men put their trust under the shadow of thy wings.
—PSALM 36:7

*I*t was a Wednesday in September. Our daughter Tamara was stranded in Anchorage, Alaska, with a newborn and toddlers Zachary and Hannah, while her husband trained at the police academy. I had come to rescue her.

One day, sunny and mellow and smelling of changing birch leaves, I took Zachary and Hannah to play in the park. Soon an older woman meandered by with a young child in tow. She nodded and smiled but didn't seem inclined to chat. Her little charge toddled off across the grass with Hannah.

Zachary and I teeter-tottered while the girls sailed down a small slide beneath the watchful eye of the unknown woman. When I twirled my grandchildren on the tire swing, the other child wanted to swing, too, and the woman came over to help. Haltingly she told me she was from Russia, visiting her daughter and granddaughter Nicole.

When Zachary tired of the swing, I went off with him to play in the sand, leaving the Russian grandmother still twirling the girls. Somehow Hannah slipped off the tire and fell backward onto the ground. The Russian grandmother was bending down anxiously over her when I scooped Hannah into my arms.

"It's all right," I said. "She's not hurt."

That's when the thought hit me. Here we are, two grandmothers, playing in the park with our grandchildren, teaching them to get along and watching out for them with equal concern.

The two of us left the park. We had met only briefly, but it was long enough for me to gain new understanding of a grandmother's mission: to help shape our world's future by sowing seeds of consideration and respect—starting in the park.

Heavenly Father, with my grandchildren in tow, lead me in Your path of lovingkindness.
—CAROL KNAPP

And he said to them, "Follow me...."
—MATTHEW 4:19 (RSV)

More than thirty years ago I faced a decision. Should I quit my salaried job at a magazine to help my husband launch a new business? On one side, a regular income in the family, work I enjoyed. On the other, challenge, risk, the excitement of pioneering together. "When I have a choice to make," our minister advised me, "I simply go to the Bible."

Simple for him, maybe—he knew the Bible inside out. But where would I even begin looking? I remembered a friend telling about getting a Bible verse over the phone when he had to make a choice. "The caller couldn't possibly have known my situation, yet the verse he gave me was my answer!" No such phone call came for me.

"I pray for guidance," another friend said, "then just let the Bible fall open." I tried this. I closed my eyes, put my finger on a page and read, "Ozias begat Joatham; and Joatham begat Achaz; and Achaz..." (Matthew 1:9).

When I laughed about this with a neighbor, Co Holby, she nodded. "That time my husband was so ill, I did just what you did, opened the Bible at random looking for guidance." Instead, Co found herself staring at the blank page between the Old Testament and the New. "The only words there were 'The Gospel.'" We started to laugh again—and then realized what she'd said. The gospel! That's where Co and I and every Christian would find direction.

Asking God for a specific verse for a particular situation, after all, is asking for a miniature miracle—wonderful when it happens, but not something I can summon on demand. My husband and I began a daily reading of the Gospels in terms of my decision, finding our fears, our egos, our hidden motives exposed to the light of Jesus' life and teaching. In the end I quit my job, but what came out of that time was something more important: a pattern for bringing every decision before Him Who followed His Father's will without fail.

Show me Your Son today, Father, as I read Your Word.
—ELIZABETH SHERRILL

The gift of God is eternal life through Jesus Christ our Lord.
—ROMANS 6:23

*W*hen I opened the box that had just come in the mail, a shock of surprise zinged through my body. In my hands lay a baby pillow made from a quilt block that had my name embroidered on it in my late mother's handwriting. The accompanying letter explained that the sender and my mother had belonged to the same women's club back in the 1930s. The members had made quilt blocks for their children, intending to piece them in a communal quilt.

"The quilt never got finished," the sender added, "but I've kept your mother's block all these years. Now I hear that you have a new granddaughter, so I've used the block to make this pillow for her."

My heart warmed with gratitude for such a kind, thoughtful gift. As I caressed my mother's embroidery, the years melted away and I sensed once more my mother's love, spanning two-thirds of a century. In memory I saw her sitting near a window in a home where we'd once lived, her brown hair and unlined face bathed in morning sunlight. Now she had moved on to live in God's home.

Precious gifts that tie the years together: a parent's love, a new grandchild, a pillow from a generous friend. And eternal life from God, our greatest Friend of all.

Thank You, Father, for letting us share in Your timeless love. Amen.
—MADGE HARRAH

They that wait upon the Lord shall renew their strength....
—ISAIAH 40:31

have been dreading this week. On Thursday the movers will come and we will be moving to a new house a few miles away. Our present home, the church parsonage, became full of contaminants after a hurricane. We'll really miss this gracious, historic, Charleston house that we've lived in for six years and where our daughter Jodi was born. Having to move is an unsettling process. Yesterday, as I tried to clean out our cluttered basement, I was overcome with frustration. Throwing on my jacket, I stormed outside and went for a long walk. It was a beautiful, crisp day. As my mind cleared and my spirits lifted, I began to notice the lovely homes and yards about me.

One yard stood out because the grass was wilted, brown, almost dead. As I drew closer, however, I saw that the lawn was actually new. Just recently, large strips of grass and dirt had been unrolled over the bare soil, then pressed down and watered so that the grass would take root. Though it looked dead and withered now, new roots were actually sprouting. Within weeks, this yard would be lush and green, too. *Just like my life,* I thought. *I'm being cut out and uprooted, so I can be planted somewhere else. I'll put down roots and grow again.*

As I walked back to the house, I said a silent prayer. I still did not look forward to the move. But I asked God, Who would be with me in the process, to help me trust Him so that I would grow strong and secure again.

Dear Father, in a world of uprootedness, may my faith in You grow deep.
—SCOTT WALKER

Now he that ministereth seed to the sower both minister bread for your food, and
multiply your seed sown, and increase the fruits of your righteousness.
—II CORINTHIANS 9:10

y father, who grew up on a farm in the Missouri Ozarks, once told me about a terrible hailstorm that shredded his young corn crop right down to the ground. "But you know what?" he finished, shaking his head in awe. "That corn came back. You see, corn grows from the inside up. Because the tiny core of each plant was still good, that corn lived, despite the pounding it had taken."

I had reason to remember Dad's story later when Larry and I faced some rough times with our children during their teenage years. There were moments when I felt pounded right down to the ground by our problems, and I'm sure Larry and the kids did, too; but I'd pray, "Lord, we've tried to bring these children up right. Please protect the core!"

With God's help, we did come through those years. Now our children have blossomed into beautiful, strong adults, while Larry and I, too, are stronger for weathering the storm. But we couldn't have done it, I'm convinced, without God's nurturing care that helped preserve the vital core in each of us where love, goodness, and hope are stored.

Father, let Your love touch the core of my being and restore me to new life. Amen.
—MADGE HARRAH

Let love be without dissimulation....
—ROMANS 12:9

*W*hen my mother was dying of emphysema two years ago, she became a hospice patient, and this sensitive, gentle group of people helped us learn how to care for her at home so she could spend her last few days in her own bed. They taught us how to make her comfortable and, more importantly, how to cope with the emotional task of facing her impending death.

One nugget of their advice vividly sticks in my mind even today because it not only guided my time with her, it continues to help me focus on the priority of being open and honest in all relationships. "Take care of all unfinished business with the people you love," a hospice nurse urged me over coffee in my mother's kitchen one morning near the end. "Say what you want to say. Do what you want to do. Today. Don't wait until tomorrow."

And so we did. Impulsively, one warm afternoon we arranged a hay ride for the whole family. We made my mother a bed of pillows, hooked up her oxygen tank, put her on, and took off through the fields, singing songs and laughing. On quieter days, I sat by her bed, taking time to thank her for lots of things I'd taken for granted before: for helping me learn to laugh at myself, for teaching me to get right back on my horse when I fell off, for showing me how to accept things in life that I couldn't change.

When she died, I was comforted in my grief. There was no unfinished business. Everything was complete.

Lord, today I want to take care of all unfinished business with
the people I love. Show me the way.
—CAROL KUYKENDALL

September 29

He asked life of thee, and thou gavest it him, even length of days....
—Psalm 21:4

*T*he dinner party brought together various branches of the family. The seats of honor at the ends of the long table went to the two eldest, my grandfather, Papa, then in his mid-eighties, and Grammy, my brother-in-law's grandmother, aged ninety-four.

Isolated by deafness, Papa had become almost morbidly interested in the details of illness, both his own and other people's. The table was buzzing with lively conversations when he shouted to Grammy, above the chattering voices, "How's your heart?"

Grammy beamed down the long table at him, a beatific smile that encompassed the entire gathering and seemed to take in all of struggling humanity as well. She answered his question with a single word, "Enlarged."

Papa did not hear, and "enlarged" was relayed to him along the seats. Sitting beside him, I shrieked into his ear, "Her heart's enlarged."

Medically, of course, a serious condition. But as I said the words, I thought they also summed up God's will for all of us as our years increase. Grammy's answer has become for me a kind of shorthand prayer. Like Grammy, let me carry my aches and ailments lightly as I grow older! Each year let me care a little less about myself, a little more for others.

Father, enlarge my heart.
—Elizabeth Sherrill

SEPTEMBER 30

Even though I walk through the valley of the shadow of death,
I will fear no evil, for you are with me....
—PSALM 23:4 (NIV)

*W*hitney has a brain tumor. She is a beautiful girl, not yet married and thirty years old. She is the daughter of friends about our ages, so I still think of her as a girl instead of as a woman. Tonight, we who are family friends are responding to a request from her parents: *Come, please, to a prayer gathering in our driveway at dusk and surround our home with your prayers.*

And so we have gathered outside Whitney's window with her parents, grandmother, friends, and neighbors. We are the people who watched her grow up, who prayed for her five years ago at the onset of this disease. We rejoiced with her a year later when the tumor seemed gone. We cried at the news of the tumor's reappearance two months ago.

Now Whitney lies in a coma upstairs in her bedroom and we've gathered outside her window, hoping she can hear our songs and feel our prayers as we light candles and lift her up on the wings of our faith. We don't understand these painful circumstances, but as we entwine our arms and form a tight circle around this house, we remember that we don't have to understand. We have to trust that God knows and cares and goes before Whitney and each member of this family, and that He will provide and be sufficient and hold up His light so that Whitney and each of us can take just one small step at a time. Always. No matter how difficult the path may be.

Father, thank You for the privilege of standing in a circle of Your love. Hold Whitney in Your everlasting arms, and give Your continued comfort to her family.
—CAROL KUYKENDALL

October

OCTOBER 1

"Lord, show us the Father and that will be enough for us."
—JOHN 14:8 (NIV)

*I*t was with misgivings that I'd signed up for the art class at our local Continuing Education center. Described in the brochure as "The Natural Way to Draw," the session was offered "for those with no previous art training."

That certainly described me. I hadn't tried to draw since grade school when I had struggled in vain to reproduce the pictures the teacher pinned to my easel. Comparing my smudgy efforts with the cat or the house I was copying, I would rip my drawing paper into a dozen despairing pieces.

Stepping into the Continuing Ed classroom now, I felt the old certainty of failure sweep over me. "There are only two rules tonight," the young instructor announced. "Never look down at your paper. And never lift your pencil from the page. Don't worry about the results."

It was a wonderfully freeing exercise, I discovered, drawing lines and loops with no concern for how the finished picture turned out. Only at the end of the session were we permitted to retrieve our efforts and look at them. I'd produced some wildly abstract designs, and a few that actually looked like a pineapple, an orange, and a banana.

It didn't matter. I was strangely exhilarated, not only because for the first time in my life I'd enjoyed an art class, but because I'd sensed God reaching out once more through words that meant more than the speaker knew. My service to Him falls so short of what I mean it to be! I get so discouraged when I compare my great intentions with the feeble results! "Don't look at results," I heard Him say. "Keep your eyes on Me and leave the finished picture in My hands."

Lord, show me Yourself today.
—ELIZABETH SHERRILL

OCTOBER 2

"Learn to do right! Seek justice, encourage the oppressed...."
—ISAIAH 1:17 (NIV)

*S*everal years ago my wife, Rosie, and I watched a TV special about all the starving children in the world. Needless to say, we both felt overwhelmed. As is so often the case when we're confronted with overwhelming need, we asked ourselves, "How can our small loaf make a difference to a hurting world?" And when we couldn't see the answer to that question, we were tempted to sit back and do nothing.

We heard part of the answer at a spiritual renewal conference we attended recently. The speaker said, "The Lord says, 'You do the feeding; I will do the supplying.'" A light came on in my mind and relief came over my spirit. I don't have to feed everyone in the world. I don't have to help everyone in the world, and I don't have to try to meet the needs of everyone in the world. I just need to be honest about my gifts and the resources that God has given me, use them faithfully when I can and where I can, and allow the great God of the universe to do the rest.

By the way, at the end of that TV show, the narrator said, "You can sponsor a child for just pennies a day." I can't feed all the hungry children in the world. Surely feeding a hundred is beyond my means, and maybe even feeding ten. But surely, from what God has given me, I can feed just one.

Lord, help me today to understand that You have asked me not to count the loaves and the fish, but to share whatever I have to reach out and touch the lives of others.

—DOLPHUS WEARY

OCTOBER 3

That you may love the Lord your God, listen to his voice, and hold fast to him....
—DEUTERONOMY 30:20 (NIV)

The phone rang last night as I loaded the dishwasher after dinner. I was glad to hear the voice of an old friend I hadn't spoken with in several months.

"How are you?" I asked as I climbed up on a stool at the kitchen counter and settled down for our talk. We had lots to catch up on, and she chatted on and on about her family, her job, and a few concerns about some personal challenges. When I hung up the phone nearly half an hour later, I felt a bit forlorn, and then realized our conversation had been pretty one-sided. She'd done most of the talking and I'd done most of the listening. She hadn't even asked me, "How are you?" By the time I turned out the lights in the kitchen, I felt a little irritated with my friend for her insensitivity.

Early the next morning, I sat at the same kitchen counter, talking to God in prayer. I chatted on and on, telling Him all about my concerns for my family and job and some personal challenges, and was about to say "Amen" when I sensed a nudge from the Lord—because our conversation had been totally one-sided. I had talked on and on about myself, but I hadn't praised God or listened to Him.

So I started back into prayer again. "How are You, God?" I asked, and then began to listen to the answers. "I am loving. I am kind. I am always with you. I have a plan for you. I am a promise-keeper. I am your provider. I am your source of strength and comfort. I am your Father. I am Lord."

When I was done listening, I added a P.S. to my prayer:

Father, forgive me for being quick to blame others for carrying on one-sided conversations, and thank You for the reminder that great blessings come from good listening.
—CAROL KUYKENDALL

OCTOBER 4

Lay not up for yourselves treasures upon earth ... but lay up
for yourselves treasures in heaven. ...
—MATTHEW 6:19–20

*W*hen I was a child during World War II, many commodities—butter, sugar, coffee, gasoline—were rationed for the "duration." That word puzzled me when I saw signs reading "closed for the duration" posted on the doors of businesses whose proprietors had gone off to war. Then someone explained that it meant until—until the war was over and those in the armed forces came home.

Meanwhile, people on the home front learned to live by that old motto "Use it up, wear it out, make it do, or do without." One thing shortages did was make people more appreciative of previously taken-for-granted things. I remember seeing a long line outside a clothing store one day and getting in it because I knew people were queuing up for something scarce. "What are they selling?" I asked a grandmotherly type in front of me.

"Nylons," she answered. "Do you need a pair?" Everyone laughed, and for a moment I was embarrassed. Thinking quickly, however, I answered that I was there to get some for my mother. Which is what I did. I don't know if I got the right size or color, but I do recall that Mother was overjoyed with my purchase.

Shortages make things more valuable—in the short run, at least. Abundance produces the opposite effect. And people sometimes act like lemmings, slaves to supply and demand. The Bible advises us not to be anxious about material needs; they will be met. And Paul, who counseled Christians to be content whatever state they were in, assured the Philippians from a prison cell that "my God shall supply all your need according to his riches in glory" (Philippians 4:19). That's a promise the apostle knew from personal experience, and one that you and I can bank on—today, tomorrow, and for the duration.

When our needs leave us despairing
Remind us, God, Who's ever caring.
—FRED BAUER

OCTOBER 5

When thou walkest through the fire, thou shalt not be burned;
neither shall the flame kindle upon thee.

—ISAIAH 43:2

I was driving to one of my favorite hiking trails in Ohiopyle State Park. Near the top of the hill, I noticed an amazing amount of smoke. I stopped beside a parked fire truck and offered to help.

A park ranger looked at me. "Okay," he said, "but please stay in the back somewhere."

The next three hours were beyond description. A yellow line of fire was coming right for us.

One of the volunteers sighed. "Start the break here," he said, drawing an imaginary line in the air that paralleled the fire's advance. He then picked up his heavy metal rake and began pulling at the leaves and small twigs. He bared the ground in an eight-foot swath, then moved a foot and began again.

I thought, *Surely we're not going to fight this fire by raking?*

We were. The high, dry brush and the steepness of the hill made raking awkward and slow. When the wind kicked up, overhead branches caught fire, carrying the flames right past our newly dug break. At one point we had to bail out altogether because no one could work through the smoke.

The fire finally slowed. We beat out the hot spots with shovels or stamped them out with our feet. After hours of backbreaking work, the fire retreated.

All over our country, volunteer fire companies are fighting for their very survival. You see them riding on their shiny red trucks, and it looks like fun—right up to the point where you clear the first few feet of earth with your rake and understand the awesome, dangerous task before you. And you hope that you're not there alone, that these strangers at your side will be there for you, as heroic and generous as the moment demands.

Lord, bless and protect all those who risk their lives to fight fires.

—MARK COLLINS

OCTOBER 6

Fear hath torment....
—I JOHN 4:18

*W*hen Shakespeare wrote that cowards die many times before their death, he was talking about me. Thanks to a busy imagination, I am a person who tends to dread the future. When I see dark clouds ahead, I'm sure they are tornadoes.

For example, I lived for years in dread of an income tax audit. There was the curriculum meeting I dreaded for a year. *I can't handle any more courses in my load*, I thought, and *I don't want to get stuck with a course I just hate*. It turned out that the committee took away two courses I hated, and gave me one new one that I always wanted to teach.

No, it doesn't always turn out this well, but it's seldom as bad as I imagine it's going to be.

In order to cope with these forebodings, I've written myself some mental memos to rehearse whenever I feel my stomach tighten.

1. Don't listen to rumors. Get the facts before you start worrying.
2. Take a "wait and see" attitude. Your fears have lied to you before.
3. Be ready to submit to whatever God wants you to do.

These guidelines don't take away my fears, but they make them manageable. I still have to talk it out with my wife and seek God's assurance in prayer. Often I find comfort in an old hymn by William Cowper.

Ye fearful saints, fresh courage take;
The clouds ye so much dread
Are big with mercy, and shall break
In blessings on your head.

Lord, I'm a coward. But if You help me, I'll not run from the future.
—DANIEL SCHANTZ

And God said, "Let the earth bring forth every kind of animal...."
And God was pleased with what he had done.
—Genesis 1:24–25 (TLB)

On the first Sunday in October the Episcopal Church of the Ascension in our town has a service called the "Blessing of the Animals." People, children especially, are invited to bring their pets to church, and in memory of St. Francis of Assisi, who dearly loved animals, there is a special time of blessing.

This year we didn't make it, my little dog and I. For close to fourteen years, she's been my constant companion, confidant, and most devoted friend, the one I trust implicitly. She's always ready to listen when I ramble on and on about this or that, or shed silent tears, sharing corners of my heart with her I wouldn't dare to share with any other. She's the only one I know who agrees with everything I say and urges me on to tell her more.

When I leave the house, her large dark eyes watch me from the window, and when I return she greets me with ecstatic joy. She asks so little and gives so much, and now she's getting old. She's getting deaf, going blind, sleeps a lot, and just can't make it up the stairs. I dread the day, the coming day all too soon, when she will no longer be here beside me.

So on this day of blessing the animals, I hold my own service. Quietly, I kneel in the garden beside my faithful friend, and, with gratitude, I thank the Lord for the loyalty, devotion, and special gift of comfort of this small dog and ask Him to give her His blessing.

Thank You, dear Lord, for the animals who are our comfort, who serve us so well and ask for so little in return. I ask You to bless them. May we pet them often, feed them well, and show them that we love them, too.
—Fay Angus

*In all their affliction he was afflicted, and the angel of his presence
saved them; in his love and in his pity he redeemed them;
he lifted them up and carried them....*

—ISAIAH 63:9 (RSV)

*L*ast Thursday our friend Ruxandra, or "Ruxy" as she is fondly called,
brought her forty-nine-year-old husband, Donald, home from the
hospital to die. Donald had fought cancer valiantly for more than a year; now he
knew his departure from this world would be a matter of a few days or weeks.

This Monday I found myself constantly thinking of them. I yearned to help,
but I didn't want to intrude on their last days together. Although I had talked
and worked with Ruxy at church, I hardly knew Donald. I had spoken with him
only a few times. Besides, what could I possibly do?

Then I remembered something I'd once heard: "When the only thing you
can do is pray, then that's the most important thing to do—and it will make a
difference!" So I began praying for my friends and found myself asking God to
send His angels to help them. I pictured invisible heavenly beings whispering
comfort to them, easing Donald's pain and strengthening Ruxy to care for him.

On Wednesday my nurse friend Barb said that Ruxy had called her with
several questions. "I've got tomorrow off," said Barb, "so I'm going to visit
them." Ah, I thought, one of God's angels!

That evening our friend Mary phoned and said that she had called Ruxy.
"She's been getting very little sleep, so I'm going over now to take the night shift."

"Oh, Mary," I said, "you're another angel God is sending them!"

"Oh, no," she protested, "you know I am no angel. But please pray for us—
that I'll be able to care for him alone and Ruxy will be able to sleep."

"I will," I promised, grateful for a way to help.

That night as I prayed, I pictured Mary ministering to Donald and Ruxy
sleeping peacefully, watched over by God's angels.

*Lord, use my prayers today to reach out Your loving arms
to those whom my own arms cannot reach.*

—MARY BROWN

OCTOBER 9

Thou shalt teach them diligently unto thy children....
—DEUTERONOMY 6:7

*I*n many ways the long-term substitute teaching job was a dream-come-true. Although the regular classroom teacher urged me to use my own techniques, we planned lessons together. I sought her approval on all new materials and assessments, since I was a guest in her classroom.

As the weeks wore on, I felt less and less like a professional educator and more and more like a clone. One Saturday morning I fumed to Dixie, a church friend of lively faith. "Why did I go into teaching, anyway?"

My wise friend listened sympathetically. "Sometimes we don't quite know why we do the things we do. We feel we've been led, then feel we aren't getting what we ought to. But you just keep at it! Remember, during those unsatisfying times, you don't know what you're giving, either."

A few weeks later at a coffee shop, I bumped into the mother of one of the pupils in my class.

"Gail! Thank you for helping Missy raise her math grade!"

"But I can't take credit," I said. "I've been with her only a few weeks."

"Yes, but she had a C before you came."

"Oh, she was probably just rusty from summer break."

"No, she had Cs all last year, too."

Still bewildered, I mumbled, "Well, I'm glad she's doing well."

As I sipped my cappuccino, I thought about what Dixie had said. Perhaps I had been so obsessed with feeling successful as a sub that I had failed to recognize small successes in my students. Once again, the kids were teaching me. Even a temporary teacher can achieve some permanent results.

Lord, give me the faith and courage to do my best,
even when I feel I make no difference.
—GAIL THORELL SCHILLING

October 10

I will sing to the Lord, because he has dealt bountifully with me.
—Psalm 13:6 (RSV)

As my husband, Larry, and our two teenage children, Eric and Meghan, climbed out of our travel trailer in the Zion National Park campground, I stopped and inhaled deeply. Apples! Piles of windfall apples under dozens of trees, filling the air with a sweet cidery odor.

"We'll cook fresh applesauce for supper!" I announced enthusiastically.

Eric looked at me askance. "Can we do that? Will the park ranger allow it?"

"Sure!" said Larry, but he decided to check, nonetheless.

"Take all you want," the park ranger said. "Every year these apples go to waste. It's as if people think apples that don't come from stores aren't any good." He explained that the trees had been planted by early pioneers, long before the area became a park.

That night we ate cinnamon applesauce beside our campfire while gazing up at a golden gibbous moon. "This is cool," said Meghan. "God has made some really neat stuff, hasn't He?"

"He has," said Larry. "Maybe we should say thanks." We paused while Larry said simply, "Lord, thank You for this bounty."

To which we responded, "Amen!"

Lord, today I will look with grateful eyes at the abundant gifts
You have bestowed upon this world.
—Madge Harrah

OCTOBER 11

Be not thou afraid when one is made rich....
—PSALM 49:16

*W*e've worked hard, but financially, it's been a tough year. So the phone call was the proverbial straw that broke the camel's back.

"Pam, did you hear about Paige? She just inherited over a million dollars from an aunt she never knew existed!"

Okay, God, I thought after I hung up, *this is a bit hard to understand. Paige has never had to work, never taken her children to church, never helped with community projects. In fact, her biggest concern seems to be her golf game. Why her, God?*

Late one sleepless night, I went out to sit on the porch. It was dark, and a breeze rustled in the trees. I thought about my life. It's a very good life. I thought of our son Brock's progress in his job, the people he's been able to help, the way he's careful to tithe his money to church. I thought of Keri, focused on becoming a psychotherapist for the right reasons. She's always doing something to make life better for someone else. I thought of my husband, David, who never says no when I come up with some idea for a project that will ultimately cost him time or money. I thought of my mother, happy and secure with her husband, Herb. The truth is, I am very, very rich in all the things that money can't buy. I wouldn't sell a single one of my blessings for a million dollars. "So why am I so angry?" I whispered to the night. And I knew exactly what I needed to do.

"God, tonight I am so ashamed. I know that You always find a way to fill my family's needs. Yet something good happens to my friend and I get angry and afraid. For a long time, I've been telling You that I want to be a person who feels joy in the good fortune of others. First, I'm going to hand my future over to You, Father. Then I'm going to show You the kind of person I want to become."

That night I slept like a baby. The next day I called Paige to tell her how happy I was for her. The words came from a light and joyful heart—and from one very rich friend to another!

Father, You have given me so much. Give me a grateful heart to share in the joys and sorrows of my neighbors.
—PAM KIDD

October 12

*M*any years ago a man from Italy boarded a ship and sailed for a New World. What fueled his great ambition to leave behind everything he'd known and cross the sea was his dream to do something new, something better. His name wasn't Christopher Columbus but Giovanni Garagiola, my grandfather. I always think of him on this day, Columbus Day, because he was also a dreamer who heard a call. He set off with the spirit of an explorer to embrace a new adventure.

Papa left his hometown of Inveruno in 1913 at the urging of friends who'd immigrated to St. Louis and found work in a local brickyard. He traveled alone with the hope that he'd work hard and save the money to send for my grandmother. But too soon World War I intervened, prohibiting transatlantic travel. Not until October 1919 did my grandmother arrive in St. Louis. Soon they started a family, bought a little house, and Papa proudly became a United States citizen.

Like Abraham, my grandfather willingly left his ancestral home, trusting that God would watch over him in his promised land. He believed that simply by coming to America he would make life better for his family. That was worth all the loneliness, sacrifice, and hardship he endured. Now, my grandfather's strength and faith inspire me to take risks to improve my world, with confidence that God will be beside me wherever the journey takes me.

Thank You, Father, for the explorers each of us has known, whose brave decisions to venture into a new world have changed our lives for the better.

—Gina Bridgeman

OCTOBER 13

So then, while we have opportunity, let us do good to all people....
—GALATIANS 6:10 (NAS)

*A*s I sat at my desk reading my mail, I absently flipped through the pages of yet one more magazine. Turning to throw it away, I noticed an article about the plight of Russian orphans. It was illustrated with a picture of a pretty seven-year-old girl with blonde hair and blue eyes. The caption said that her name was Julia and that she had been deserted by her mother on the streets of Moscow in the midst of a winter storm. For a few brief seconds, I gazed into Julia's eyes and then I dropped the magazine into the trash can.

As I got up to put on my coat and go home, I thought about Alan and Susan Nelson, a young couple in our church. The Nelsons had often talked with me about their desire to adopt a homeless child. *Russia is a long way off,* I thought as I shut and locked my office door. But as I walked to my car, Julia's eyes kept staring at me. Finally, I turned and went back to the office, retrieved the magazine from the trash can, circled Julia's picture, and mailed the article to the Nelsons.

That happened more than a year ago. Tonight my wife, Beth, and I drove with the Nelsons to the Dallas/Fort Worth airport to meet the plane bringing their newly adopted daughter Julia from Russia. Watching that little girl walk off the plane and into her new parents' arms was one of the most moving experiences of my life. And it would never have happened if I hadn't listened to that inner voice nudging me.

I guess I'm slowly learning not to throw away the opportunities that God sends my way, not to doubt God's ability to make good things happen in the most far-fetched of situations. Julia will always remind me of what God can do if we give Him an opportunity.

Father, let me see the opportunities You put before me this day and allow You to work through me. Amen.
—SCOTT WALKER

OCTOBER 14

"Exalted be God, the Rock, my Savior!"
—II SAMUEL 22:47 (NIV)

*J*t was my favorite Sunday of the month: the Sunday the children's church worshiped with us. I always love their exuberance, their smiling faces, their incessant wiggles. But today I was almost too tired to enjoy them. It had been a week of deadlines and late nights, of worrying about a sick friend and hassling with a troublesome neighbor. I was exhausted!

But as the congregation sang the praise chorus "The Lord Liveth," I noticed one child in particular belting out the words. Each time we came to the chorus, he loudly sang, "Let the God of my salvation be exhausted." *Exalted*, I thought. *It's supposed to be exalted. Imagine God being exhausted!* And in that instant I knew: God didn't want me exhausted, either. He wanted to exalt me, to lift me up in His love and strength. To help me mend fences, meet deadlines, cast my cares on Him.

I sang as loudly as my little friend the next time the chorus came around: "Let the God of my salvation be EXALTED!"

You are exalted above all creation, Lord! I come to You with my weariness and worrisome ways. Draw me into Your presence. Exalt me!
—MARY LOU CARNEY

OCTOBER 15

I plead with you to be of one mind, united in thought and purpose.
—I CORINTHIANS 1:10 (TLB)

*I*n 1999 I got to attend my friend Winnie's wedding in Kuala Lumpur, Malaysia. I took a bus from Milwaukee, Wisconsin, to Chicago, flew from Chicago to Narita, Japan, caught a plane to Singapore, was met in Singapore at midnight by Sreela, a friend of Winnie's whom I had never met, and taken to Sreela's uncle's home to spend the night. At nine o'clock the next morning Sreela and I took the bus from Singapore to Kuala Lumpur, where at long last I met up with Winnie.

The whole week was filled with meeting people from India, China, Japan, and London who'd come in for the big wedding. Winnie's mother (who is Chinese and doesn't speak English) and I communicated with hand motions, pidgin English, and lots of smiles. She told Winnie it was like a duck talking to a goose, but somehow we managed to communicate.

I made friends with Nilo, a young Indian woman, Muslim by religion, who was raised in Malaysia, married to an Englishman and for the past ten years had been living in London. Nilo and I, who were both staying at the bride's apartment that week, laughed our way through a day of shopping at the Central Market and Chinatown. We attended the wedding together, enjoyed the eight-course Chinese dinner at the reception, then joined the dancing in the two long lines of folks so diverse in their ethnic backgrounds that it looked like a gathering of the United Nations.

I'm planning a trip to London to visit my new friend Nilo and I'm encouraging her and Sreela, as well as the bridal couple, to visit me in America. And these days I strike up conversations with people of all nationalities. I meet them in restaurants, shops, the theater, or at church. I figure if I could have so much fun with strangers who live nearly ten thousand miles from me, I could surely get to know a few people right here in America who hail from other countries.

Lord, give me courage to reach out to people who may seem very different from me but are my neighbors just the same.
—PATRICIA LORENZ

OCTOBER 16

"Son of man, look with your eyes, and hear with your ears, and
set your mind upon all that I shall show you...."
—EZEKIEL 40:4 (RSV)

I got into the office extra early this morning so I could work on this devotion before the business day began. As soon as I turn on my computer, I get an e-mail from my sister-in-law Toni in Michigan, asking if I would mind looking for a first-edition Steinbeck novel she wanted to give my brother for his birthday. "Sure," I type back. "No problem."

Now to get to work. I'm not a line into it before the phone rings: a subscriber complaining that she keeps getting billed even though she has a canceled check proving she's paid up. I explain that I'm just the editor and supply her with the number of someone I know in customer service.

All right, back to work. But, no. Colleen, one of our editors, storms through my door with her coat still on. Her three-year-old, Louisiana, bit another child this morning at day care and Colleen is beside herself. "I can't believe my daughter is a biter!" she sputters.

No sooner has Colleen left than my assistant, Tina, arrives. She's dying to tell me a joke she heard at dinner the night before. I don't normally go for jokes, but this one truly surprises me and I laugh very hard—so much that I have to call my wife, Julee, at home and tell her.

Of course, my devotional time is shot. Another morning wasted by interruptions!

Yet look: Toni reminded me that my brother's birthday was around the corner. A subscriber offered an unsolicited compliment about the magazine. I was able to help calm down a dismayed mother and friend. To top it off, I actually heard a funny joke. Not a half-bad way to start the day.

And who knew I would actually get a devotional out of it?

God, thank You for all the wondrous details of life all around me,
clamoring to be noticed and overflowing with grace.
—EDWARD GRINNAN

OCTOBER 17

But where shall wisdom be found? and where is the place of understanding?
—JOB 28:12

*T*he past several weeks have found me again taking my number at the local Department of Social and Health Services office. Frustrated and demoralized each time, I've come home and recounted to my mother the red tape I've encountered. Yesterday, describing yet another bureaucratic runaround, I suddenly remembered something my son said thirteen years ago.

We were in the process of moving from Seattle to Bellingham, Washington. To ease the transition, a friend bought each of my children a new outfit to wear on their first day in their new school. A couple of items, however, were too small or too big, and because I was swamped with the many details of the upcoming move, my sister Tresa volunteered to take them back to the store and find something that would fit.

A few days later we were all driving to the Seattle Center for the last time—my sister, myself, and my three children. Tresa, sitting in the front passenger seat, got to telling me how irritated she'd been while trying to get the clothes exchanged. If it wasn't one thing, it was another! She was getting herself all worked up, reliving the ordeal, when suddenly eight-year-old Phillip popped up from the backseat. "Auntie Tresa," he said quietly, "it sounds like you're still there, standing in line at the store."

There was stunned silence from the passenger seat. Then Tresa burst out laughing. "You're so smart, Phillip! I am still there, aren't I? I'm holding on to those silly old clothes when I should just be happy it's over!"

All this came back in a rush when I heard myself going on and on to my mother, except I could hear Phillip talking to me this time. "Mum, it sounds like you're still there, standing in the line at DSHS."

But I'm not there, am I? Thanks, Phil!

Dear Lord, when I wear myself out going over unpleasant things, remind me
I can choose to let the misery go and move on.
—BRENDA WILBEE

OCTOBER 18

He kept him as the apple of his eye.
—DEUTERONOMY 32:10

*W*e were visiting our friends Jen and Rob in their New York City apartment, oohing and aahing over their new baby, who'd just been christened. I noticed their four-year-old, Rebeka, standing to the side, her arms folded across her "I'm the Big Sister" T-shirt. She wasn't smiling. As an older sister myself, I could relate to that feeling of not being the center of attention. So I knelt, draped a hand over Rebeka's shoulder, looked her in the eyes, and said, "You know, when you were a tiny baby like that, we all oohed and aahed over you, too."

She flashed me a skeptical look. Tilting her head, she said, "Oh, I was never tiny like that."

Surprised, I said, "Of course you were! Everybody in this room was created by God, and we all began as tiny babies."

"Even you?" She still looked unconvinced.

"Sure." I lowered my voice. "Even your parents were tiny babies once."

At that she laughed loudly and said, "Oh, I can't believe that." As she ran off, I could hear her murmuring, "Linda's telling stories, Linda's telling stories!"

I chuckled at Rebeka's skepticism, but it reminded me of just how amazing that particular story is. There's no better time than at the beginning of a new life to marvel at the changes we all go through.

Dear God, thank You for Your love that follows us throughout our lives.
May I never lose my sense of wonder at how wonderfully
You bring us from babyhood to adulthood.
—LINDA NEUKRUG

Jesus said, Suffer little children, and forbid them not, to come unto me:
for of such is the kingdom of heaven.
—MATTHEW 19:14

Jonathan, an insatiably curious, skinny, sandy-haired ten-year-old, frequently buzzed into my Sunday school kindergarten class from his classroom next door. On this particular Sunday he stopped in front of Hannah, who was drawing a picture, her long, dark braids touching the table. "What's this?" he asked, peering over her shoulder, tapping the paper with his finger.

"This is Billy, my cat," Hannah said solemnly. "He died and went to heaven. He's waiting there for me."

Jonathan scrunched down over the table and, in a moment of uncommon quiet, studied the picture. "That's good," he said, and buzzed on out of the room.

Billy, who'd been run over by a car a month earlier, was frequently the subject of Hannah's pictures and prayer requests. Knowing he was still hers in heaven bridged the gap his passing had left in her life here.

Some weeks later I received terrible news: Jonathan had died suddenly of a brain aneurysm. That Sunday our class gathered somberly. We talked about Jonathan. I asked the children if they'd like to draw pictures of heaven. They nodded and went to work.

Fifteen minutes later, Hannah handed me her finished picture. Amid green grass and yellow flowers, a gray-and-white stick-figure cat bounded toward a stick-figure boy with familiar sandy hair. "I gave Billy to Jonathan," she whispered, "so he has his own pet up there."

Lord Jesus, help me to prepare for Your kingdom by generous giving.
—SHARI SMYTH

...Having been firmly rooted and now being built up in Him and established in your faith....

—COLOSSIANS 2:7 (NAS)

I was admiring the beautiful hardwood pews that a carpenter friend builds for places of worship. He told me he personally selects the trees from which the pews are made. "The cost is considerable," he said. "First of all, I have to travel by plane halfway across the continent to where the trees grow. Then I must hike for days through hardwood forests on the stormy side of the slopes."

"Why the stormy side?" I asked.

"That's where trees develop deep roots and firm cell structures because they must grow strong enough to withstand the prevailing winds. By comparison, the trees on the sheltered side of the slopes have shallow roots and a coarse grain."

Last year the prevailing winds were blowing rather fiercely on my side of the slope. There were family decisions to make, problems complicating my course of action, and upheavals in my work schedule. My inclination was simply to give in to self-pity and wait for the pressures to slack off. But they didn't.

Instead, I found myself praying—really praying—for the courage to meet problems head-on, for the grace to confront difficult situations, for guidance in establishing a time-management plan.

At the end of the year, I was not only standing a little taller and a little straighter, I had gone down a whole lot deeper with God.

Lord, You not only created trees, You were raised here on earth by a carpenter and know the value of growing on the stormy side of the slope. Use the winds in my life to help me grow strong in spirit.

—ALMA BARKMAN

There is one glory of the sun....
—I CORINTHIANS 15:41

I was married on an autumn afternoon in a little A-frame church overlooking Kalispell Bay on Priest Lake in north Idaho. I remember kneeling at the altar, feeling the sun streaming through the glass and warming my back and shoulders. Several years ago, when my husband and I went through a shaky period in our marriage, I sometimes thought about the feel of the sun on my back that day, as if God's touch had rested there. And in that remembered moment I could hear Him encouraging me: *Steady on, girl, steady on.* I did hold steady, and the problems eventually disappeared.

Two winters ago, on our first morning in our new home in Minnesota, I woke at dawn to sit by the bedroom window and give thanks to God. I felt grateful for the freedom our house and acreage afforded after cramped townhouse living. But I felt doubt, too. The house had cost more to build than we'd expected and there were other expenses still ahead. *Have we acted impulsively?* I wondered.

Suddenly, at the horizon, a huge red sun seemed to surge up out of the ground beside a stand of oaks, just beyond a small hill. I started to cry at the unexpected beauty. As it rose higher, I felt a deep conviction that we were doing the right thing by investing in this house and land, to enjoy it and use it for whatever God had planned. His voice was there in that awesome sunrise, giving me hope and saying, *Welcome, neighbor!*

Lord, I wait eagerly for the sound of Your voice in sunrises and sunsets yet to be.
—CAROL KNAPP

OCTOBER 22
FIRST DAY OF FALL

I will put in the wilderness the cedar, the acacia, the myrtle, and the olive; I will set in the desert the cypress, the plane and the pine together; that men may see and know, may consider and understand together, that the hand of the Lord has done this, the Holy One of Israel has created it.

—ISAIAH 41:19–20 (RSV)

Poking into the reasons why leaves turn colors in the fall, I discover that they don't turn colors at all—they lose the green that comes from being flooded with chlorophyll in spring and reveal their true colors, which are, depending on the species, flaming orange, stunning purple, shouting red, searing yellow.

I didn't know that. It's sleight of leaf, as it were, a deft trick by the tree that senses the seasonal shift in amounts of light and water and pulls back the green force for a season.

I sit and ponder trees for a minute and begin to see them as perhaps God and children do—really tall plants, verrrrry slow acrobats with enormous stiff brown fingers, patient and wonderfully sensitive woody creatures who eat sunlight, drink rain, totally understand soil chemistry, and house animals ranging in size from bacteria to boys.

Dear God, thanks for trees. Nice job of creation there, for without them, we would be desert dwellers always and, all told, there's a lot to be said for treedom.

—BRIAN DOYLE

Such as I have give I thee....
—ACTS 3:6

*W*hen I was seventeen, I had open-heart surgery. For a time, I felt self-conscious about my scar, but after a time, the feeling faded. Unfortunately, so did the feelings of gratitude that my operation had at first kindled in me, gratitude toward the doctors and nurses and my family and friends, who'd visited me faithfully.

Then one day I was reading a magazine article on the "blessings of the twentieth century." To my surprise, there was open-heart surgery, along with microwave ovens and television. I got the chills when I realized that if I'd been born just a half-century earlier, the operation that healed me (I'd been born with a hole in my heart) wouldn't even have existed.

I wish there were something I could do to express my gratitude, I thought. But to whom? And what? I couldn't afford to donate a wing to a hospital! The very next page of the magazine held my answer: "Only two percent of those eligible donate blood. You can help—give blood." Who, me? Suddenly, giving back didn't seem to be so urgent. *Wouldn't it hurt? Or take hours? Besides, they wouldn't take my blood, would they?* Well, they would and they did—and it was *easy!* It took about fifteen minutes, it didn't hurt me at all—and I got to guzzle all the oatmeal cookies and apple juice that I could. The nurse slapped a heart-shaped sticker on my sweater: "Be nice to me," it said. "I gave blood today."

"Thank you," she told me.

"Thank *you!"* I said, and I meant it. It felt good to give back.

God, is there something I'm grateful for in my life—my family, job, friends?
Today, let me find a way to give back.

—LINDA NEUKRUG

And I will pray the Father, and he shall give you another Comforter,
that he may abide with you for ever.
—JOHN 14:16

I glanced at the clock on the bedside table. The bright orange numbers read 3:25 AM. Slipping quietly from the bedroom so as not to disturb my husband, Larry, I moved silently into the living room. My thoughts seemed almost as dark as the shadows I found there, and my hand moved automatically to the switch on the floor lamp. I was tired, but my mind wouldn't let me rest. I lay down on the couch, mulling over the affairs of the day.

My son Jeff was in a struggle to pull his life back together following a recent divorce, and I keenly felt his pain and loneliness. My parents, who own a large turkey farm, seemed always to have too much work to do and not enough time to do it. Neither had been well, and I was concerned about their health. I was also concerned for my poor mother-in-law, who was in the grip of a serious depression that had affected her entire family. Tonight I couldn't help but wonder what the future held for these people I loved.

As those dark thoughts clamored in my mind they seemed to chill the very air around me. Glancing up behind me on the couch, I spotted the soft throw that is always folded there. *Pull the comforter over you,* I said to myself. But as I reached up to tug at the throw, I was suddenly struck by the phrase I had just used. Why, of course! What other possible answer could there be for any of life's problems than to pull the Comforter over me?

Snuggled inside the folds of the warm throw, I finally closed my eyes. I could rest now. I had been reminded that the affairs of the day, as well as the people I love, were also resting . . . safe in the arms of the Comforter.

Father, when I rest in You, my yoke is indeed easy, and my burdens are light.
—LIBBIE ADAMS

Neglect not the gift that is in thee....
—I TIMOTHY 4:14

J met a friend at the supermarket. "How's retirement?" I asked. "How're the first four months of freedom?" He frowned. "All right, I guess." Then, "There's nothing to do!" Nothing to do? Really?

Socrates gave his wisest philosophy at seventy.

Plato, a student at fifty, did his best teaching after sixty.

Goethe wrote part of *Faust* at sixty, the remainder at eighty-two.

Noah Webster compiled his monumental dictionary at seventy.

Gladstone was Britain's prime minister at eighty-two.

Grandma Moses' first public showing of her paintings was at seventy.

Helen Hooven Santmyer had her best-selling novel published at eighty-eight.

Maybe we aren't as talented as these seven, yet retirement brings a gift: the gift of time, with endless choices on its use. Time to learn, to explore, to listen, the opportunity to be a living example of poise and tranquility. Time to gain a new sense of calm, quiet trust, to grow closer to loved ones, and to serve the Lord and His children.

Nothing to do? Retirement from work is not retirement from life. It only means more of His gift, time. Aren't we told, "Withhold not good from them to whom it is due, when it is in the power of thine hand to do it" (Proverbs 3:27)? Well then, let's get going!

Dear God, there is *so much to do in Thy name.*
Don't let me waste a precious moment.
—OSCAR GREENE

OCTOBER 26

Praise be to . . . the God of all comfort, who comforts us in all our troubles,
so that we can comfort those in any trouble with the comfort
we ourselves have received from God.
—II CORINTHIANS 1:3–4 (NIV)

*Y*ou don't know me, and I hope you don't mind my calling," a woman told me when I answered the phone one Saturday morning, "but someone gave me your name." Her voice broke. "My teenage daughter has the same problem your daughter had." Immediately, a strong bond of shared experience connected me to this stranger and my heart hurt for her as she began to describe her daughter's autoimmune disease. You have the disease for life, and for self-conscious teenage girls, it is particularly life-altering.

"I don't know what to do. I don't know how to help her," this mother told me. For nearly an hour I listened and tried to encourage her. As we talked, I reached into a file drawer and pulled out some papers with names and phone numbers and pieces of information I had gathered two years earlier. I tried not to offer too much advice. I remembered that when I started down this same path with Kendall, I couldn't take in too much advice at once, but before we hung up, I encouraged her to call me anytime.

"Thank you," she said.

"Thank you, too," I said, though she probably didn't understand what I meant. When this disease struck eighteen-year-old Kendall and she lost all her hair, I couldn't imagine any good coming out of the struggle. But now Kendall is off at college, and she has hair on her head. Although we live with the ongoing reality of the disease, we have passed through the place where this other mother and daughter now find themselves. I now understand one of God's truths more clearly: Our pain is not wasted when we can reach around and comfort another coming along behind us on the same path.

Father, thank You for the comfort that comes in comforting another.
—CAROL KUYKENDALL

OCTOBER 27

The Lord shall preserve thy going out and thy coming in
from this time forth, and even for evermore.
—PSALM 121:8

*H*ave you ever felt sometimes that your life was on a runaway course, that you were headed for a smash-up if something didn't happen soon to prevent it? Well, I have, and it's scary. But I came across something not long ago that has helped me ever since.

It was while my husband, Larry, and I were traveling over Loveland Pass in Colorado that I noticed a sign that said Truck Ramp, 1/2 Mile. When I questioned Larry about it, he said the ramps are for vehicles that lose their brakes on the steep mountain roads. Soon we came to the ramp off the main road, an incline that angled up the side of the mountain and ended in a soft dirt bank where a runaway truck could slow to a halt without injuring the driver. *What a good idea!* I thought. If only there could be a spiritual ramp for people like me when life feels out of control.

That night, reading in the motel's Gideon Bible, I came to Psalm 121:1–2, "I will lift up mine eyes unto the hills, from whence cometh my help. My help cometh from the Lord, which made heaven and earth." The psalm goes on to outline all the ways the Lord helps those who put their faith in Him. I nodded, reading those words. Do I have a place of refuge I can run to when I feel my life getting out of control? Yes, I do!

Lord, today I put my trust in You.
—MADGE HARRAH

OCTOBER 28

Be strong and of a good courage... for the Lord thy God,
he it is that doth go with thee....
—DEUTERONOMY 31:6

*J*oan, my neighbor, had had her life torn apart. For twenty-two years she was an executive's wife. She was confident, secure. But after her husband's sudden death, everything frightened her— the phone, the man from the oil company, cars, overhanging trees in the dark. She stopped driving, stopped going to the grocery store. Eventually she even stopped going out for the mail.

Psychiatrists have a term for Joan's suffering: agoraphobia, fear of open spaces. But I knew a better term from reading the Psalms. Joan was walking through the Valley of the Shadow of Death. No one knew how to help Joan. Then one night, I heard a knock on my back door. It was Joan, breathless with terror. "My daughter's sick. Can you come over?"

It was only the flu. A pot of chicken soup saw the little girl through. But Joan had made the more drastic step toward recovery—she had sacrificed her fear for love! A month later, I saw Joan sweeping her front porch. Then going down the driveway for the mail. Her greatest triumph that year was coming over for coffee. We sat for an hour over doughnuts while she told me about driving a camper to the Grand Canyon one summer when her daughter was a baby. After that, we made regular trips to the grocery store together. And then she found a part-time typing job in the neighborhood.

If you, like Joan, are caught in depression's net, don't despair. Start untying the knots one by one. Remember that very often the first step out of the Valley of the Shadow of Death is to forget yourself and reach out to another.

Today, Father, help me walk out of the shadow into light.
—LINDA CHING SLEDGE

OCTOBER 29

God will redeem my soul from the power of the grave: for he shall receive me....
—PSALM 49:15

hat fall morning it was brisk outside, the first really cold day of the season. I glanced at the thermometer in the window: thirty-nine degrees. I turned to the newspaper for the forecast: It wouldn't even get up to fifty. Time for the winter wardrobe. I searched the back of the closet for my tweed jacket. Brown with autumnal highlights of gold and red, it was the perfect thing for an October day.

As I walked to the train, I took a look at the garden in front of our apartment. The hydrangeas were turning copper, the mums a brave yellow and the little Japanese maple at the end of the drive had already blushed red. Soon there would be no flowers, no leaves, and the only bit of color would be the big red bow on the wreaths put up at Christmastime. I found myself yearning for spring.

I put my hands in my jacket. When did I last wear it? Probably last winter or on one of the cold days of early spring. But what a difference there is between a cold October day, when the summer is past, and a day in March, when spring is just around the bend. There's something sad about saying good-bye to those vibrant colors when they won't be back for six months.

Then I felt something in my pocket and took it out. A dried palm branch woven in the shape of a cross. I suddenly remembered the last time I wore this jacket: Palm Sunday. That day in church, as I listened to the extraordinary story of Christ's suffering, I wove this cross from a green palm frond. Then Easter came with its bright promise of everlasting life, and soon spring followed. I put the cross back in my jacket and kept it there. Easter has a message I need all year long.

Lord, I turn to You for the promise of new life.
—RICK HAMLIN

It is a good thing to give thanks unto the Lord....
—PSALM 92:1

One day my pastor asked me to pick up an eighty-eight-year-old member who needed a ride to church from her nursing home. I dreaded the assignment because most of the elderly I knew were worriers and complainers, ever ready to enumerate in detail their pains and problems. But I had to admit Ellen was different. As we drove to church, she told me how thankful she felt that she could walk with a cane. "When I came here five years ago," she explained with a wrinkled smile, "I was on a walker. So I guess I'm making progress. Also, I weighed eighty-eight pounds then and now I'm up to a hundred and four." On our next trip, I discovered she knits scarves, gloves, and sweaters and then gives them away. And that she plays the piano for eight religious services at the home. She confided she was blind in one eye but praised God for excellent vision in the other.

One day I got a bright idea: to introduce Ellen to some church shut-ins. *She'll be a good example to them,* I thought. Sure enough, they perked right up when Ellen was around. Her attitude was contagious. "Be thankful for what you have," she would say, "and what you don't have won't bother you so much."

Then one day I was grumping to my wife about something when I suddenly thought of Ellen. And laughed. There I'd been complaining about older people—for complaining. Now it was clear to me. Complaining has less to do with age than with attitude. Being thankful is something that can keep anyone from nine to ninety from complaining. Including, I realized shamefacedly, me.

Lord, keep me too busy counting my blessings to complain.
—SAM JUSTICE

October 31

When I was a child, I spoke like a child, I thought like a child,
I reasoned like a child. . . .
—I Corinthians 13:11 (RSV)

*E*ven as an adult, I've always had a lot of fun with Halloween. It was originally adapted by the Celts in the ninth century for the Christian celebration of the eve of All Saints' Day (November 1 began the Celtic New Year). But today, for most kids—and us kids-at-heart—it's really a great big dress-up-and-pretend day. I can close my eyes and see a towheaded boy of four decked out in Superman duds, wearing blue leotards and flapping a red cape. Not a vision my now-teenage son Phil would care—or dare—to repeat! And once when I attended the kids' costume parade at their elementary school, I dressed as a nurse and poked them with fake shots as they walked by. Their exaggerated squeals let me know they liked a mom who could still play their games.

Another less-considered side to Halloween is the opportunity to befriend other people's children, exemplified by my husband's uncle Earl. He began on a small scale with individual bags of treats when our costumed tribe first stopped by his apartment. Each year the bags bulged bigger. Then he began serving simple refreshments, which eventually escalated into a full-blown party thrown just for us. It was the highlight of our evening until we moved away. Uncle Earl faces a life-threatening illness now. Our seventeen-year-old daughter, Tamara, recently expressed her feelings in a postcard: "I'll always remember the Halloween parties you gave for us, Uncle Earl. Thank you."

Halloween doesn't have to be sinister. By carefully choosing our approach, we can treat ourselves to some healthy fun and a stash of sweet memories.

Father, help us enjoy the children in their make-believe delight,
And coax a smile from us "big kids" on this fun October night.
—Carol Knapp

November

NOVEMBER 1
ALL SAINTS DAY

*As for the saints who are in the land, they are the glorious ones
in whom is all my delight.*

—PSALM 16:3 (NIV)

*I*t was the first All Saints' Day after my first husband Jim's death and I
was keenly aware of "the saints who have gone on before." I was also
becoming well-acquainted with "the saints who are in the land." Alongside my
tears and memories of Jim, I began to think about some of the people whose
thoughtful, loving gestures were helping me to cope with life.

There was my sister Lin, who came to live with us that first year, helping
with my three young children—doing everything from plumbing to bedtime
stories. And Ann, my friend, who listened to my grief by the hour and seemed
always willing to lend a hand. Ted, who spent an evening helping the kids
carve pumpkins and, a few weeks after their daddy died, took them shopping
for Mother's Day gifts. There was Stephanie, who in those early weeks of our
enormous loss, appeared on my doorstep every Friday noon with a hug and a
simple bouquet of flowers.

The saints in the land, the glorious ones, in whom God delights—my life
has been full of people like that and I'm grateful for an opportunity to remind
myself that the saints of God are many and surround me today.

*O Lord of the everyday details, I'm grateful for all those saints who have touched
my life. Help me today to see and to do those small things for others
that so delight You.*

—MARY JANE CLARK

"He must wash his clothes, and he will be clean."
—LEVITICUS 13:34 (NIV)

New Market, Virginia, has its own fall festival days. Our first year here, I was delighted to find that I could set up a table on Congress Street and sell things. It was a wonderful way to meet new people.

One woman introduced herself as Jane DePreiter, the president of the Chamber of Commerce. She pulled up the extra chair I'd put out for visitors, and we began to chat. I told her that although I loved our new home and our new town, some unexpected circumstances in my life were creating a very difficult time. "New learning is coming slowly to me. I feel so frustrated and inadequate. I wish I would hurry up and get changed—I'm driving me crazy!" I said with a laugh.

Jane commiserated. "That reminds me of something I learned not long ago when I was upset about a situation in my own life. I couldn't seem to get a handle on what was happening to me and why I felt so irritable and out of control. Then one day I was leaning over my washer, shoving the last of the clothes in as the cycle began and it was as if the Lord spoke to me. I suddenly realized that, like my clothes, sometimes I have to get agitated to get cleaned!"

Lord, when I'm in one of those frustrating, irritating, nerve-wracking times, help me remember that the end result will be a much-needed cleansing and fresh breezes blowing through my life.

—ROBERTA ROGERS

NOVEMBER 3

Thine heart was lifted up because of thy beauty....
—EZEKIEL 28:17

*I*t seemed almost like a finger beckoning me outside. I went to the hall closet, pulled out my husband David's blue fleece jacket, and wrapped myself in its safe softness. Outside, the day was brisk. Rain was on the way. I walked back toward the creek where a row of maples and sycamores had shed a lovely, yellow-brown carpet all along the bank. A red leaf swirled in the stream below.

Funny, I thought to myself, *I used to dread fall, and now find myself drawn to this season of change.* Once autumn seemed an ending, but today I sensed a sort of rebirth: a pattern. A perfect plan. Beautiful leaves, falling, mulching together in the ground, dying so they might live again. The leaf that floated past my window suddenly seemed an invitation straight from God. *Come, step back into life,* it beckoned, *where the seasons come and go and God makes everything beautiful in His time.*

I found myself impatient to get back in the house and attack the work that waited on my desk. Thanksgiving and then Christmas lay ahead. I had a lot to do.

Father, let me rest awhile in Your perfect plan and then
step joyfully into the new day that waits.
—PAM KIDD

Don't you know that a little yeast works through the whole batch of dough?
Get rid of the old yeast that you may be a new batch without yeast....
—I Corinthians 5:6–7 (NIV)

For days I had been testing and retesting a unit that adjusted the air intake on aircraft engines. The performance of the unit was erratic and the test results were inconsistent. At the time, I was a working leader in development testing where troubled parts were returned for observation. These parts had passed inspection, but now they weren't working normally. Engineers with complex instruments joined me and for one week we tested without an answer.

Finally a gentleman with tousled hair and a crumpled suit entered the test lab. He appeared to be deep in thought as he examined the errant part. After a few minutes of silence, he said, "Do you have one that works?" I nodded. "Let's try it," he said. I did, and it worked perfectly. Then the man reached down to the floor and gathered some lint between his fingers. The amount was so small I could hardly see it. He sprinkled the fibers into the unit. "Give it a whirl," he said. I did, and the part functioned as erratically as the rest had. The man turned and left without introducing himself. Later I learned he had a doctorate in engineering design.

When I find myself angry or sad as I go about my tasks, or if my prayer life seems to be drying up, I think back to our problem with that errant part. Sometimes the source of my problem isn't an obvious error or a structural flaw. Sometimes it's as simple as a cross word with my wife, Ruby, or a quiet time I've skipped or a bad night's sleep. As simple as a pinch of lint.

Dear Father, help me to avoid the little things that lead me away from You.
—Oscar Greene

NOVEMBER 5

*Let us not become weary in doing good, for at the proper time
we will reap a harvest if we do not give up.*
—GALATIANS 6:9 (NIV)

W hen my father had emergency gallbladder surgery, I stepped into
the temporary role of running the household and caring for Mom,
who was confined to a wheelchair. There was so much to remember—feed the
dog, water the plants, exercise Mom's legs, cancel the hair appointment, switch
Mom's eye patch every few hours. I fell into bed exhausted, then remembered
that I'd forgotten to brush Mom's teeth. *I'll never be able to keep this up,* I
thought wearily.

The next day I noticed that one of Mom's medications was running low. Dad
had managed to tell me that he orders medicine by mail and that the necessary
forms and instructions were in a file marked "Medical." I pulled open the file
cabinet in my parents' bedroom, searched through it three times, and found
only files for the organizations Dad supports.

"I give up," I muttered in frustration as I stumbled out of the bedroom and
down the hall. Then I noticed another file cabinet in a small spare bedroom. I
went through it eagerly, but I didn't see the "Medical" file. Then I yanked open
the top drawer again, and my eyes fell on a file marked "Perseverance." Curious
about the odd title, I pulled out the file. It was a talk Dad had given at a retreat. I
flipped to the last page and saw these underlined words: "We can persevere
because Christ and the Holy Spirit will enable us."

I put the "Perseverance" file back in the drawer. Almost immediately I found
the file I was looking for, right there in the top drawer where it had been all
along. "I guess I can do this job, Lord—if You'll enable me," I said. And I closed
the file drawer, having found what I was searching for—and also something I
desperately needed.

Lord, thank You for the strength You give me to accomplish the hardest tasks.
—KAREN BARBER

Getting wisdom is the most important thing you can do! And with your wisdom, develop common sense and good judgment.
—Proverbs 4:7 (TLB)

I was surprised to find a piece of paper with the heading "Mertilla Township: Mill Levy for Roads" among the ballots I was given on Election Day. My husband, Don, and I had discussed candidates for judge and county commissioner while we drove the fifteen miles to Plains, our polling place, but he hadn't mentioned a mill levy. If there had been a story on it in the newspaper, I'd skipped it. After marking the other ballots, I scanned the mill levy petition. One thing was obvious: Voting YES would raise my taxes. I checked NO without bothering to read the full text.

"How did you vote on the Mill Levy?" I asked Don on the way home.

"Yes, of course!" he told me, surprised that I'd asked.

"Well, I voted no!" I said. "Our taxes are already way too high!"

"Did you actually read the petition?" Don asked. "We'd pay less than fifty-five dollars each year—not much compared to getting that east road built up and graveled."

When we heard the results that night, the Mill Levy had been defeated—by one vote.

Were there other times I'd been uninformed about the issues and had neglected to pray for wisdom before casting my vote? I didn't have to go far into my memory. I'd supported an official whose views were hostile to the poor. I'd helped our church elect a leader without the skills to take us through difficult times. And because I didn't bother to learn about the Mertilla Township Mill Levy, our east road continues to be nearly impassable after a hard rain.

Lord Jesus, help me to vote with an informed mind and a compassionate heart, trusting that my choices will be pleasing to You. Amen.
—Penney Schwab

November 7

She is clothed with strength and dignity; she can laugh at the days to come.
—Proverbs 31:25 (NIV)

At ninety-seven, my great-aunt Anna was still enthusiastic about life. Born in Russia twelve years before the Revolution, she survived three terrible wars and a flight for her life that took her across Europe and ended in a pioneer settlement in Paraguay. Then in her early fifties she emigrated to Canada, where she started over again. "I've had a good life," she'd exclaim.

Anna had not lived in Canada long when one day, on her afternoon off work as a cook in a nursing home, she and her friend Lena walked three miles to my mother's house. After a delightful visit and the usual *vaspa* (evening meal), they were ready to walk back. "It's too dark for you to be walking," my mother said. Anna and her friend allowed my mother to call a taxi.

The two women were huddled in the backseat when they suddenly heard a man's voice. After a few moments, the driver answered.

"Who's he talking to?" Lena whispered in her native German.

"Another man," Anna whispered back. "He's got another man in this car. They're up to no good!"

As the darkened countryside flitted by and nothing looked familiar anymore, the women became convinced that these men had evil intentions. Why else would one of them be crouching so low that they couldn't see him?

"When he slows at a stop sign," Anna whispered, "be ready to jump."

Suddenly the car stopped. The driver got out and opened the passenger door.

"Here you are, ladies, safe and sound at the Menno Home," he said in perfect German.

"Later I learned about two-way radios," my great-aunt laughed. "I also found out the taxi driver goes to my church."

Instead of being embarrassed, Aunt Anna saw humor in the situation. And come to think of it, many of her stories ended with a good laugh. Laughter is a great way to get over the potholes of life. My great-aunt seemed to know that.

Dear Lord, send me on my way today with a sense of humor.
—Helen Grace Lescheid

November 8

Now I know in part; but then shall I know even as also I am known.
—I Corinthians 13:12

Across the crowded hotel lobby, I saw the pastor of the church I had attended as a child. I had last seen him in 1969 when I was eight years old. Even though it was now three decades later and his face had been altered by the passage of time, he was unmistakable.

I knew he would need help to remember who I was, so I began to rehearse an introduction: My name is Dave Franco. My mom and dad were part of your congregation at Alamitos Friends Church during the sixties. Their names are Ruben and Sally Franco. My sisters, Laura and Karen, were friends of your daughter's, and I knew your son Mickey.

Feeling sufficiently prepared, I made my way across the lobby to say hello to my dear old pastor. As I approached him, his eyes caught mine, and before I could open my mouth, he said, "David! How wonderful to see you!"

Thirty years had passed. He had looked into thousands of different faces since then. I had changed from a boy to a man nearly forty years old. And still he knew me. What a welcoming feeling that was!

I think that's something like what it will be like when I get to heaven. The Lord knows me even better than I know myself, and when I finally approach Him, He'll give me the warmest welcome of my life.

Lord, I can't wait to feel Your arms around me.
—Dave Franco

November 9

The Lord is nigh unto all them that call upon him … in truth.
—PSALM 145:18

The most important weekly meeting I attend at the office has no formal presentations, no overhead projectors, no budget proposals. People don't argue their positions or make impassioned justifications for their departments. Those of us who come to the conference room sit around a large table and pick up a handful of letters. In silence we read.

"My grandson needs a raise at work," a grandmother writes. "Even with overtime he's not able to support his family. Please pray for him."

"Last year I was in the hospital for five and a half weeks," says another letter. "I now have an apartment, but it does not allow pets. My twelve-and-a-half-year-old dog has been with a foster family for more than a year. Please pray for me as I speak to my landlord. Wiggles is very well-behaved."

The greeting on one note makes me smile. "Hi, Spiritual Siblings!" it says. Another letter is painfully succinct: "Keep my mind intact." I find myself moved by another's plea: "I'm so lonely. I haven't met anyone who wants to date or take out a fifty-three-year-old woman. Help me to pray."

The ideal words come from a cheerful soul who says, "I live on two acres and love to mow the grass. (I have a rider.)" I read her prayer aloud: "I have faith in Jesus. For He's there on my good days; He's there on my bad days; He's there all the time." What a reminder for starting out my week!

By now you might realize I'm writing about the Guideposts Prayer Fellowship. We gather in our offices on Monday mornings at nine forty-five to pray for others. With every letter, I find myself fortified. It's a meeting of spiritual siblings worldwide.

Lord, be there on my good days; be there on my bad days; be there all the time.
—RICK HAMLIN

NOVEMBER 10

But I trust in your unfailing love; my heart rejoices in your salvation.
—PSALM 13:5 (NIV)

For many years of my life my dad helped and looked after me. And for the past several years I have looked after him. He has Alzheimer's disease and lives in a nursing home near me. He no longer knows me, but I visit with him anyway, although it's difficult to find things to say. He has no memory of his life at all. When he catches a glimpse of himself in a mirror, it frightens him because he doesn't recognize the man he sees.

During the past year, my dad has had pneumonia three times. This last time has been especially difficult for him. He's very weak and occasionally needs oxygen to help him breathe. He has a living will, so nothing drastic will be done to keep him going. All anyone can do is try to make him comfortable.

At first I had a hard time dealing with the fact that I couldn't do anything to help my dad. All I could do was hold his hand and pray as I watched him drift off into sleep. Finally, just the other day, I realized that I had a problem: My will was struggling with God's will. What I needed to do was let go and turn this over to God—because my father's life was in His hands, not mine. At that moment I prayed again, but this time for myself. I asked God to help me release my dad into His loving hands. And almost immediately I felt at peace. I still do.

I know now that when I sit beside my dad's bed, I am not supposed to do anything. God is his caregiver—and mine.

Dear Lord, there are so many of us caring for loved ones who are ill. Be with us in our helplessness and comfort us with Your love. Amen.
—PHYLLIS HOBE

November 11
VETERANS DAY

I will make every effort to see that after my departure you will always be able to remember these things.

—II PETER 1:15 (NIV)

*W*e really celebrated Veterans Day when I was growing up. My father would put out the flag on the front porch, step back, put his hand over his heart, and bow his head for a few moments. Then my parents would go to church to pray for all the friends they'd lost in World War II, and for all those whose lives were still darkened by the shadow that terrible war cast over a whole generation of Americans, a generation that saved the future.

World War II dominated my parents' consciousness. The day after Pearl Harbor, my father, a naval reservist, requested active duty but was turned down because of arthritic knees and stomach ulcers. We lived in Philadelphia at the time, and the navy officer who rejected my dad said, "Maybe if the Japanese capture the Liberty Bell, we'll have to use you."

That didn't stop him from doing his part. My parents had a sleek little inboard motorboat they kept moored on the Delaware River, and on weekends when the weather was fair Dad would take it out into the Atlantic and patrol the shoreline, looking for German U-boats, Mom steering while Dad swept the horizon with his binoculars. Once, Dad thought he spotted a periscope and radioed the sighting to the Coast Guard—but it didn't come to anything and probably wasn't taken very seriously, since U-boats weren't known to lurk around the mouth of the Delaware. He took a lot of ribbing about that in later years, but Dad didn't care. He'd done what he could to help fight a war that he understood had to be fought.

Some people might think that Veterans Day isn't relevant anymore, but I think they're wrong. I'm going to make a real celebration of it again. I'll start by putting out the flag.

God, protect our nation and shed Your grace on us this Veterans Day.

—EDWARD GRINNAN

Bear ye one another's burdens, and so fulfill the law of Christ.
—Galatians 6:2

My seventeen-year-old son, Drew, is growing up quickly in so many ways. Now a senior in high school, he recently spent a week in Mexico City working in an orphanage. Today he showed me some photographs he had taken of the kids with whom he worked.

One of the photographs captures the playful delight of children in every city and culture. It's a picture of a twelve-year-old boy giving his ten-year-old friend a piggyback ride. Both boys are thin and ragged but are smiling from ear to ear.

Gazing at the photo, Drew said, "Dad, you don't understand this picture. That's Juan and Mario. Juan is the kid who's giving Mario a ride. Juan was born blind, but he can walk. And Mario, who is on his back, is paralyzed. He can't walk, but he can see. So Juan gives Mario rides and Mario gives Juan directions. They've worked out quite a system. They're a team."

As I looked up at my son, I knew that he had been initiated into the sad world of human suffering. But I also knew that he had discovered the beauty of the human spirit, of one person helping another.

All of us are handicapped in some way. We have our weaknesses and limitations. But all of us have the ability to give what we have in the service of others. We can help the lame to walk and the blind to see and feed thousands with a few fish sandwiches. This is the spirit of Jesus. And this is the source of miracles.

Dear Father, take my strengths and my limitations and use them to help others. Amen.
—Scott Walker

NOVEMBER 13

Whatsoever ye do in word or deed, do all in the name of the Lord Jesus,
giving thanks to God....
—COLOSSIANS 3:17

I'm in the basement, radio on, folding laundry. It's a contemplative act, with its own rules.

First rule: Look for towels, sheets, and blankets to fold quickly into squares. In the hands of a master, the folds fairly fly. You want to get off to a good start, to have the feeling of work being done efficiently and the towels build up into an impressive stack of folded stuff.

Next: kid stuff. Might as well concentrate on what is most plentiful, and with three small children there is an eye-popping number of shirts, pants, socks, hats, sweaters, sweatshirts, and diapers. With baby stuff you enter the dream zone, when your mind sails to Italy and walks the sunny rows of the vineyard contemplating the exact right day to begin harvest while your hands lift the shirt, snap it straight, fold sleeves in, fold belly up, reach for next shirt.

Then wife's stuff. Mostly shirts and jeans, but hey, here's a bra! How do you fold a bra?

My stuff: A hundred years ago, when I was young and single, I didn't wash anything; I'd actually leave things out in the rain on purpose. Then I started washing unmentionables. Then everything else. But what self-respecting guy folded his own stuff? Now I fold my own stuff, with affection and respect, savoring each hardworking garment, some of which have been with me half my life.

This is the prayer of the laundry room, which is really the prayer of the small daily act. And what are our days but a whole motley pile of small daily acts— each a prayer, if only we can keep attending to its inherent holiness.

Lord, give me the sharpness of eye and width of heart to spy Your grace and
humor in what seem to be the smallest and most insignificant corners of my days.
Yea, even unto the finding and folding of socks hot from the dryer.
—BRIAN DOYLE

NOVEMBER 14

"Unless you change and become like little children, you will never enter
the kingdom of heaven."
—MATTHEW 18:3 (NIV)

On the wall above my desk, I've taped a wonderful snapshot of a chubby-cheeked, three-year-old cherub, wearing a fluffy pink tutu and confident smile. Her name is Gracie, and her mother sent me the picture because I told her that Gracie had become my symbol of what it means to keep a childlike heart.

I was attending a Sunday after-church brunch with a bunch of adults I hardly knew. We all seemed a bit self-conscious as we sat knee-to-knee, balancing paper plates of food on our laps and making small talk. Then Gracie arrived in her pink tutu.

"It's her favorite outfit right now," her mother explained as Gracie paused at the door, and then floated into the room, totally free from self-consciousness or self-centeredness. As I watched Gracie that day, I admired the ways she responded to the world with such joy and exuberance. And now, as I look at her picture above my desk, I vow to do the same, especially now that I'm past the fifty-year mark in my life. "Maturity is the process of becoming childlike," someone once said. Part of my vow is to be more playful. Though I probably won't show up in a pink tutu, I do have a collection of hats I can sometimes wear for fun, including one that has flashing lights, another with clapping hands, and one that has a halo.

I also vow never to lose a *wow!* response to evidences of God's goodness, like arching rainbows, fluffy snowflakes, exquisite little ladybugs, and gooey cinnamon rolls.

And I don't want to let self-consciousness grow bigger than self-confidence, so I vow to trust that where I am and who I am is delightful in God's eyes. If I start forgetting any of these childlike goals, I have that picture of Gracie, my heroine in her pink tutu, right above my desk to remind me.

Father, show me how to keep a childlike heart in this aging body.
—CAROL KUYKENDALL

Truly the light is sweet, and a pleasant thing it is for the eyes to behold the sun.
—ECCLESIASTES 11:7

Driving the Southern California freeways during rush hour is a test of true grit and something to be avoided if at all possible. I had deliberately timed my return home from a conference in San Diego to miss the traffic. I was whizzing along, making good time, when, suddenly, coming around the turn that feeds 57 North westward onto the 210 freeway, I found myself caught in a hideous backup. *Bother!* I thought. *Now what?*

By the time I had inched my way around the bend and was driving west, I had my answer. The long line of cars had all slowed down and were crawling along so that their drivers could see one of the most magnificent sunsets I have ever experienced. I joined the drivers who had moved their cars over to the right shoulder to stop and catch the wonder, mesmerized by the brilliant light that filled the sky with reds and gold and surreal electric pinks.

It didn't last long, probably no more than five or ten minutes. Then came the gray of dusk. As suddenly as we had been caught up in the glory of a celestial light show, we were once again earthbound. Those of us parked on the shoulder revved our engines, turned our wheels, and jostled our way back into the rush of the traffic.

I didn't think a sunset could get any better than the ones I'd seen over the ocean in Hawaii, but here in midst of the stress-filled California rush-hour traffic, God splashed a canvas across the sky of such dazzling glory that freeway drivers slowed, pulled over, and bestowed the accolade of a pause that, in our best Hollywood tradition, applauded "Bravo!"

How magnificent is Your handiwork, Lord God of creation!

And how much more will be Your glory when I see You face-to-face!
—FAY ANGUS

November 16

They helped every one his neighbor; and every one said to his brother,
Be of good courage.
—Isaiah 41:6

I love getting e-mail, especially when it's like the one my husband sent me recently. "Thanks for being my parachute packer," was all it said.

Attached to the e-mail was a story about a navy pilot whose plane was blown apart in Vietnam. He was able to eject from the plane, and his parachute settled him slowly to safety on the ground. Years later, as he was dining in a restaurant, a man wandered over to his table, called him by name, and said, "You flew jet fighters in 'Nam and were shot down!"

"How did you know that?" the ex-pilot said, startled.

"Because I packed your parachute!" the other man said with a grin.

The ex-pilot grabbed the man's hand and thanked him profusely. "If that parachute hadn't worked, I wouldn't be here today!"

The story made me think about those who, largely unseen, provide the emotional, physical, and spiritual "parachutes" that we all need every day. My husband's six-word e-mail was sweet recognition of the little things I do for him that most of the time go unnoticed, but that keep his life from crashing out of control.

Who packs your parachute?

Lord, I'm praying today for the people whose words or deeds help keep me afloat, especially _____.
(FILL IN NAME)

Help me to show how much I appreciate them.
—Roberta Rogers

I am weary with my sighing....
—PSALM 6:6 (NAS)

*S*ometimes a disappointment comes along that knocks me for a loop. It's been that kind of week: disappointment in a loss, disappointment in a dashed opportunity. Such experiences leave me depressed, angry, and sad, in the depths of an emotional ditch.

Today, I am trying to decide whether or not I will crawl out of that ditch. Somewhere from childhood I hear my mother's voice: "Scott, you cannot always control your circumstances, but you can control your attitude." I bet she heard those words from her mother, too.

Old saw or not, it's true: I do have some control over how I will feel and act today. I can decide to crawl out of my ditch of despair or lie in my pain a while longer. I do have choices.

Granted, I have learned over the years that grief can only be healed by expressing my emotions and feeling my pain. I also know that I cannot rush this process. But there comes a time to get on with life and enter a bright new day.

Today, I'm going to find ways to clamber out of my ditch. I'll take a brisk walk, have lunch with a buddy, and clean off my messy desk. And if I have time, I'm going to do something good for somebody floundering in a ditch deeper than my own.

These are all things I can do today. Tomorrow will take care of itself.

Dear Father, give me the courage to make decisions. And grant me the strength to climb out of the ditch. Amen.
—SCOTT WALKER

If your brother is distressed because of what you eat, you are no longer acting in love. Do not by your eating destroy your brother for whom Christ died.
—ROMANS 14:15 (NIV)

*O*ne of my favorite snacks is gorp—a carryover from spending summers at camp in Maine. I now make this mixture for my children, adding some marshmallows and M&Ms to raisins and peanuts.

At a recent playdate, I set out a dish for the children. Within minutes, the mother of one young guest scooped up the dish and placed it out of reach. "I hope you don't mind," she explained, "but my daughter is highly allergic to peanuts."

Later that day, I was reading Romans 14, where Paul says not to argue over food. Apparently, it was common for first-century Jews and Gentiles to disagree over what foods were appropriate. But that was a long time ago, so these verses never seemed applicable to me. Now, one sentence really struck me: "If your brother is distressed because of what you eat, you are no longer acting in love." So if peanuts bother my daughter's friend, then we don't eat them around her, period.

Whether it's friends struggling with bad habits or neighbors dealing with temptations, there are plenty of places for me to double-check that my behavior isn't causing someone to stumble. I'm sure it was there in Romans 14 all along, but it took a little gorp for me to see past the peanuts.

Heavenly Father, thank You for the nuggets of truth hidden beneath the surface of Your Word.
—WENDY WILLARD

NOVEMBER 19

The Lord will be your everlasting light, and your God will be your glory.
—ISAIAH 60:19 (RSV)

*W*hether we get our biblically allotted three score and ten or a few years more or less, we're constantly reminded of our mortality.

In November 2001, North America was a prime viewing area for the Leonid meteor shower, dust particles from the comet Tempel-Tuttle that orbits the sun once every thirty-three years. To see this heavenly show, my wife Shirley and I set our alarm clock for 4:30 AM and went out on the dark Gulf of Mexico beach behind our house in Florida. There, under a breathtaking, starlit sky, we oohed and aahed as countless meteors, like diamonds on a string, flashed by in every direction. I'd never seen anything like it. One father was reported to have told his young son, "The stars are so happy, they're dancing." So it seemed.

Is it presumptuous of me to say that many of us who saw this meteor display will not be around for the next one in 2034? I think not. For those who believe that God made the heavens and earth and everything therein, that is not a troubling thought. His Word promises another life to follow. And just maybe those who aren't here to watch the next Leonid meteor shower will have an even better view from above.

Remind me, Lord, as your child, the best is yet to be,
In a heavenly promise named Eternity.
—FRED BAUER

November 20

Now faith is the substance of things hoped for, the evidence of things not seen.
—Hebrews 11:1

There were six or eight of us on the playground that day, and we decided we wanted to organize a game of football. The only problem was the football itself—we didn't have one. "I know," one of us said, "let's just pretend we do."

The game worked pretty well for a while. The quarterback would wind up, pretend to throw, and at the other end of the field one of us would jump up, pretend to make a catch, and dance around victoriously. Then, inevitably, arguments started up.

"Hey, you don't have the ball. I do."

"No you don't. I intercepted it!"

"Did not!"

"Did, too!"

Even at age nine, my friends and I were discovering that our imagination, which up until then had made the world such a magical and obliging place, was starting to let us down. Little did any of us know just how much worse it was going to get—that in adult life, wishing a thing were so won't work for even a second, much less the space of a few football plays.

Of course, I also didn't know then that when God brings us out of the innocence of childhood, He also gives us gifts to make up for what He takes away. I think the reason that moment on the playground still stays so fresh in my mind is that the faith I hold as an adult is both so like and so unlike that invisible football. For though faith can't be seen, and others may even doubt its existence altogether, it is in truth the most real and lasting thing I carry with me.

Dear God, help me remember that my faith rests on the rock of Your faithfulness.
—Ptolemy Tompkins

Weeping may endure for a night, but joy cometh in the morning.
—Psalm 30:5

*W*hen my grandmother died, unexpectedly and away from home, I experienced a deep feeling of loss and a lack of closure. She had always been there when I needed her. Now she was gone, and I hadn't been able to say good-bye. A few days after the funeral, my sister Debbie came across a letter Grandmother had written to me. It was a single handwritten page, with no indication of when it had been sent. But to me, the words seemed to have come from heaven.

> Dear Libbie,
>
> I miss all of you down there. Not that I'm lonely or homesick; every day is a good one. Everyone is so helpful and kind. Just remember, when you are blue or lonely, you are not alone. Just stop for a moment and thank God for all things as they are, for they are working out something beautiful in your life. You may not see it today, but tomorrow is coming, and the sun will rise and shine down your path. Keep sweet. God loves you, and I love you.
>
> Your grandmother

Neither Debbie nor I really knows when this letter was written. I think Grandmother sent it to me in 1981, while my husband, Larry, was away for a year on Okinawa with the US Navy. I have no memory of receiving it, and it doesn't matter now. What really matters is that God knew it would comfort me, and He saw that it was delivered right on time.

Father, You really do work in mysterious ways. Thank You for the wonders You perform in my life.
—Libbie Adams

NOVEMBER 22

It is a good thing to give thanks unto the Lord....
—PSALM 92:1

*I*t seems to take hours for everybody to get seated on Thanksgiving. The steaming mashed potatoes fog up people's glasses, the stuffing spills off the serving platter, the dish of cranberry sauce gets passed around, there's a request for salt and pepper from one end of the table—sometimes two tables in our cramped dining room. And then, something that's a tradition in our house: There's a clink of a spoon against a glass for silence. "Pam, do you want to start?" I ask. Pam, an old friend, is good at setting the mood.

"I'd like to say how grateful I am for my mother and what she gave me when I was growing up," she begins. The opportunity is passed around the table, just like that dish of cranberry sauce. From five-year-olds to ninety-five-year-olds, everyone gets to express what they're thankful for. The litany is wide-ranging, from a winning soccer season and the life of a pet rabbit to good health. Tears well up behind the fogged glasses. The teenagers roll their eyes at first, then rise in eloquence to the occasion. I start worrying that the succotash is growing cold and the pie will burn in the oven. But blessings must be said. We are a group of many faiths, and one or two with no declared faith at all. But thanksgiving runs deep.

Lord, I'm thankful for this day when thankfulness is on everyone's lips.
—RICK HAMLIN

NOVEMBER 23

...And another glory of the moon....
—I CORINTHIANS 15:41

Four children in as many years had transformed our house into a neighborhood zoo. But whenever the moon shone on a summer evening, God wooed us outside for an hour of "hush." We'd sit on our kitchen chairs and make up songs about the beautiful things He has made. Sometimes we danced slow twirls across the lawn. Our zoo became a peaceful little backyard chapel.

Years later, after we'd moved to Alaska, I was driving my teenage daughter Kelly home from volleyball practice down a deserted country road. We were both tired, but the bright moon lulled me to a stop along the roadside, and I switched off the van's headlights. Out of the stillness, Kelly quietly recited a line from Alfred Noyes's *The Highwayman*, a poem she'd memorized in sixth grade: "The road was a ribbon of moonlight over the purple moor...."

I was amazed Kelly still remembered the poem and that our wayside pause had prompted her to recite it. Complete contentment filled me. All that the moon meant to me—peacefulness, mystery, purity, loveliness—was present there. It was our backyard chapel all over again. The yard was bigger, and mother and daughter were older, but the God Who had spoken His serenity to me then still sounded exactly the same.

At day's end, Lord, when my soul needs quieting, You whisper
Your peace by the light of the moon.
—CAROL KNAPP

Blessed are all they that wait for him.
—ISAIAH 30:18

*G*ood morning, Father.

Today I have come perfectly prepared to spell out the needs of my friends and family—a young mother fighting depression, a challenging decision for Brock, traveling mercies for Keri, David's concern over our savings balance—and to give You some suggestions about how to answer those needs.

But now, considering just Who I stand before—the Great I AM, for Whom no words exist, the Creator Who spun our world into being and spread universes beyond universes in space—I step back in awe. It's time to abandon my "here's how You can best answer my prayers" instruction sheet.

Remember how, as a child, I always had my Christmas letter written and ready to go by the first of November? Inside the envelope was a carefully printed list of all the things I wanted. I'd walk out to the mailbox, slip the letter inside, put up the red flag, and that was that. Ahead was the anticipation of waiting until Christmas morning. I didn't worry a minute until then. Because, always, under the tree in the living room, the answer waited. Never exactly what I listed in the letter—always better.

I'm not going to worry today, Father, about the long list of concerns and hopes and needs I had planned to recite. You have already read them on my heart. So I let them go, send them straight to You. For once, they come with no instructions, because today I'm going to trust. Today, I'm going to take great pleasure in the anticipation of Your answers to my requests—never exactly what I included on my list—always better.

Amen.

—PAM KIDD

NOVEMBER 25

Casting all your anxiety upon Him....
—I Peter 5:7 (NAS)

*T*he branches of the fir tree scrape against the windowpane, needling me to get out of bed. It's a sure sign that a blizzard has blown in very early on this November morning. I look out the window where the only sign of life is a tardy flicker that missed fall migration. I feel helpless watching that beautiful bird scavenge in vain for berries among the vines. *What do flickers eat, anyway?*

I put on my parka and boots, drop some suet into a mesh bag, and scoop up some birdseed. As I push open the storm door, it scrapes away an arc of snow from the drift on the back step. Sinking deeper and deeper into the drifts, I plunge along to the bird feeder and then retrace my steps. Stamping the snow off my boots in the back entrance, I worry whether the flicker will be able to withstand the storm. Surely such weather will prompt it to fly south. If not, I hope it will eat the food I've put out for it.

As I turn on the radio, the morning disc jockey is cautioning his listeners to take the storm in stride. "Remember, folks, not everything in life is fixable, so don't sweat it." *He's right, Lord. There's nothing more I can do.*

While waiting for the blizzard to blow itself out, I make a big pot of coffee. And then during my quiet time, I mentally release that stormbound bird into the hands of God.

Lord, I waste so much time worrying over things I can't help. May I spend that energy carrying them to You in prayer.
—Alma Barkman

NOVEMBER 26

The Lord is my shepherd....
—PSALM 23:1

*L*ord, I am so *confused. My life seems like a series of accidents. I'm getting nowhere.*

I am the Shepherd. You are a lamb. It's not your job to know the way, but to follow Me. Through all the twists and turns, I am leading you in paths of righteousness. You'll see when you arrive.

But, Lord, I'm falling behind financially. Who's going to pay all these bills?

You shall not want. Your daily cup is running over. Remember when I fed you in the presence of your enemies? And the time I anointed your head with healing oil, when you were very ill? Trust Me, one day at a time.

But I'm getting older, God. Sometimes I wake in the night, thinking about dying.

Even when you walk through that dark valley, I will be there with you. I've already been through death, and I know the way. When you come out on the other side, it will be to dwell with Me in My house forever.

But I get so weary, Lord. So very tired.

I know, and I want you to lie down in green pastures. I can restore your soul, if you will give Me a chance. But you continue to worry and work as if I were not here, and as if everything depended on you alone.

Doesn't it?

Not at all. I am leading you for My name's sake, not because you are so wonderful. My name is "the Good Shepherd" and I intend to keep My good name by caring for you. It's what I do.

But I have so many regrets. Things I said and did that fill me with shame.

Just settle down. My goodness and mercy have been following you everywhere. I am healing those old wounds and cleaning up the messes you made. Leave the past—and the future—to Me. Pay attention to this day—it's the only one you have for sure.

Lord, help me to go forward in faith, knowing that You,
the Lord of all the times, are leading me on.
—DANIEL SCHANTZ

NOVEMBER 27

Jacob kissed Rachel, and lifted up his voice....
—GENESIS 29:11

M y friend's wife had passed away a year before. He still missed her deeply and liked to reminisce about the many years they'd had together.

"What I guess I miss most," he said one time, "are the little pats." When he saw I didn't understand, he explained, "She had a habit of touching me lightly whenever she passed. A few taps on my shoulder as I sat reading. A slight pressure on my arm as we stood waiting for a table in a restaurant. Little things that those around us didn't notice, but now I realize how much they meant to me. Because I know now that each touch was saying, 'I'm here, and I'm so glad you are here.'"

How wonderful and valuable are the little things we do for those we love! Small things, like words of encouragement, smiles, an unexpected hug, a touch to let them know how happy we are that they are a part of our life, that we depend on them, as they can depend on us. These tender reminders of our love mean much more than gifts of furs, jewels, or other material things. For gifts like these can't be bought. They are without price. They are the links that bind hearts and souls together.

God, let me recognize and appreciate the many small signs of
Your love for us all, and then pass them on.
—WALTER HARTER

There is no fear in love; but perfect love casteth out fear....
—I JOHN 4:18

My little son Geoffrey has a love-hate relationship with monsters. Also trolls, goblins, giants, and abominable snowmen. His fascination with terrifying beasts is a way of dealing with his fear of the unknown—the big scary grown-up world. I used to worry until I saw that he not only brings monsters to life in his mind, he conquers them too.

Here's how. He learns everything about one monster, reads books on it, decorates his room with pictures of it. Then when the monster is conjured up in all its glorious fearsomeness, Geoffrey climbs into my lap and says, "I'm scared."

"Okay," I say. "Here's what we can do." And we both think of ways that the monster can be caught, vanquished, banished by force, by trickery, or by simply repeating the words, "Go away. You aren't real." And we say a little prayer: "God, chase the monster out of my head." Then Geoffrey takes down the pictures and piles up the books to be returned to the library. With my help, he's tamed this monster—until the next one comes along.

The system works for any monster-sized worry. The next time you are overwhelmed with anxiety, visualize your worst fears; write down their names. Facing your fears directly actually makes them less terrifying than pretending that they don't exist. Having named them, you can work to conquer them. One way is to use prayer as a weapon. Ask God to turn those fearsome monsters aside.

Right now.

> *Dear God: I have monstrous fears. They are _____ and_____ . Chase them from my mind and heart.*
> —LINDA CHING SLEDGE

NOVEMBER 29

For in him [God] we live, and move, and have our being....
—ACTS 17–28

*M*ost of us are disturbed when someone we know commits suicide. It's not a comfortable subject to talk about, I know, but it's becoming increasingly prevalent in our society, especially among our young. Not long ago I went to see a longtime ailing friend, who smiled and said, "I want to say good-bye—I won't be here the next time you come." True to her word, an hour later she was taken to the hospital as a result of an overdose of sleeping pills. She never regained consciousness.

After someone close commits suicide, it's hard to know what to do. There are so many questions: "Since the Lord brought us into the world, shouldn't only He take us out?" or "Why weren't our love and caring enough to prevent this?" I had these very thoughts when my friend died, and after a lot of soul searching and grief, I finally asked myself what I could do now that she was gone. And then I understood that out of love for my friend, there was only one thing I could do to commemorate her: *to continue to affirm life vigilantly.* Affirm my own life—by taking care of my health. Affirm the lives of friends and family—by loving and listening. Affirm all life—by giving, by reaching out to help shoulder a fragment of the overwhelming burden of the world's pain and sorrow.

No, I know I can never bring back my lost friend. But I can join the never-ending struggle for goodness and life. And, with ever-present gratitude, take the best possible care of my Creator's gift of life to me.

Lord, in the face of sorrow and sadness, we say yes to Your gift.
—SAM JUSTICE

NOVEMBER 30

Let this mind be in you, which was also in Christ Jesus: who, being in the form of God, thought it not robbery to be equal with God: but made himself of no reputation, and took upon him the form of a servant....

—PHILIPPIANS 2:5–7

The first glimpses of Christmas in New York bring me great angst. Lights and wreaths and ribbons start sneaking out well before Thanksgiving and the heralded arrival of Santa, courtesy of Macy's. My mind overflows with obligations and worries. I find myself turning away from that initial splash of red and green and wishing it was still the red, white, and blue of July Fourth when the year still held such promise!

But I have an antidote. It's a memory from a December day the year after I graduated from college. In the grip of wanderlust, I had gone south, through the Caribbean to Central and South America. I was picking my way through a bustling little marketplace high in the Ecuadorian Andes at the far edge of the northern hemisphere. Natives had traveled many rugged miles to display their wares on blankets and in makeshift stalls, as they had been doing for centuries.

Beneath a tree at the edge of the market I saw what looked to be an old baby doll resting in a pile of straw and cloth, almost as if a child had abandoned her toy. When I looked closer, I noticed a crude wooden cross stuck in the dirt and a plain box, which my companion explained was for donations for the needy. No blinking lights, no jolly St. Nicks, no midnight madness sales. Not even the figures of Mary and Joseph or the wise men. Just the Christ Child and the simple message that He was among us.

I didn't know at the time how persistent a memory it would become, that simplest of Nativity scenes in the Andean marketplace. But today, when the frenzy of this season gets to me here in New York, I think back to it and consider what it said to me.

Lord, You came among us in humbleness so that we would be humbled. In the celebration of Your birth, I will not forget that.

—EDWARD GRINNAN

December

DECEMBER 1

O Lord, open thou my lips: and my mouth shall show forth thy praise.
—PSALM 51:15

*T*he letter came on the stationery of a pottery barn in Vermont. "You probably won't remember me," the woman wrote, "but I want to thank you for your part in launching this business."

I read on in bewilderment. A pottery business in Vermont? We'd met, the letter continued, at the Mohonk Mountain House some years ago. I remembered the occasion very well—a Wildflower Weekend at a nature preserve in upstate New York. But there had been eighty or more flower enthusiasts taking part, and I didn't recall this particular woman.

She, however, remembered a remark of mine on one of the guided walks. The leader had pointed out a cluster of bluets at the edge of the woods that, unlike their vigorous cousins carpeting the meadow, were stunted and colorless. "They just got started in the wrong place," he said. And I, apparently, had commented, "It's a good thing people can pick up and move."

"Your words were like a shaft of light in a dark place," the woman wrote. Miserable in a desk job in the city, she'd eventually sold her condo, moved to Vermont, and turned her ceramics hobby into a full-time business.

All this, I wondered, from a throwaway remark I can't remember making? But of course, mine was just a tiny piece in a design only God saw whole. The plan for her life was His, that shaft of light on her path, His words to her alone. The significance of my comment was beyond my knowing. What I do know, what this letter tells me, is that the role each of us is given to play in the lives around us is greater than we dream.

Remind me during the year ahead, Father, that You can reach out to
Your children through anyone at all . . . even me.
—ELIZABETH SHERRILL

December 2

He has sent me to proclaim release to the captives and . . . to set at liberty those who are oppressed. . . ."
—LUKE 4:18 (RSV)

*T*he wall clock was ticking away my father's life.

I was a helpless twenty-one-year-old, sitting by the white mounded bed that was slowly swallowing his great body into that sea, or heaven, where independent oil operators go when all the wells are dry and the last field pump has ceased.

And then the pump seemed to come alive, in a frenzy to get the last drop out of life. He groaned, and a hooded Sister of Charity appeared from nowhere and took his ham-like hand. "Can you hear me?" she said gently.

"Umm." He nodded, his eyes still closed.

"Have you ever accepted Jesus as your Savior?"

He shook his head slightly.

"Would you like to?"

Silence.

As he decided, my mind flew back down the years to our childhood Depression dining table: my eyes wide as Father took us on imaginary flights to Paris, the Grand Canyon, Hollywood—places he'd take us really "when our ship comes in!" But the ship of hope he'd seen so vividly had disappeared in a gray fog of unpayable bills and unspeakable fears.

"Do you accept Jesus as your Savior now?" the soft angel voice of the sister said.

"Oh, yes, I do!" he whispered, nodding, much to my surprise. Then he sat up in bed, wide-eyed with wonder.

"I see a ship!" he said.

And then he fell back and disappeared from my life and sailed into the "otherwise" with Jesus.

Lord, thank You for reaching out, past doubt and failure, to take our hands and lead us home across the sunset waters. Amen.

—KEITH MILLER

December 3

For how great is his goodness, and how great is his beauty!...
—ZECHARIAH 9:17

I've always loved to travel, but I haven't been able to for the last few years. My friend Sue McCully, on the other hand, has always dreamed of traveling, but didn't have the chance until she recently retired from teaching school.

Sue's face was radiant as she described her adventures. "In England, I saw the beautiful white cliffs of Dover. Pilots returning from dangerous missions during World War II said they always knew they were safely home when they saw those gleaming cliffs."

"On our trip to the Holy Land," she whispered, "I walked where Jesus had walked and I prayed where He had prayed. I saw the olive trees and the pomegranates that the Bible speaks about. Oh, it was all so wonderful, so beautiful!" She paused, closed her eyes briefly, and then continued. "In Greece, I relived the second journey of Paul, and in Rome, I had an opportunity to see St. Peter's Church."

Sue's most recent trip was to Colorado, where she sat, warm and snug, before a floor-length hotel window and admired the crystalline brilliance of winter glistening in the snow. "Many people were sledding, and on a distant pond, I could see others ice skating. But I wasn't about to risk my old bones on any of that! So I sat and marveled at the loveliness of it all. And then we were almost home again. The automobile carrying us covered familiar ground, and soon we were crossing the Tennessee River. Then we turned into the driveway of my house and there was the sweet sense of love awaiting me inside the front door."

She reached for my hand and we two sat very still, each in her own heart thanking our wonderful Lord for the beauty He's given His people.

Father, You have so generously blessed us, including those who go and then return to tell the stay-at-homes so that all may rejoice in Your lovingkindness. Amen.
—DRUE DUKE

DECEMBER 4

The inward man is renewed day by day.
—II CORINTHIANS 4:16

The morning before my birthday, I stand in line under the big renewal sign at the Department of Motor Vehicles. I've been whisked through the eye test, had a photo snapped so quickly it felt like an ambush, and now find myself in a bit of a bottleneck waiting for a clerk to certify the paperwork and take my check.

I keep thinking about that word *renewal*. It seems an unlikely description of the process a dozen of us are going through, moving sleepily from station to station (we're the ones who are convinced that the earlier we get here, the faster we'll be out), studying the newspaper and sipping coffee from Styrofoam cups.

The older I get, the more I think of my birthday as an unwanted reminder of the inexorable aging process. I glance at my four-year-old license picture. Not a bad shot, I muse. As a rule I am very critical of myself in photos, a kind of reverse vanity. Four years from now, will I look at the ambush photo taken today and think, *Not bad?*

The thought strikes me: *When I look at my life today, when it counts most, can I help but think, Not bad?* Things have changed in the past four years, certainly, and most of what has come to pass couldn't have been foreseen when I last stood here in the DMV renewal line. And life will change more in the four years to come. But today, standing in this line on a gray, sleepy morning, waiting for a free clerk, I can't help but feel grateful for God's careful guidance and for what I believe is my increasing awareness of it. In that respect, I know I am different. I am four years closer to God.

I look up again at the sign that says renewal and smile. Not bad.

Lord, in Your presence my life is a process of rebirth in You.
—EDWARD GRINNAN

"For the Son of man also came not to be served but to serve...."
—MARK 10:45 (RSV)

*A*ccording to a friend who is a member, a local church, St. George's, recently had a debate about their budget for the new year. Instead of giving the receipts from their annual rummage sale to the town's soup kitchen, some people wanted to use the proceeds to carpet the sanctuary. One of the old-timers said those favoring new carpet needed to remember the church's mission. Then he told them this story.

Because they lived on a dangerous coastline, the villagers of Rockymoor constructed a hut on the shore and bought a boat to go to sea whenever a ship went down and sailors needed rescuing. Over the years many lives were saved, and the little outpost became famous. They bought bigger boats and constructed a larger building, which became a sort of clubhouse for members. But gradually the members tired of going to sea and risking their lives, so they hired trained crews to do the rescuing. And that sufficed until one day a large shipwreck occurred and the crews brought many cold, dirty, half-drowned survivors to the clubhouse. Afterward the place was a mess.

"I think we need to build a shower outside to clean up the victims before we bring them in," one member suggested. "Otherwise, we're going to ruin the place, and who will want to be part of our club?" An argument about priorities ensued, and eventually the organization split in two. About half the members went down the way and built another lifesaving station. It was a ramshackle place, and they were short of equipment and expertise, but the rescuers were dedicated and they saved lots of lives. Their operation grew and became famous, and they enlarged their building and formed a club, and...

What did St. George's do? They decided to forego new carpet this year, at least, in favor of the soup kitchen. The vote was 47 to 42.

In the new year, Lord, alert me when I forget my true mission:
To bring Your bidding to loving fruition.
—FRED BAUER

December 6

*"He will be great, and will be called the Son of the Most High . . .
and of his kingdom there will be no end."*
—Luke 1:32–33 (RSV)

*T*he journey that began the December night I received my child's frightening medical news continued into the next summer. One evening I was sitting at the end of a dock beside a clear mountain lake. A few last rays from the setting sun tinted the scattered clouds, which earlier had brought a light rain. I was praying yet again for my child. Suddenly, I flung my open arms to the sky and spoke to Jesus with complete conviction: "If You have allowed it, then I can trust it." It was my way of giving up my child to Him—of giving up my desire to say how this should end.

No sooner had I spoken than a magnificent rainbow formed right before my eyes, filling the sky with color. I wanted to leap into the air and run under that rainbow, treading the clouds. I still had no answer for our family's crisis, but I had hope.

Six months later, after another Christmas celebration of the miracle of the Christ Child, our own child received miraculous news of perfect health!

Even in the dark times, Mary had a hope anchored in that first angelic promise, "Of his kingdom there shall be no end." I believe this hope supported her from the flight into Egypt clear to the foot of the Cross. For all her joy in holding her Bethlehem baby, I picture her most keenly—even at Christmas—rushing into the outstretched arms of her risen Son.

*Jesus, You give such hope and power and purpose to Your people! The tiny flailing
fists of Bethlehem have become the strong arms of my salvation.*

—Carol Knapp

DECEMBER 7
PEARL HARBOR DAY

*And thou shalt rejoice in every good thing which the Lord thy God
hath given unto thee....*
—DEUTERONOMY 26:11

ny of us old enough to remember December 7, 1941, can tell you exactly where we were—in what room, with what people—when President Roosevelt's voice came over the radio with the news that the Japanese had attacked Pearl Harbor. My father called us into the kitchen where radio reception was best: my mother, my nine-year-old sister, my eleven-year-old brother, and me, age thirteen. I remember my sister's round, frightened eyes watching Daddy's face.

"Daddy," she whispered, "are we in the war now?"

We'd heard about the war for a long time. For two years newspapers and newsreels had shown terrifying pictures of the fighting in Europe and Asia. We'd flattened our tin cans and rolled the tinfoil from our chewing gum into silver balls for our armament factories. Every week my Girl Scout troop had baked brownies to raise money for Bundles for Britain. But the war was far away, fought in places with strange names by people none of us knew.

My father looked around at us all before answering.

"We've always been in the war," he said at last. "Any war is our war."

Any war? Anywhere? Ours, too? A mysterious, unseen connection between us and everyone else? I didn't know then that this was a God sighting—perhaps my first intimation that there was a God. We were not a religious family. Years later when I learned the prayer that begins "Our Father," I remembered Daddy's words: "Any war is our war." And I knew the reason why every person's suffering is also mine.

Father of us all, help me to love the brothers and sisters I have not seen.
—ELIZABETH SHERRILL

DECEMBER 8

*T*here is a place in New York City that I never go to, or merely pass by, without my spirit being renewed: the massive marble edifice of the New York Public Library at Fifth Avenue and Forty-second Street. It's not that I remember the exhilaration of some successful research I've accomplished there, or the pleasure gained from any number of special exhibitions I've visited. No, I refer to those two stalwart guardians flanking the front steps, on duty in summer's heat and winter's cold, twenty-four hours a day: two majestic concrete lions.

The lions and I go back to the days when I was a student in college. I would come to the library for special reading and occasionally take a break in the sunshine on the steps outside. I would see them lying there, two creatures at ease, their tails quiet and their front paws stretched out before them, with heads held high and a look of satisfaction approaching a smile on their faces. They were not intimidating, but they were not a child's plaything. They had dignity.

"They seem almost alive," I mused to a fellow nearby, one of many taking the sun for one reason or another.

"They are alive," he replied. "They're alive for me, at any rate. They're here to give me hope. And they have, repeatedly." He pointed to each lion and introduced me. "This one is Fortitude and that one is Patience."

Now, whenever I see a bird alighting on one of the lions' heads, I see that the lion doesn't mind. One Christmas years ago someone set fire to the wreaths around their necks, but the lions retained their composure. (Fortunately, after years without them, the wreaths are back.) And whenever I am near the library, no matter my frame of mind, I look and am invigorated by the fortitude of David and the patience of Job given me by my two friends of the lion heart.

Lord, protect these sculptures as though they were truly beasts of the earth.
—VAN VARNER

DECEMBER 9

Then Joseph being raised from sleep did as the angel of the Lord
had bidden him, and took unto him his wife.
—MATTHEW 1:24

*I*n my early twenties I wrote a Christmas play that was published in a
magazine. Shortly thereafter I received a phone call from a Sunday
school superintendent. "We would like our junior high group to put on your
play and we're wondering if you'd direct it for us."

I'd never directed anything in my life and Christmas was only six weeks
away. But the superintendent said that they would get the costumes and assign
the parts. All I had to do was show up.

I did. And what I found terrified me: fifteen seventh and eighth graders
jumping over benches, throwing paper airplanes, shouting, laughing. The
rehearsal was abysmal. The kids wouldn't settle down. Joseph, a big guy with
flaming red hair, was the ringleader. Clowning, making faces, he egged the
others on. The only one who was serious about her part was Mary, a sweet,
brown-eyed girl with long hair.

"If these kids don't settle down, we're not going to be able to do the play," I
said to the other teachers at the end of the evening.

"Let's pray," the superintendent said. So, forming a circle and holding
hands, she led us in a prayer for a miracle.

Two more awful rehearsals passed. But each time the superintendent said,
"Let's pray. God can work a miracle."

And He did. At the fourth rehearsal, Joseph was transformed. He'd fallen
in love with Mary. Shuffling and awkward, he gazed adoringly at her and she
at him.

We'd asked for a miracle; we got one. But as so often happens, God made it
out of what was already there: a boy, a girl, and adolescent hormones.

Lord, thank You for answers to prayer that sneak up on us from right under
our noses. Just like the first Christmas.
—SHARI SMYTH

Good tidings of great joy, which shall be to all people.
—LUKE 2:10

*L*ast Christmas my wife, Joy, and I wanted to plan a family trip. Our boys were twenty-three, twenty-one, and nineteen, and we figured we might not have many more Christmases when we were all together. I assumed the boys would want to go skiing as we had often done before, but when we asked them, they said in unison, "Let's go to the beach!"

"The beach? How could you have Christmas at the beach?" I grumbled. But my objections were drowned out by a trio that soon became a quartet as Joy reverted to her Southern California upbringing. So I asked some well-traveled friends where we should go for sun, sand, and adventure.

We finally hit on Ambergris Cay, an island off the coast of Belize in Central America. Warm sun, beautiful reefs for snorkeling, trips to the mainland to see Mayan ruins, crocodiles and monkeys...it sounded like fun, but not like Christmas, so on the plane trip down, I read the Christmas story in all four Gospels, trying to find a way to connect beaches with Bethlehem.

Ambergris Cay was a paradise. On our first night we walked to town to find dinner, and Nathan pointed to a big sign by a restaurant door: NO SHIRT, NO SHOES? NO PROBLEM! "See, Dad," he said, "they'll take anybody here, even wackos who wish they were skiing!"

Nathan's words brought to mind a phrase from Luke's Gospel: "Good tidings of great joy, which shall be to all people." Like the restaurant, Jesus takes anybody. A bunch of guys smelling like sheep at the door? Great, send them in. A grumpy Minnesotan pining for snow? That's okay, Jesus will give him six days of love and laughter with the most precious people in his world and hope he gets the message that Christmas is about people and not places.

*Lord, thank You for coming into the world in a way all of us
can take into our hearts and make our own.*
—ERIC FELLMAN

DECEMBER 11

A plane slid off the runway." My sister Lori's voice was tense. "I'm watching it right now on TV." It wasn't our parents' plane, but the winter storm would only worsen by the time theirs left for Bermuda. My sister, still fixated on the jetliner perched precariously at the runway's end, said what we were both thinking. "It's a sign."

We were very big on signs in my family. We always searched for a sign when making important—or not-so-important—decisions, from which college to attend to whether the car would make it home without stopping for gas. Of course, we were convinced these signs came right from God.

Now, Lori and I feared the runway mishap was a sign that our parents shouldn't go. Six hours later, I was convinced of it as I hung up the phone after hearing from airport operations that my parents' plane was still on the runway, three hours behind schedule.

Didn't they see that plane go off the runway? I fumed frantically to myself. *Why don't they just come home?*

To pass the time before I called the airline again, I began thinking about signs. True, our family had always relied on them, but had we only sought those we expected? While panicking over the skidded plane, I'd not considered any number of other signs, like the professional, helpful airline staffers who'd been calm and informative every time I'd called. Or that my parents had driven to the airport without mishap. Or that no one on the "de-runwayed" plane had been injured. Or even God's presence with me now.

I dialed the airline number again, but before I could even say hello, the customer service representative said, "Marci, they're in the air!"

Lord, help me remember that You ask me to walk by faith,
and not by sight—or signs.
—MARCI ALBORGHETTI

For he that is mighty hath done to me great things....
—LUKE 1:49

*J*enny is an unprepossessing child. Shy, awkward, a little ungainly, she seemed an unlikely choice for Mary in the church Christmas pageant. No parent was heard to complain, but then our pageant has always had its casting irregularities (including the boy who insisted on playing a camel one year).

That morning, there was the usual display of nerves and high spirits, the flashing of cameras, the last-minute tweaking of a halo, the mouthing of a well-rehearsed line. I went to my spot in the gallery to watch. The Annunciation came early in the pageant. A teenaged boy wearing sneakers underneath his white robe told Mary that she would bear the Baby Jesus. Jenny, dressed in blue, walked down the center aisle and responded, "My soul doth magnify the Lord, and my spirit hath rejoiced in God my Saviour" (Luke 1:46–47).

Jenny's voice was strong and confident, filling the church. Her diction was crystal clear. To my amazement and to everyone else's, she went on, "For he hath regarded the low estate of his handmaiden...." She was going to recite all ten verses of Luke's Song of Mary (1:46–55). We sat on the edge of our pews. Before our eyes, Jenny was transformed from a nine-year-old wallflower to a brave, commanding soul. Never missing a beat, she made her way through the entire speech. When she was finished, the congregation burst into spontaneous applause.

Better than any preacher, Jenny had given us the message of that moment. God could take a young peasant girl and make her the mother of His Son. God could transform a life into something awe-inspiring.

Take my life, Lord, and let it be changed by You.
—RICK HAMLIN

DECEMBER 13

Then the shepherds went back again to their fields ... praising God for
the visit of the angels, and because they had seen the child....
—LUKE 2:20 (TLB)

id you put up a tree?" my sister Amanda asked when we visited by telephone the week before Christmas.

"Don did. And, yes, it's a six-footer." My husband, Don, and I have argued over tree size for thirty-eight years, the length of our marriage. Our family can tell by the size who chose the tree. "My other decorations are up, too, such as they are. I envy those talented people who carry out a Christmas theme!"

"I have a theme," Amanda said. "It's called 'Early Attic.'"

"Since I don't have an attic, I guess my theme is 'Terribly Tacky,'" I responded.

Later, I walked around the house and studied the decorations. The Nativity on the piano was made from cornshucks, not porcelain, but it reminded me of the stable and the humble surroundings of Christ's birth. The cut-tin candleholder came from our church bazaar and shone as brightly as the star over Bethlehem. And the ornate stick-on window Nativity (number seven in a magazine list of "Ten Trashiest Decorations") had stunning colors that brought to mind the rich gifts of the wise men.

Then there was the tree, which even at six feet could barely contain all the ornaments. We bought the tree-top star the Christmas after we married; we were in North Carolina, miles from friends and family. Michael's and Rebecca's Sunday school craft projects adorned the lower branches. Halfway up was the plaster-of-Paris bell Patrick made in kindergarten; it hung right above paper decorations made by his three sons.

I didn't need talent or creativity or more money. I didn't even need a theme, because I already had one: Jesus. The ornaments and decorations are merely reminders of Him and His love. I looked over my beautiful Christmas house one more time, then went to the telephone to call Amanda.

Jesus, help me to remember it's You I'm celebrating this and every Christmas!
—PENNEY SCHWAB

Seek that ye may excel to the edifying of the church.
—I CORINTHIANS 14:12

I had a mild case of the Christmas "blahs." Preparing for Christmas at home and at our ministry, Mission Mississippi, was getting me down. I wouldn't have minded sleeping right through till December 26.

Then, two days before Christmas, my telephone rang; on the other end was my friend Shelby. "Dolphus," he said, "do you know a place where my family and I could go to help on Christmas morning? We would love to serve at a homeless shelter or help someone working with the poor." Shelby and his wife have two sons and a daughter; perhaps they were looking forward to Christmas at home, so I asked him if he was sure this was what he wanted to do.

"Yes, Dolphus," he answered, "we all really want to do this."

I hung up the phone and thought for a few minutes. Then I began to call people I knew until I found a mission in Jackson that needed volunteers. I called Shelby back and gave him the news. "Praise the Lord!" he said. "We'll have the privilege of serving others this Christmas rather than concentrating on ourselves. And it will be a great opportunity for us to teach our children about the real meaning of Christmas."

Shelby and his family were reaching out with more than a dollar in the kettle or a check to a charity—as good as those gifts are—to share food and their own presence with the hungry. What a beautiful way of "doing Christmas"! And not only were they helping the people they'd be serving, they had helped me, too, by the example of their caring.

Lord, help me to take my eyes off of myself and to seek ways to remember Your special gift—Your Son.
—DOLPHUS WEARY

December 15

Now when this was noised abroad, the multitude came together, and were confounded, because that every man heard them speak in his own language.
—ACTS 2:6

I was twenty-two years old, I had just graduated from college, and I was spending the year in Italy teaching English as a foreign language. For Christmas I visited a French family who had been friends with my family in California for years. I was so thrilled with the sights of Paris and so proud of my independence that I don't remember being particularly homesick. It was only on Christmas Eve that I wished that I could be flown home for just a few minutes, to sing carols at our half-timbered church, to embrace my old high school friends beneath the palm trees outside, to worship in a familiar way.

My French family were Huguenots, part of the Protestant church that dates back to John Calvin in the 1500s, and on Christmas Eve we went to their small church in a Parisian suburb. There were a hundred people there at most, with no choir, and an organ that wheezed and squawked through the hymns. Worst of all, I struggled to comprehend the French of the service, always finding myself stuck on a phrase, translating in my head as the rest of the congregation moved forward.

For Communion we stood in a circle and passed the elements one to another. The papa of the family (as I called him) was on my right, and when he turned to me with the wine, saying, *"Le sang de Dieu, eh?"* I suddenly understood. Yes, this was the mystery of faith, as hard to translate as a page of Proust, and yet completely comprehensible when it was shared between two who believed in Him. "The blood of Christ" was a concept as clear as day in Papa's foreign tongue.

God, give me understanding.
—RICK HAMLIN

December 16

The darkness and the light are both alike to thee.
—PSALM 139:12

*A*fter the bad news came, I went outside and took my usual path through the woods, not headed anywhere, too stunned to pray or even to cry. Someone dear to me had died, needlessly, senselessly, and the shock was like a physical blow.

Before, in times of great stress, the woods had spoken to me of a world of beauty and serenity, far removed from the ugliness we humans create. That morning no such comfort came. On the contrary, the peace of the woods seemed an affront to the cruel realities of life. The fluttering leaves, the silly chirping birds, were irrelevant to human suffering.

I glanced up through the branches at the blue, uncaring sky and stopped short. High above me, the upper trunk of the tree was split in two. One of the halves ended in a jagged stump, perhaps the result of a long-ago lightning strike, while new branches from the surviving half filled in the empty space. Slowly I walked on. A few yards farther, the heart of a chestnut oak was eaten away with disease, a thin outer layer soaring skyward around a hollow core. Here insects had left a gall wound, there a branch was missing. Everywhere I looked were signs of trauma and loss. But all these were living trees, drawing life from the sun, giving it back as food, oxygen, shelter.

It was far from the time when my own wound would grow a protective shell. Farther still until I could turn my healing into help for others. But what I'd seen that morning was loss and gain, not as opposites, but as the seamless fabric of life itself.

Father, help me also to see the dark threads as part of Your design,
and so learn to trust You in all things.
—ELIZABETH SHERRILL

DECEMBER 17

"For to the snow he says, 'Fall on the earth'... that all men may know his work."
—JOB 37:6–7 (RSV)

*O*ne Sunday afternoon in December our church holds its annual Bethlehem Day. With temperatures in the seventies in Arizona, we turn the courtyard outside the sanctuary into our idea of old Bethlehem. Families enjoy Christmas music and cookies while little costumed shepherds and angels tromp on the straw-covered ground from one craft booth to the next, making star-shaped candles or a clothespin Baby Jesus in a wooden manger.

The day is usually sunny and bright, but a few years ago an uncharacteristically blustery morning had turned cold by afternoon. And as my little daughter Maria and her Sunday school choir rehearsed "Away in a Manger," I looked out the windows of the choir room in delighted shock. A soft, wet snow was falling, blanketing Bethlehem Day in dazzling white.

"It's snowing!" someone shouted, and folks ran to the windows and then outside, giddy at this incredible sight. It's hard to say who was more excited, the kids or the grown-ups, as we stood with our arms outstretched, heads tilted toward the sky, and mouths open, literally drinking in God's wonderful surprise. The snow in Phoenix lasted only a short time, but it brought a joy that carried well beyond the day.

Christmas began with a wonderful surprise from God, too. The world awaited its Messiah, but no one expected a tiny baby to be the One. Christ's actual birth was a small moment, unnoticed by all but a few shepherds. But the joy He brought into the world is everlasting. And unlike our once-in-a-lifetime desert snowfall, Christ comes again and again—each year at Christmas, and every time we invite Him into our hearts.

Come, Lord Jesus, as I stand with my arms outstretched, ready to welcome You.
—GINA BRIDGEMAN

DECEMBER 18

Blessed be God, even the Father of our Lord Jesus Christ, the Father of mercies, and the God of all comfort; who comforteth us in all our tribulations....
—II CORINTHIANS 1:3–4

*H*eavy snow was falling that night as we drove toward New York City. John's father had died of a heart attack an hour earlier. *What can we possibly say to Mother at such a time?* we wondered in the midst of our own shock.

She met us at the door to their apartment at Union Theological Seminary where Dad taught. After dinner that evening, she told us, they'd gone for a walk in the snow. Two hours later, Dad complained of pain in his chest. The doctor had arrived too late. We groped for words of comfort, but none came. At last, feeling that we'd failed her, we went to bed.

The following morning the doorbell rang at seven. Standing in the hallway was Reinhold Niebuhr. A fellow professor at Union, this renowned theologian was well-versed in the mysteries of life and death. He would be able to put into words all that we could not. A minute passed. Two minutes, while my expectation mounted. "Well, Helen," he said—the very first words he had uttered. Silence fell again. Five minutes...ten full minutes had elapsed, and still this gifted preacher had not shared his words of wisdom.

After fifteen minutes, the stillness of the room began to seep inside me until a wordless communion seemed to enfold us all. When the clock chimed the half hour, Dr. Niebuhr stood up and let himself out. And still John and Mother and I sat silent. Not until the undertakers arrived just before eight did any of us speak, and then only to deal with the logistics of death. Later John and I would find the words of love and honoring that need to be spoken in their time. For now, though, it was enough that we were there.

We had learned the power of silence from one of the great speakers of our century. Niebuhr had not come with words, no matter how lofty. He had brought instead the best, the costliest thing one person can give to another. He had brought himself.

Thank You, Lord, that You are Emmanuel—God with us.
—ELIZABETH SHERRILL

Thou openest thine hand, and satisfiest the desire of every living thing.
—PSALM 145:16

*T*he Paris doctor warned us that the baby would never reach full term. In fact, he said my own life could be in danger. And so, after three years of roaming Europe as travel writers, John and I hurried home to the specialist my anxious family had located in New York, only to confront a second crisis. Two major New York newspapers had recently folded; scores of expert writers were out of work. Every job John applied for had been filled. Doctors' bills were mounting and the one resource we had, our writing experience, was worth nothing. The one resource, that is, that we knew about. We had yet to experience the sustaining power of God.

Our anxiety had reached the desperation point when John found a stop-gap job. Just until something better turned up, he was to be a reporter for a little sixteen-page religious pamphlet named *Guideposts*. "Religious?" I asked incredulously. "Did you tell them we don't go to church or anything?" He had, but the editor, a man named Len LeSourd, had simply smiled. "God has a plan for you, John, no matter how hard you try to hide."

The baby was born, full-term and healthy—our son John Scott, now a grown man. And John and I were launched on the biggest travel adventure of all: the journey of the spirit.

Father, give us faith to trust in Your provisions all along the way.
—ELIZABETH SHERRILL

"He has helped his servant Israel . . . as he spoke to our fathers. . . ."
—LUKE 1:54–55 (RSV)

*I*t must have been difficult for Mary to share her newborn son so soon after He arrived, but the shepherds were right there on her doorstep within hours. From the beginning, Jesus belonged far beyond Mary's little family. He had come as Savior of the world!

On my dresser I used to have a small brown ceramic plaque with 1939 on the back. On the front, precise block lettering read *Jesus Never Fails*. Squeezed beneath that was a portion of Hebrews 13:5, "I will never leave thee, nor forsake thee." I learned about the plaque from my aunt, my father's sister, who mentioned it to me at his graveside. He had given it to her when she miscarried her first baby.

Several years later, after my aunt's death, I asked her daughter if I might have the plaque. I greatly treasured it as something that came from my father's heart. Sometimes I would trace the lettering with my fingers and pretend I was reaching back in time to touch my dad.

Then the cousin who had given me the plaque lost her son in an accident. It seemed only right that this gift, given by my father to her mother years ago, should pass from me to her and again offer its comfort.

I finally sent the plaque just before Christmas. I remember sitting in front of our Christmas tree holding that little package in the palm of my hand and crying until the Christmas lights became a blur. I was crying because I knew I had to give it up—and for my cousin's pain. But mostly I was crying for all the generations of my family's tears.

Then I thought of the shared faith in Christ that I knew ran far back in our heritage. Deeper than our individual or collective sorrow was that River of Life flowing through the tears. And that faith—not the plaque that was merely one of its expressions—was what I needed to hang on to.

Oh, God, thank You for sharing Your very self with me in Jesus.
—CAROL KNAPP

DECEMBER 21

Now the God of patience and consolation grant you to be likeminded
one toward another according to Christ Jesus.

—ROMANS 15:5

You know something that sends up my blood pressure? It's being put on hold and kept there for long periods when I'm trying to conduct business over the phone. Recently when I called to make an airline reservation, I was placed on hold for a full eight minutes (I timed it by the clock). Later I described to a friend how I had sat there listening to that awful canned music while the heat in my veins slowly rose to a boil.

My friend heard me out, then said, "I used to react the same way, until I came up with the idea of *holding-pattern prayers.*" She went on to explain that when she's placed on hold now, she begins by praying for the overworked person on the other end of the line. If the waiting continues, she progresses to prayers for friends and family. "The time speeds by," she concluded, "when you spend it with the Lord."

Since then I've tried her technique and it helps not only my blood pressure, but my prayer life as well. The next time you're put on hold, maybe you'd like to try some holding-pattern prayers.

No matter when I call You, Father, You're always ready to listen.
—MADGE HARRAH

DECEMBER 22

Thou shalt love thy neighbor as thyself....
—LEVITICUS 19:18

*E*arly on a Saturday morning at the start of winter, my husband and I woke up in a lovely, old-fashioned bed-and-breakfast room. We were due at a prayer breakfast in what seemed a very short time. I took the plunge, jumped out of bed, and ran over to the window. There was snow—lots of it—and our car, parked beneath the window, looked like an igloo. "Edward, get up," I urged. "We don't even have a scraper."

We began to get ready in disgruntled haste, not at all the right frame of mind for gathering to pray. And I was responsible for the opening words. Suddenly, I heard an odd rhythmic noise, like a distant lawn mower. Hairbrush in hand, I walked over to the window. There below me was the hooded figure of a fellow guest whose acquaintance we had made only briefly the night before. As quietly as he could, he was cleaning the snow off our car windows. He had already finished his own car parked next to ours.

I drew a deep breath as I let the curtain fall into place. Someone, almost a stranger, without fuss was smoothing our path that early morning. Scraper in hand, he was loving his neighbor in practical fashion. Clearly he planned to drive off unseen. I had no difficulty with that day's opening prayer, entitled, as it happened, "For Others."

Dear God, bless those who care for others in so many ways
and ask for no reward.
—BRIGITTE WEEKS

Blessed are they that put their trust in him.
—PSALM 2:12

Neither of us wanted to love or trust the other. We'd both been hurt too deeply. Yet we stood there staring at each other, each of us ready to turn and run. Total strangers, we had met unexpectedly. I made the first move. "Come on." He was reluctant. I put my hand out...something powerful clicked between that stray collie and me.

I'd never wanted another collie after my beloved Mollie had been killed. It was obvious that this giant of a dog had been hurt, mistreated, even abused. While he devoured the food I set before him, his untrusting eyes never left mine. I put him in the backyard and locked the gate, half excited over finding him, half fearing that I'd love him too much. The pads of his feet were torn and he was desperately tired. He collapsed in sleep.

Whenever one of my sons left the gate open the dog dashed out and ran out of sight. Time after time we chased him and brought him back. Then, after a year, the gate was left open one day and he just lay there, inside the gate, inches from it, looking at freedom with what appeared to be an amused, satisfied expression in his big brown eyes. Soon after, I began walking Caleb on a leash, knowing he was strong enough to break away in a moment if he chose to.

God seemed to speak gently. *You used to be like Caleb, running from help, from love, even from Me. You wanted your "freedom" to do things your own way. In desperation you finally discovered My love and relaxed, rejoiced, remained. I'm glad you decided to come unto Me, for like Caleb, you were weary and heavy-laden.*

I took the leash off Caleb and he turned and ran back to our house, through the open gate into the backyard.

Master, forgive us when we are afraid to trust You. Teach us to love and be loved by You.
—MARION BOND WEST

"My soul magnifies the Lord."
—LUKE 1:46 (RSV)

I didn't know it was to be, after fourteen years, my last Christmas Eve in Alaska. Yet had I known, I wouldn't have changed a thing.

After a wonderful dinner with friends at their alpaca farm, I slipped outdoors in the chilly night air to spend time alone with God under the stars and to enjoy the woolly animals quietly bedded down in their lean-to shelter near the house. The earthy aroma of hay filled my nose. More than a dozen alpacas followed me curiously with their intelligent big brown eyes. They weren't the traditional ox and donkey, but the scent and feel of the scene transported me to that first Bethlehem Christmas Eve.

All at once I began to sing "Away in a Manger" softly to the animals. This roused the inquisitive rooster, who fluttered out from his crumpled bed of straw beneath the deck. He strutted about, pecking at bits of hay in the snow. My song ended, but I couldn't stop praising God.

I looked up at the stars and called out, "Glory to God! Peace on earth! Christ is born!" Suddenly the rooster stopped his pecking and crowed three times, as if he were repeating my praise. We kept it up for several minutes, until I was bursting with such laughter and rejoicing that I ran inside to share it with everyone.

Was there, I wonder, a rooster in the hay the night Jesus was born? If there was, did he let out a zesty crow at the young Savior's first cry? It's something I'd like to ask Mary. Somehow, I don't think she would find my question strange at all.

Jesus, You are so glorious that all creation sings Your praise!
—CAROL KNAPP

"He has filled the hungry with good things...."
—LUKE 1:53 (RSV)

For my husband, Terry, and me and our four children, Christmas was always a gift of joy—tramping through the snowy woods to cut our tree, twisting candy cane cookies in the kitchen, filling the house with candlelight, wrapping presents (always leaving a few unlabeled), guessing who the "mystery" presents were for. But at last there came a Christmas that was very different.

My husband had accepted a job promotion that moved us far from our now-grown children. We were strangers to Minneapolis, our new hometown, and it was almost December 25. Our tiny temporary apartment was so crammed with boxes that we couldn't put up a tree. Out on the road we saw car after car loaded with college students heading home for the holidays. Our hearts filled with a deep loneliness for our own children. We longed for Christmases past.

"Well, Lord," I prayed, "You are the meaning of Christmas, and we still have You." Then my brother called with an invitation to his home in Colorado. We accepted gratefully. The decorations were different, the tree was charmingly artificial, and the children weren't ours, but oh, what a good gift that Christmas was for two empty nesters learning to live by themselves again.

On the first Christmas morning Mary held everything she—and we—would need for her—and our—whole life in her arms. God's Son had come to satisfy every hunger of the soul, as she had proclaimed in her song. And in obedience and faith, she had given the world its Savior, the one Good Gift from Whom all other good gifts would come.

Jesus, on this Christmas day, fill my soul with Your presence,
the Good and Perfect Gift.
—CAROL KNAPP

December 26

Be patient....
—I Thessalonians 5:14

We were driving through the Wichita Mountains Wildlife Refuge in southwestern Oklahoma. My friend Ginny was at the wheel and I was the navigator, with a road map spread across my lap. Although we still had a few more hours of daylight, I was anxious to get to the next big town where we planned to find a motel, go for a swim, and have a good dinner.

"Let's not take too long going through this park," I said. No sooner were the words uttered then we rounded a bend in the road and got caught in a jam—a bison jam! There they were, about forty huge black beasts, most of them standing still right in the center of the road. At first I was entranced. *They'll move soon,* I figured. But they didn't. They just stared at us belligerently. "Honk the horn," I ordered. Ginny did. One cow moved, but not as we hoped. Instead, she went down on her knees, folded her hind legs under her massive body, and settled down for a rest. I became more and more exasperated.

We discussed trying to go up onto the grass and drive around the animals, but the slope was much too steep. "No use fussing and fuming," Ginny said. "There's nothing to do but be patient and wait." So that's what we did. We settled down. We studied the animals. We admired the scenery. We talked about the wonders of God's creations. Finally, after about fifteen minutes, "Belligerent" (as we had named her) rose up and moved over to the side of the road. Other bison followed, leaving enough room for us to drive past.

Today, back in the concrete city, whenever I get impatient about temporary roadblocks in my job or in my private life, I remember those bison. It's God's way of telling me, "Stop fussing and fuming. Be patient. Take time to look around and admire the wonders of My world."

Dear Lord, patience is such a difficult virtue. Help me to practice it.
—Eleanor Sass

Pray one for another, that ye may be healed....
—JAMES 5:16

I've been practicing something new that I've just got to share with you! In January, as I was sorting through the Christmas cards I'd received, I found myself with a dilemma I have every year: what to do with the snapshots of families, friends' children and grandchildren, and other loved ones tucked inside the cards. I delight in receiving the photos, but after the holidays I don't know what to do with them.

This year I had an inspiration for keeping the gift alive. I decided to use them as bookmarks. In addition to marking my stopping place, I also use the pictures to mark special pages I want to come back to later. Each evening before I start to read, I look at the picture that is marking my place and pray special blessings upon that person. After finishing the book, I go back and pray again for all those people whose photographs are marking special passages. Then I leave them in the book, to be found sometime later.

During the past week I've been rereading a book I first read in February, so I've prayed another time for my nephew David and his family, for the cute little granddaughters of my high school friend Jeri, for a *Daily Guideposts* reader named Laurie, even for "Poor George," the fluffy white dog of Janelle in California. I feel a special bonding now with friends' children I've never met, a renewed closeness to old friends I haven't seen in years, a personal relationship with readers I may never meet. It has enriched my prayer life in a deep way, and it's going to become a tradition with me!

Thank You, God, for new ways to pray for lives that touch mine.
—MARILYN MORGAN KING

"Ask where the good road is, the godly paths you used to walk in, in the days of long ago. Travel there, and you will find rest for your souls...."
—JEREMIAH 6:16 (TLB)

I've always considered myself to be forward-moving, flexible, adaptable, and living on the innovative edge of life, but lately I find myself clinging to the comfort of the old and familiar.

Perhaps that's why I'm looking at my new Bible with apprehension. I certainly need a new Bible, but months after having received it, it is still pristine, beautiful, and virtually untouched. I know that all my favorite passages of Scripture are in there, exactly where they ought to be, but I can't seem to find them. So I continue to reach for the Bible that has been the most familiar of all my companions for more than forty years. Its pages are held together with sticky tape, its binding is falling apart, and snippets of inspiration clipped from here and there or given to me by those who know me best are stuffed between its pages. With scribbled notes in its margins and underlined passages, I can find anything I'm looking for in less than half a wink!

Sure, bring on an exciting, new, innovative year, but it is with a thankful heart that I find myself singing "For Auld Lang Syne" (For Days of Long Ago). I'm grateful for the comfort of familiar names on greeting cards, familiar faces that jump out at me from a crowd of strangers, familiar things (especially my Bible), and places, all of which chronicle my life with the sweetness of memories shared, disappointments prayed over, friendships kindled, and love celebrated.

For the paths of yesteryear, thanks, dear Lord. For the road that lies ahead, strength.
—FAY ANGUS

The Lord is my rock, and my fortress, and my deliverer.
—PSALM 18:2

A few years ago my husband faced serious surgery. For a time, things were uncertain, especially the biopsy results, and I grew very fearful. The evening before the surgery, my daughter Ann plopped her beloved replica of Noah's ark in my lap. "It's torn," she said. The ark was stuffed pink calico with pockets that held a menagerie of tiny animals. I pulled out the sewing basket to repair the split seam.

I hadn't thought about the story of Noah in years, but now it came rushing back to me—how Noah, facing a storm, built the ark, trusting in God rather than giving in to fear and doubt. How he climbed aboard and rode out the storm, persevering for forty rocky days. After that he sent out a dove, not just once but three times, hoping for land.

Through that calico ark, it seemed as if God was helping me to face the storm in my own life. And we did come through it. One morning after many rocky days, the doctor pronounced my husband as good as new. We hadn't been beaten down with fear; rather we were held up by God's love.

And now I share my "Ark Lesson" with any of you who are storm-tossed today.

1. Build an ark of trust. Put the situation completely in God's hand, trusting in Him rather than the negative voices of fear.
2. Ride out the storm. Hold onto God's strength no matter how rocky the circumstances become.
3. Send out doves of hope. Keep believing there is a solid new beginning beyond the storm. There is—in His care.

Father, surround this reader in Your Love, comfort him (or her) in stormy crossings, guide him (or her) safely to the other side. Amen.
—SUE MONK KIDD

December 30

I was walking to my car in the parking lot of our local hardware store when my bad leg (I'd had polio years before) buckled under me and I fell, packages of potting soil and fertilizer spewing in all directions. An elderly man helped me to my feet and, after I'd assured him that I wasn't hurt, he helped me gather my scattered purchases and stow them in my car.

Of course I thanked him, but in the excitement I forgot to ask his name. I was so grateful for his kindness that I wanted to meet him again and thank him properly, so I placed an advertisement in the local newspaper: "Will the gentleman who helped a lame man in the parking lot of the hardware store please telephone this number?" It was a month before he called. He had been away on family business, he told me, and it was pure luck that a friend to whom he'd mentioned the incident had saved my ad to show him. He stopped me as I started to thank him again. "There's no need to thank me," he said. "I was only doing what my employer would have wanted me to do."

"Who is your employer?" I asked.

"God," he answered. "Isn't He yours, too?"

Well, I'd never thought of it that way. But it's true for all of us, isn't it? No matter who signs our paychecks, we're all working for God, not just from nine to five, but twenty-four hours a day. That means we're on call to "do good unto others" all the time. It's something we don't have to think twice about. And isn't that a nice way to make a living?

Father, help me to be a good employee of Yours—all the time.
—WALTER HARTER

He maketh me to lie down in green pastures: he leadeth me
beside the still waters. He restoreth my soul....

—PSALM 23:2–3

When I was a boy growing up in the Philippine Islands, New Year's Eve was always a time of intense celebration. Filipinos and Chinese love fireworks, so my friends and I would buy bags full of firecrackers and skyrockets and spend the night in deafening explosive delight. My mother always worried that I would blow my fingers off; my dad just sat back and chuckled, wishing he were a boy again.

Now my New Year's Eves are a quiet time for meditation and contemplation. I love to build a big fire in the fireplace, feel its warmth, and stare into the flames and embers. With a cup of coffee in hand, I reflect on the events of the past year in the world, in our country, and in my own life. Slowly, a sense of gratitude wells up within me as I realize that God has guided me through another year. As I face the future, I'm reminded that whatever happens, God, my Good Shepherd, will be walking with me.

Watching the fire, I become aware that I've begun to softly hum a hymn, Joseph Gilmore's "He Leadeth Me."

He leadeth me! O blessed thought!
O words with heav'nly comfort fraught!
Whate'er I do, where'er I be,
Still 'tis God's hand that leadeth me!

As we celebrate New Year's Eve together, Gilmore's words, written more than a century ago, are words of faith and hope for all of us: "Whate'er I do, where'er I be, still 'tis God's hand that leadeth me!"

Happy New Year!

Father, I trust You to be with me in all events of life. May I follow You and
never fear, for You are my Shepherd and I shall not want. Amen.

—SCOTT WALKER

A Note from the Editors

We hope you enjoy *365 Spirit-Lifting Devotions of Comfort*, created by the Books and Inspirational Media Division of Guideposts, a nonprofit organization. In all of our books, magazines and outreach efforts, we aim to deliver inspiration and encouragement, help you grow in your faith, and celebrate God's love in every aspect of your daily life.

Thank you for making a difference with your purchase of this book, which helps fund our many outreach programs to the military, prisons, hospitals, nursing homes and schools. To learn more, visit GuidepostsFoundation.org.

We also maintain many useful and uplifting online resources. Visit Guideposts.org to read true stories of hope and inspiration, access OurPrayer network, sign up for free newsletters, download free e-books, join our Facebook community, and follow our stimulating blogs.

To learn about other Guideposts publications, such as our best-selling devotional *Daily Guideposts*, go to ShopGuideposts.org, call (800) 932-2145 or write to Guideposts, PO Box 5815, Harlan, Iowa 51593.